DARE THE NIGHT

"*Dare the Night* is the compelling story of Michael Cross, who became visually impaired at eight years old. With courage and determination—and the support of his family and teachers—Michael defies the darkness to navigate his new world. An inspiring autobiography of resilience and endurance, this book is a must-read for everyone."

—**DR. NED VANDERS**, retired superintendent of Catholic Schools, the Diocese of Austin

"One does not simply overcome tragedy and sadness but rather adapts in a positive or negative way to the situations these obstacles create. In *Dare the Night*, Michael chooses to lean into the positive. Compelling and inspiring, this book is filled with joy . . . [and] advocacy for those who have experienced vision loss."

—**MARILYN DUBBERLY RHINEHART**, former vice president of instruction, Johnson County Community College, Overland Park, Kansas, and former dean of women, North Harris College (now Lone Star College–North Harris)

"Taking readers along every step of the way, *Dare the Night* is a story of courage, determination, anger, strong faith, great grief, and—most of all—unconditional love. Michael Cross paved the way for those who will follow him, both with and without disabilities."

—**KAY GUYNES**, lifelong friend and classmate

"With something for virtually every reader, *Dare the Night* tells the story of one person and his family overcoming great challenges with persistence and faith. It offers snapshots of American history—from the medical system of the 1950s to family vacations in the 1960s, student life in the 1960s and 1970s, to the horror of gun violence in the 2000s. This book made me laugh, cry, reminisce, and think. I highly recommend it to the reading public."

—**E. A. PUFFE**, freelance copyeditor and proofreader (thirty-eight years), publisher contributions include University of Texas Press and SMU Press

DARE THE NIGHT

My Life, the Way It Happened

MICHAEL R. CROSS

TCU
Press

Fort Worth, Texas

Library of Congress Control Number: 2025012190

TCU
Press

TCU Box 298300

Fort Worth, Texas 76129

www.tcupress.com

Design by Ashley Muehlbauer

I dedicate this book to my parents, Harold Ray Cross and Regena Cross, for their unwavering support; to my brother, Tracy, for his example of resilience; to my sister, Kay, for her wonderful spirit and help to Mother; and to the memory of our younger son, Anthony Michael Cross, who waltzed through his days, greeting life with a bear hug.

Contents

Preface

I started writing this book over ten years ago. The story revolves around my loss of vision at age eight. For the rest of my life, I confronted one question that I could never escape: Would I allow blindness, the night that swallowed me whole, to keep me from pursuing a future of my choosing? Would I allow it to imprison me, or would I accept the challenge as a dare? Would I dare the night? The way to face the dare was ever changing. Could I be nimble enough to respond to the challenges as they evolved? Luckily, I didn't have to face them alone. This is not just my story, but the story of the family that supported me and my brother, who was dealing with a very different disability.

Acknowledgments

When I set out to write this memoir, I realized that without help, this would be a skewed version of what happened to me. We are all the product of genetics, obviously, but also of our interactions with the people around us. This narrative, although it mentions others, focuses on me and my immediate family. I consulted four people to present a more complete picture of my life: my brother, Tracy Alton Cross; my sister, Regena Kay Hayter; my mother, Regena Dale Cross; and my aunt, Betty Blassengame.

My mother died shortly after reading the first chapter. Thereafter, my help was considerably limited. Aunt Betty's recollections, as a younger sister, supply some of what Mom didn't live long enough to contribute. My father, Harold Ray Cross, died long before I wrote this memoir, and his appearances in these pages are few, but his influence on me is unsurpassed. He was the bedrock character in the background. I strive, but I have little hope of being as good a man as he was. My greatest tribute is to my mother, the virtuous and industrious wife described in the book of Proverbs. Without her dedication to her family, we would all have been lost, and my successes, such as they are, instead would have been failures.

I would like to acknowledge the individuals whose support has also contributed to this work. E. A. Puffe was the first person to edit this manuscript. Her guidance has been invaluable. Also, Marco Roc, my TCU Press editor, is a steadying hand. Thanks to both. Finally, I owe a great debt to my wife, Karen, who saw the worth in my story, who urged me forward when she thought I had more to say, and who is the most important person in my life.

Chapter 1

Nightfall

I couldn't take my eight-year-old eyes away from the gun barrel. It began spitting bursts of blue flame, and the night was filled with the cries of desperate men, the crash of battle, and the flash of explosions. I nearly jumped off the edge of my seat. *To Hell and Back* was the name of the movie, and Audie Murphy and his army buddies rushed the enemy lines. I watched spellbound as Audie crashed into a room and riddled a mirror with machine gun bullets. He had just killed his own reflection in the glass. A buddy in the room just behind Audie Murphy said, "Well, I never saw a Texan outdraw himself before." For the rest of the film, Audie Murphy did amazing things, causing him to end up as the most decorated soldier in US history. These images from the Capitan Theater in Pasadena, Texas, are among the brightest and most indelible from my childhood because it was the last movie I ever saw. Night was already descending on my color-splashed, carefree days. Yes, Audie escaped his hell to once again tramp the fields where he and my mother, Regena, had picked cotton together as kids. But unlike Audie Murphy, I would never escape the shadows and the battle poised to swallow me.

It began in late spring with headaches that grew increasingly stronger and more devastating. After a few episodes Mom was worried enough to take me to the family doctor. I sat in the waiting room so the doctor could talk to Mom privately.

"Well, Mrs. Cross, I don't think his headaches are real. He is trying to get attention because right now his little brother is the center of concern. By the way, how is Tracy coming along?" He looked down at his notes. "We took his leg cast off about nine weeks ago."

Regena Cross perked up. "He is walking again, but it took a while. He's a cheerful little boy, playing and coloring in his book. But something is wrong. He's the prettiest baby I've ever seen. His eyes are blue. Even the whites of his eyes have a blue cast. For that matter, his teeth look blue, too."

The doctor made a note. "Next time you bring Tracy in, I want you to point that out to me. How did he break his leg again?"

Mom bristled. "He sat down on the toe of his dad Ray's shoe, and screamed. When he kept screaming, I thought a safety pin must have opened and jabbed him. But the safety pins were okay, and when I opened his diaper, his leg was swollen. I knew it was broken, but I was watching when it happened. Nobody was touching Tracy."

The doctor rose to leave. "That is very unusual, but freaky things do happen. This is why Mike is having headaches; he senses your worry but interprets it as a loss of standing in the family. Just let time pass, and it will sort itself out."

As it turned out, he had another dumb thing to say. "And as far as Mike is concerned, pay a little more attention to him, and I think he'll stop having headaches." On that note, the office visit ended, but my headaches did not. It must have entered Mom's mind that at this rate, with her two sons grabbing all the attention, she might expect her five-year-old daughter, Kay, to play out a death scene that would make Katharine Hepburn jealous. But Kay didn't do that; she wasn't a demanding child.

Although Tracy had started walking again, our home life didn't return to normal. Even though Mom went out of her way to spend more time with me, my headaches were no longer mild. By August I had seen three doctors, none of whom found any reason for alarm. Their only concern was that Mom believed that my headaches were real. The third doctor said, "He has pinworms. All you people in the South have pinworms." By then I was going through the house closing doors and pulling the window blinds because light hurt my eyes. My headaches had a definite center—at the base of my skull. Once they began, they intensified until I vomited and blacked out. I stood frozen, wherever I happened to be, clutching my neck to ease the spasms and waiting for the headache to peak. During these times, my vision disappeared instantly under a black snow flurry, and I lost consciousness. Between these bouts I felt fine, but the bouts were coming more often.

Trying to bring some normalcy back into all of our lives and worried that Kay wasn't getting enough attention, Mom and Dad decided to give her a bicycle for her sixth birthday. On the big day, Kay and Dad came home from Sears with a shiny blue one. We all started blowing up balloons and setting up tables full of party favors and treats under the carport. Dad took time out to give his excited daughter pointers on how to keep her new toy upright. The party was small, attended only by the kids that played at our house every day: two little boys from next door, my friend Charlie Kissenger, and

Barbara Beerbower, the only girl in the neighborhood who was Kay's age. Everyone was having a good time when I left holding my head. I didn't even stay for the root beer, cake, and ice cream. Mom knew I never would have passed that up. She didn't need any more proof that my symptoms were real, and my problems were serious. So ended the party, but more than that, any pretense of normalcy. Three days later, Kay successfully rode her bike for the first time. She mounted it to visit Barbara, who lived on the far corner of the street. Barbara, on her own bike, waited for her to get started. Kay coasted down the sloping driveway, turned right onto the sidewalk, and peddled away after her friend.

I wanted to be normal, so much so that I tried to hide the attacks from the other kids. But when I went rigid and blacked out during a wrestling match with my friends, it was out in the open. At first Charlie and Gary thought I just wanted out of the contest. I don't know why they thought that, since I wasn't losing the match. I went limp in my opponent's arms, and we both collapsed in a heap. A couple of kids realized something had happened. Gary and Royce taunted me with cries of "chicken!" I slowly got up off the ground and started dragging myself home. Someone tackled me from behind, slamming me face-down on Charlie's concrete driveway. My head exploded in pain. When I came home holding my head and screaming, Mom was terrified. This incident convinced her there wasn't much time left. She saw me wasting away, and she couldn't find a doctor who could reach a diagnosis. Finally, just before Labor Day, Dr. Herndon, an ear, eye, nose, and throat specialist, agreed to see me. So Dad took the day off from his job at the Port of Houston to drive us into Pasadena. When I staggered into the waiting room, Dr. Herndon was talking to the receptionist. He looked at me, went white, and called us into his office immediately. I don't remember much of that office visit. Mainly, I remember being embarrassed when the doctor had me strip naked and try to walk a straight line. I failed miserably, weaving and stumbling around all over the place. After I dressed, Dr. Herndon laid me on a table, turned the lights out, and shined a bright light into my eyes. It hurt. He left and returned with two other doctors. No one spoke. The two doctors examined me in turn, looked at each other, and said, "We agree with your diagnosis." I didn't witness the conversation in the doctor's office because I was sent back out to the waiting room, but I heard about it years later.

Dr. Herndon was visibly shaken and angry. This was 1955, and men typically didn't show emotion, not in Texas anyway. "How dare you bring a dead child into this office! It's too late to save him!" If Mom had been terrified before, she now felt the world crumbling around her. Both sons had been stricken in six months' time.

"His father and I haven't been ignoring Mike. We've been to three different doctors. You're number four."

"And what did they tell you?" And so she told him. "Well, he doesn't need a tonsillectomy. These men were all stupid! He's having headaches, his eyes are dilated, and he has trouble walking. Unbelievable!"

He was worked up, and Mom was near tears. "Now wait a minute, they belong to the same AMA you do!"

At that, he threw up his hands. "Oh, forget I said anything. I'm sorry, Mrs. Cross. I can see you did what you could. I'm not going to hide anything from you. Mike won't survive brain surgery. But if by chance he does, and if his tumor is where I think it is, he'll never see anything again." Mom was shattered. "Today is the Friday before Labor Day. I'll give you four names. They're all very good surgeons. Any name on this list is the right choice." Mom's world was destroyed. I was oblivious to everything, and no one was going to tell me what was going on.

When Dad pulled up in the Chevy, we got in, and Dad looked at Mom. "What is it?"

She shook her head and looked away. "Not now."

Dad's brother Wesley and his wife Lilly had driven in that morning from Fort Worth, so I could hardly wait to get home. Grandma Cross lived in the garage apartment behind us, and they would be back there with her, Kay, and Tracy. When we got home, Mom climbed the back porch to the kitchen, while Dad and I walked back to Grandma's apartment. The day was hot, and all the windows were open. Everyone was talking when we heard crying. Dad, Wesley, and Lilly suddenly left, and Grandma looked concerned. When they walked into the bedroom, Mom was lying on the bed crying. She got up and faced them. Frightened, they knew the news about me was not good.

"There won't be any more crying," she said.

Dad put his arms around her and said, "What is it, Regena?"

Mom asked, "Where is Mike?"

Dad said, "He's with Grandma. What is it?"

"Mike has a brain tumor. Dr. Herndon thinks Mike will die on the operating table."

They all froze in shock. There was nothing to say. "Here's how it's going to be. We're not going to tell Mike he's going to die. These are his last days on earth. He's going through enough. Telling him won't help, and it would ruin what time he has left." (Now if there's a psychologist reading this, I'd say I was okay with Mom's decision. It would have done me no good at all to know. There were no loose ends in my life I needed to attend to because I had barely begun life.)

The next night, I slept on the screened-in porch for some relief from the heat. But there was no relief for me. I think somebody lay down beside me, but I can't be sure. The tumor inside my skull was trying to push my brain through my face, and as I found out later, it was the size of a tangerine. Fortunately, I was under nine years of age, which meant that my skull was still malleable. So when the tumor pushed, my skull was flexible enough to give way. The world had become a searing headache, too intense to allow any intrusion into my consciousness. Eventually, the tumor stopped pushing, and the world returned to me. This kept happening all throughout the night.

The next morning I vomited again, so we didn't go to church. A few feet away in the kitchen, Mom decided not to wait until Monday. She called George Ehni, one of the names on the list of surgeons, and described my symptoms and Dr. Herndon's diagnosis to his receptionist. She hung up and waited.

The phone rang, and Dr. Ehni's gentle voice came on the line, "Mrs. Cross, can you bring him to Methodist Hospital this morning?"

She looked at Dad and whispered, "We need to go to Methodist Hospital now."

Dad said, "Thirty minutes."

"Yes, we can be there in thirty minutes."

While Dad helped me get dressed, Mom called her parents in Corpus Christi to get help with Kay and Tracy. At the time, none of us knew that Tracy had osteogenesis imperfecta, otherwise known as brittle bones or chalk bones. He only had a mild case, yet he would break his legs seven more times, eventually ending up permanently in a wheelchair.

Grandpa Richards, whom everybody called A.P., said into the phone, "You can't let them cut that child's head open!"

"Daddy, if they don't do it, he'll die a horrible death right in front of us." Before driving to Houston, A.P. sat down on the couch and cried.

Kay and Tracy didn't come with us to the hospital. That seemed strange to me, but I couldn't keep my mind on anything except how I felt. Finally, we got out of the car and went into this big building where another doctor asked me more questions and watched me walk. He sent us upstairs, where I was ushered into a room. There was a teenager there who had fallen out of some bleachers and hurt his neck. Visitors came to see me. Charlie Kissenger and Bobby Graph were underage and couldn't come to my room, but they sent me a handwritten newspaper they were starting. There was a line in there about me. It said, "Mike Cross is 'shick' in the hospital." I laughed at the misspelling, but that started another headache.

On Wednesday night, two men came and shaved my head. No matter how much I begged, they wouldn't stop. Those two male nurses didn't take sadistic pleasure in violating me, but I didn't believe it at the time. "Come back and wash the soap off my head," I shouted. And they did, while I cried. There were other children with brain tumors on the same floor, and that prepared Mom for her ordeal. Mothers whose children were Dr. Ehni's patients were very supportive of each other. A twelve-year-old girl had had a section of her brain removed, yet she was up walking around and seemed to notice everything. One boy had malignant brain tumors that kept coming back, no matter how many times they were removed. He just lay there, unable to move or speak. I was with Mom when she visited him. He was like a statue lying there, unresponsive to us or the world around him. I still didn't know what was about to happen. It hadn't yet dawned on me that this boy and I shared something. Mom told me later, "I prayed all night long: 'Please God, if it's malignant, don't let him wake up.'" She couldn't stop thinking about the little boy down the hall.

Thursday, I was in surgery for eight hours. The lab test performed days later showed the tumor to be a cerebellar astrocytoma, not malignant but so fast-growing that hardly anyone survives it. Its growth accelerates rapidly, and the window of opportunity to recognize it in time to save a life is very small.

When I woke from surgery late that afternoon, Dad was to the left of my bed sitting on a ledge, drinking what I took to be a Coke. The room was very dim. My world never again looked bright and beautiful. I had lost half my vision in eight hours. Three years later, my loss stood at 98 percent. "Hi, Dad," I said. He immediately called Mom, who came to the foot of my bed. Although my recognition of Dad meant that I could see, they both wanted to know just how much. And yet it hurt too much to answer their questions—just saying hello almost took my head off. My head and neck were packed in ice to hold down the swelling.

Sixty-six years later, I still remember the pain vividly. If you have ever hit your "funny bone," you have felt hot, searing fire crawling up and down your arm. My head and neck felt like that twenty-four hours a day for two weeks. In 1955, the typical eight-year-old didn't know enough to ask for more painkillers; anyway, I certainly didn't. I just accepted it as my fate. Because of the intense pain, I was afraid to move or talk or even eat. That month Mom practically lived at the hospital. One day, when the pain had somewhat abated, my bed had been rolled down the hall into the TV room. One of the nurses must have had a bad day because when she came to change the sheets on my bed, she put her hand behind my back and pitched me forward onto my knees. My neck and head flopped forward as if I were a rag doll, and I screamed. That was the single most intense pain I have ever felt in my life. Mom came running. I didn't know what went on around me because I was transported to some fiery place where I hoped never to go again.

It takes three months to form a new habit, and I had a whole world to change. I hadn't yet confronted the new me. Losing my vision wasn't the only change I would have to adjust to. My neck was as weak as a newborn's, forcing me to lie in bed for a month. I never recovered complete motion in my neck because Dr. Ehni had fused some of the bones in it. Initially, I was incapable of leaving a wheelchair, and when I eventually was, I found that my balance had been affected, a problem that plagues me even today. It forced me to walk with a wide stance like Charlie Chaplin. I can't balance on one leg. Staircases are especially dangerous—if I don't have a handrail, I will fall. As soon as I lift a foot from the ground, I'm off-balance. So I refuse to go up or down steps without a rail or someone to hang on to.

I would find out over the coming year that I could see my handwriting, but only if my nose was almost touching the paper. The fine motor skill in my hands was diminished, especially the right hand. My handwriting became, and still is, atrocious. I was no longer ambidextrous. And how ambidextrous was I? Two years before, in the first grade, my teacher had suspected me of cheating. The two sets of handwriting on my papers slanted in different directions. One day as she watched, I got tired and switched hands. Today, I sign my name with my left hand. Years later Mom would tell me that there's a higher incidence of brain tumors among ambidextrous people.

When I was strong enough, I went downstairs in a wheelchair to see Charlie. Although I was happy to see him, I sat bandaged, not moving or talking because I was still very weak. Charlie's eyes got really big, and he was uncharacteristically quiet. What he saw when he looked at me didn't equate to his version of being sick. You would think he was looking at an Egyptian mummy come back to life. So when Charlie did speak, it was almost a whisper. I guess seeing a playmate with a bald head scared him. In a place where practices like bandaging, shaving heads, and using wheelchairs are common, you try to avoid drawing attention to yourself. On the way home, he told his parents, "Oh, Dad, Mike looks hurt bad."

It's hard for me to measure my emotions when I look back at the summer when I was eight. Was I that boy, in 1955, who could see? As I write this in 2020, I've been blind for sixty-five years. A major part of my identity had disappeared, and the consequences for me were radical. What future did I lose? I can't answer. I can only speculate about where the things in my life may have led me had I not lost my vision. What was unusual about me? Nothing, except I had an eye for color and a strong desire to draw and paint what I thought was beautiful. But that included everything—I thought it was all wonderful. My earliest memories with full vision date back to 1949, when I was two years old. There are three memories that will come to me readily until the day I die. These memories are, in some primal way, a link between who I am and who I could have been. Standing as burned-out bridges to a future I would never have, these three memories are among my strongest.

The earlier two memories are especially beautiful. I was alone in both instances, and there was no sound associated with either. These are snapshots excerpted out of what will forever be, to me, a golden time. Whatever scheme the mind uses to select a moment in time to retain, I'm certain these are the best from that world. When I was two, Dad taught school in Tyler, Texas. One spring morning I mounted the steps to an abandoned trailer behind the house we rented. As I stood on a chair that was leaning against the front door and looked through the glass pane in the door, the sun was rising behind me. Rays of light streamed over my shoulder and illuminated the large room. There was a sink directly across from the front door and off to the right was a table and chair. I gazed spellbound as dust particles rotated and glided in a fairy dance. The glint of the sun silvered the gossamer galaxy where a spider sat watching. That moment in time and the little boy remain forever captured in his web.

The next snapshot, from two years later in Commerce, Texas, when I was four, is also an early-morning scene. It had recently rained, and the gutter was full. The sidewalk where I knelt, staring down at a tadpole, was in the cool shadows. I couldn't take my eyes away from the tear-shaped jewel moving lazily from one morsel to another. It was a magical image of tiny shifting things.

The third memory is from the day after I went to Dr. Herndon's office. Reeling between denial and acceptance, Mom wanted some way to gauge how much vision I was going to lose. She had some "before and after" descriptions of things around the neighborhood that she wanted from me. On this day, we had walked to the corner where, as requested, I turned and faced the opposite corner. She pointed out a tree a block away and asked me to describe everything in detail. What I saw is incredible to me now; I described the pattern on a bird's wing. One feather was fluffed up and out of place. The texture was crystal clear. It is hard for me to relate to the boy who saw that. A month after surgery, I once again stood on the corner describing things to Mom, and this time I understood why she was having me do this. I looked for that tree a block away, but I couldn't see it.

As I read over these three snapshots, I recognize them as my memories, but they don't touch me. They are, at the same time, my memories and not mine at all. Whenever they visit my dreams, they are not an occasion for sorrow. And yet, it is strange to think that I once was someone else. That someone else had a love of color. Today, my memories and dreams are not brilliant; they are faded and drab. As art walked out of my life, I tried desperately to hang on to it. Art was no longer a way to explore the world. I've talked to other artists who have lost their vision, and now, I have two questions: For us, is art an attempt to recover something from the past? Is it an attempt to see things the way we saw them, in a past we may not even remember?

None of my art survived, except for one pencil drawing. I drew a self-portrait when I was twenty-five. It was the last image I ever rendered. I drew it from a photograph which I examined with a strong magnifying glass. My tunnel vision was so narrow, I could only see small portions of it at a time. The whole experience was so unsatisfying that I turned my back once and for all on what could have been. (But by this period of my life, I was moving in a different direction, away from art.) In addition to writing with both hands, as a child I drew and painted with both hands. When my first-grade teacher looked at my papers, she perceived two styles. None of my early art exists to be examined for style. If I hadn't had a brain tumor, would my paintings look like they had been done by two people?

Self-portrait of Mike, drawn at age twenty-five, 1972. Author's collection.

Chapter 2

Homecoming

Kay entered first grade the week I had brain surgery. Her first month was an ordeal. Mom was at the hospital almost all the time, and Dad worked long hours. So Grandpa Richards drove up from Corpus Christi to drop Grandma Richards off. Kay and Tracy were happy because they didn't get to see them except on long holidays and during summer vacation. Grandpa (A.P.) stayed one night. Grandma planned to stay for three weeks, doing the cooking and cleaning. Kay needed a mother for emotional support while she adjusted to the scary new world of first grade. Grandma tried to fill the gap, but it wasn't the same as having a mother.

A.P. went back to his job on the Missouri Pacific Railroad and to be with Betty, their eighteen-year-old daughter who was a freshman at Del Mar College. But he was back almost immediately—Betty got strep throat and missed the first two weeks of college classes. Grandma Richards went home, and Grandma Cross stepped in to do the chores. She related to adults better than to children, which is why Grandma Richards had been the first choice to help out. Because Grandma Cross was older and had less energy, she was overwhelmed. Kay wasn't watched as closely as Tracy, leaving her relatively ignored. Two years earlier, when I had opened my bright-red *Dick and Jane* primer, the family had gathered around to hear me read. But Kay coped alone with a demanding new world. No one was there to listen to Kay read about Dick and Jane. She went to bed every night dreading the next day. At last, I was released from the hospital, and Mom came back into Tracy's and Kay's lives.

And then, the homecoming. It wasn't yet real to me that my long nightmare had come to an end. Late that afternoon Mom and Dad drove me home. Then, with assistance, I mounted the front steps, and a room full of aunts, uncles, cousins, and grandparents welcomed me home. Seeing all those faces, even if they were much fuzzier than they used to be, lifted my spirits. At last, the crowd of relatives departed. Wanting to make the whole day a celebration, Mom made our family favorite: hamburgers with her special relish, made with mustard, onions, pickles, and tomatoes; and for the final touch, Southern fried potatoes—a dish that later we would realize was French fries. Everyone in the family was making an effort to please me. Tracy's broken leg had mended, and he was walking again. Wearing a shirt and diaper, he looked up at me with a big smile on his face. Always shy, my sister Kay approached me as if I were made of china. She saw a very different brother. I was only now finding out how my body worked. I had no stamina, and my movements were unsure; and so, on that first day, I didn't act overjoyed. In truth, I was afraid that if I smiled, the dream would shatter, and I would wake up in the hospital. My energy drained quickly, and I went to bed early.

Mom helped me do everything. Kay wasn't the only one who treated me cautiously. Everyone else did too. In fact, I treated myself as if I were brittle and didn't know when I would break. A big piece of my skull where my head and neck joined was missing. An angry scar crawled up the back of my neck, and it was all the more prominent because I was completely bald. The area that was no longer protected by skull was never far from my thoughts. I did everything slowly, conscious always of whatever might touch me there. The recently traumatized nerves in my neck still objected to sudden head movements. The pain streaking up my neck could be so intense that I blacked out. So, I was very careful getting into bed. I sat on the edge and braced myself for the next step. Lying down was going to be tricky, and I had to think it through. I didn't want to lock my hands behind my head—the missing chunk of skull made that area tender. I was afraid even to turn my head. The consequence of even slight neck movements was unthinkable. That day, a month after surgery, a careless quick turn of the head still sent a lightning bolt up my neck. For the first time in my life, I went through a checklist. I didn't know the word "physics," but I knew I wanted a hand under my head pushing straight up against its weight. After putting my right hand to the side of my head, I started to lean toward the bed. When I hit the pillow, I was lying on my right side. So far, so good! Then I rolled very slowly over onto my back and breathed a sigh of relief. No pain! The first time I tried to lie down after surgery, I had chosen the wrong maneuver and had lain straight back onto the pillow. The nerves in my neck had screamed bloody murder for a long time. The lesson had been harsh: I couldn't do anything without considering consequences. As I lay there between clean sheets, looking over in the pitch black at the bright yellow slit of light under the door and listening to the soft murmur of Mom's and Dad's voices, I finally allowed myself to believe I wouldn't wake up in the hospital. There would never be music so beautiful as those voices whispering peace to me from the other room. My world was safe again; the nightmare was over.

That night I slept the sweet sleep of one who had been rescued from a great tragedy. Next morning, I awoke to a world that seemed both old and new. Drifting gently into consciousness, I realized how very quiet it was. I heard none of the hospital sounds or smelled any hospital odors. Hoping that I wouldn't see anything to dispel the peace I felt, I opened my eyes. A large object was at the foot of the bed. I couldn't make it out, and sat up to take a closer look. It was Tracy's playpen. I took in the rest of the room. Why was it so dim? I looked at the window and the streak of light on the wall opposite. From its position, the hour was late. Today was a weekday, so Dad was at work doing whatever he did at the Port of Houston. The bedroom door was closed so I wouldn't be disturbed, but I could hear Kay talking to the baby. There were two doors to the bedroom, and the one leading off toward the kitchen wasn't closed. The clang of pans and the splash of water were a familiar background to Mother singing softly to herself. I reached sideways for my clothes, but I couldn't see my hand as I felt around. Something clattered to the floor. I had to look straight at my hand to see it. My peripheral vision was gone. I no longer heard dishes bumping against the sides of the sink. Footfalls came down the hall into the room where I lay.

"Good morning. It's a beautiful day, and I saved you a plate of pancakes." When Mom leaned over to kiss me, the wet dish cloth draped over her arm and soaked the front of my pajama shirt.

"Hi, Mom."

Tracy toddled through the door on his chubby little legs. Mom whirled and caught him up in her arms. Since Tracy had broken a leg earlier in the year, Mom had become quick to catch him when she thought he might be about to fall. Kay came quietly into the room and said hello. With three people in the room, I didn't want to get out of bed—I didn't have any pants on. "Come on, kids. Let's let Mike get dressed," Mom said, as I pulled the sheets up.

Once alone, I stood on one leg to put my pants on, and I immediately toppled backward onto the bed. Oh, my neck! A few minutes later, I tried again to balance on one leg but couldn't. So, I thrust my legs into the pants sitting down, then stood on both to finish dressing. On the way to the kitchen, I kept swaying and put a hand on the wall to steady myself. Once safely in my chair at the table, I was eager to look around at the small kitchen I hadn't seen for a month. I could still see the refrigerator, the counter and sink, and the cabinets above the counter, but many of the details were missing as if they had been airbrushed out. The sunlight shining through the blinds made brilliant bars across the table. I couldn't see past those bars. I tried to understand what I was seeing; it looked like those bars were between me and the table. After staring at the scene for a while, I asked Mom to shut the blinds. She paused and looked at me for a long time. When she shut the blinds, the bright streaks disappeared; the table and my breakfast popped into view. I was glad to be home, but there were some weird things happening. Worried by this, Mom got on the phone, but I didn't listen to what she was saying.

I was staring hard at the kitchen, when Kay approached and said she was glad her big brother was home. Tracy was down on the floor, playing with a metal car and making motor noises. Kay's wide eyes reminded me that I was bald, and I got up to go look for the hat Dad had bought for me. I was extremely embarrassed about my bald head and neck with its long, ugly scar. I looked and looked for the hat. When Kay handed it to me, I was upset that I had not been able to find it. Kay, who is very attuned to the feelings of others, started to tear up, thinking she had done something wrong. I hurriedly put my captain's hat on and told Kay she hadn't done anything wrong. With the hat on my head, I calmed down. Tracy picked up on Kay's emotion and started to howl. Mom came in and asked what was wrong. I guess she saw the look on my face and the hat pulled down abnormally far on my head, because she picked Tracy up and led Kay away for a talk. I had escaped a frightening world, but there were some things I didn't like about this one. That hat stayed on my head, even when I took a bath.

Over the next few weeks, I got stronger and didn't wobble quite so much when I walked. At first I stayed in the house, playing with Kay and Tracy and watching TV. But I couldn't see it unless I put my face so close to the screen that everybody complained. Even sitting close, Mickey Mouse cartoons seemed very grainy with lots of detail missing. I started back to school in late October but couldn't keep up. Mom and Dad pondered what to do next. Our next-door neighbor, Lillian Schreiber, arranged to be my homebound teacher. She hoped to catch me up with my third-grade class at Briscoe Elementary. I had missed about six weeks, and it was soon apparent that my vision loss wouldn't let me catch up, so the attempt was dropped. Lillian and her husband had no kids of their own, but they really wanted children.

Sunlight streamed into the playpen next to the window. A little boy stood there, clutching the rails, looking out. A tiny visitor hopped onto the window sill and peered through the screen at Tracy. The squirrel had come every day for the past week. Looking directly into Tracy's face, it fluffed its tail and chattered excitedly. The child squealed in delight and cooed in his musical little voice. Fascinated by each other, they conversed for quite a while. A board creaked somewhere in the house and the squirrel looked around in alarm. It hopped down and was gone. The next day, it was back, and Tracy grew to expect its appearance. The days got cooler, and Mom didn't raise the window, but the squirrel came anyway, putting his nose against the screen. Inevitably, one winter day, the visits ceased, never to resume.

Halloween rolled around, and I went to the Briscoe Elementary Halloween Trick or Treat party. For a costume, I wore a gorilla mask with matching black shirt and pants. So that no one would mistake me for a giraffe, there was a gorilla pictured on the front of my shirt. Still too fragile to participate in the vigorous activities going on all around me, I walked the halls with feeble steps. Mom and Dad stuck to me closely, fearing that someone would run into me and knock me down. Mom saw my first-grade teacher; otherwise we saw no one we knew. We stayed a while longer, then left. Until then, I had hopes of rejoining my class. At home that night, I felt that I had lost touch with everyone I knew. I was beginning to realize that when an illness or an injury leaves you different, people will avoid you. Because my education was already at a standstill, everyone agreed that I should take the rest of the school year off to make my recovery easier. My doctors hoped during that time to stabilize my failing vision.

One November morning, we heard Tracy calling us from behind the closed door to his room. Mom was busy in the kitchen, so I opened the door and went in. Tracy was standing up, holding onto the rails of his playpen. I can say now that I didn't know my brother until that moment. He wore a big smile on his cherubic face; I could hear it in his voice. He was holding something out to me in his little hand. "Cherry," he said. Why would Tracy have a cherry? My vision may have deserted me, my brain certainly had, but there was nothing wrong with my sense of smell. I was all set for the taste of cherries! My hand was halfway to my mouth when the smell hit me. In the same instant, I realized the thing in my hand didn't feel like a cherry. Tracy was still smiling, looking straight at me. This event shaped our relationship for years. What a sucker I was!

My voice rose in an affronted tone, "Mom! Tracy handed me some poop and told me it was a cherry!"

I wanted to disown my hand. I couldn't hold it far enough away from me. I tried to get away from it, but it didn't work. My escape route was driven, not by my vision—it had let me down—but by my nose, my only friend at that moment. I moved quickly backward, tripping over a chair. Unfortunately, my hand followed me. I tried to get up without touching anything with my handful of poop, especially myself. I continued to wail, which brought Mom at a run. She hadn't understood my cries, so I repeated this crime story. Oh, it wasn't to be tolerated! My mind shut off all input from my hand. Since I couldn't get away from it, I tried ignoring it. I was about to dump it in the playpen with Tracy when Mom grasped my forearm with one hand and captured the poop in toilet paper using her other hand. As she marched me into the bathroom, Kay followed, asking what the problem was. Mom stuck my dirty hand under the bathtub faucet and turned it on. I held my fingers as far apart as I could. A one-year-old baby had just played a trick on his eight-year-old brother. How embarrassing! Life is full of lessons. I had just learned one: When Tracy tries to hand you anything, don't take it! Did I learn a lesson where there was no lesson to be learned? Perhaps the squirrel had offered Tracy an acorn, and he had adopted this etiquette from the animal kingdom. Maybe my little brother was innocent. Yeah, and maybe the sun rises in the west! One question still lingers: Why did that squirrel really stop visiting Tracy? Did he grow up and lose interest, or did Tracy give him a cherry?

Almost always in the house with Mom and Tracy, my days were empty. Adding to the loneliness, Kay was at school. Daytime TV didn't hold much interest, because it was full of dull shows for adults. So, I was permitted to play in the front or backyard, always under Mom's watchful eye. Our immediate neighbor to the right was Lillian, but in the house to our left was a family with two boys, neither old enough to attend school. James, the older of the two, spent lots of time at our house. Nailing boards together, Dad fashioned me a crude battleship. Its gun turrets were wooden blocks, with two nails sticking out as guns. This was a pretty hefty wooden ship. About this time, Mom allowed me to have a kitten, which I named X10 Peachy. One day in the backyard, X10 climbed an oak tree to get away from James. Upset, he wanted the cat down. He screamed his frustration. "Come down, cat, right now!" Strong for a five-year-old, James picked up the wooden ship and hurled it at the cat. I was unfortunately standing under the tree. The battleship came down onto my head. I screamed and briefly lost consciousness. I say briefly because I was still on my feet when I regained consciousness. Mom arrived in a panic, and James's mother, Millie, rushed over and hauled him away. The board didn't hit me edge on, but its flat surface drove down all across the top of my head. When it hit me, it jammed my teeth together and the next instant everything went black. In mystery novels when the hero gets knocked out, the author always says he or she saw stars. Well, I saw flashes of light, sparks leaping away from me in every direction. Of course, it really hurt in that instant before I blacked out, and it still hurt when I regained consciousness. Mom sat me down at the kitchen table and called Dr. Ehni, my brain surgeon. The wooden battleship had impacted the crown of my head, not the incision on my neck. The doctor asked Mom to check my eyes to see if they were dilated. When she said they weren't, he instructed her to watch me but didn't think she needed to bring me to the hospital. For months, Mom banned James from our property.

I don't want to leave the impression that Millie was a bad neighbor, because she was in fact a very good one. One crisp day shortly after Halloween, Mom walked with me two blocks to Motts, a five-and-dime store. She had left Tracy in the care of Grandma Cross, who lived in the garage apartment behind us. We browsed around in Motts, eventually buying some licorice and a wax harmonica. As we emerged from the store, a jeep pulled up, parking directly in front of us. Millie got out and hurried up to Mom.

"Regena, Mrs. Cross is in the back seat with Tracy. He fell and broke a leg."

Mom was cool under pressure. She put me in the front seat with Millie, and got in the back and carefully took Tracy away from Grandma Cross. Grandma was in tears. She kept apologizing. Tracy had tripped over the back foot of a rocking chair and had fallen onto the concrete floor. (After that incident, Grandma Cross was afraid to keep him.) Millie dropped me and Grandma off at home and went to the hospital with Mom. The doctor wanted to put Tracy in traction, but we couldn't afford the medical device. Dad was a good carpenter, a good car mechanic, and an all-around handyman. Welding together nine strips of metal tubing, he fashioned a traction device, resembling a pup tent. Imagine two triangles standing upright and facing each other. Then imagine that the corresponding vertices of the two triangles are connected by long metal tubes. Tracy lay across the flat bottom of this tent-like device with his leg pointed toward the ceiling. At the foot of the traction device, a five-pound weight hung from a pulley. A thick cord tied to the weight ran through the pulley and over to Tracy's leg. It worked well. The first few days were especially hard on all of us. Tracy cried himself to sleep, and woke up and moved his leg, not remembering the break. He then jerked into full consciousness, causing himself intense pain. Those screams were enough to curdle your blood. In time, he was more careful on waking, and Tracy's cheerful nature reasserted itself.

Thanksgiving was hard that year, but Mom and Dad tried to make it festive for us kids. I suppose by this time Mom and Dad were feeling snakebitten because of all the emergencies. We usually spent Thanksgiving in Corpus Christi, visiting Mom's parents, Grandma Richards and Grandpa A.P. (No one ever called him anything but A.P., never Alton or Preston.) That year we didn't go to Corpus, because Tracy in his bulky cast made travel complicated. Instead, Mom's parents came to Houston. Kay and I were A.P.'s first grandchildren, and Tracy was number five. Having two grandsons struck down in one family really affected A.P.—he was deeply pained by the events of the last three months. Seeing Grandma and A.P. always lifted our spirits. For a while we forgot our troubles.

Thanksgiving was over, and we again faced our problems. Mom took me to Louis Gerard, a well-known ophthalmologist. He decided that in order to halt—or at least slow—the decline in my vision, intervention was needed, and soon. The problem was that the blood supply to my optic nerve had been severely reduced by the damage done during the brain surgery. The plan was to speed the circulation, primarily through intravenous glucose feedings three times a week. In addition to the IVs, I would have to take niacin tablets, also intended to speed up the blood flow. These pills produce a hot flash that lasts about thirty minutes. I left Dr. Gerard's office in the Herman Professional Building in blissful ignorance of these decisions.

On the way to the bus stop to return home, I did something I am very ashamed of. We had just walked out of the Herman Professional Building when a boy and his mother passed us, moving toward the building we had just left. The boy was very overweight. Looking back, I assume his weight was due to a medical condition. When he got close, I saw him and laughed. Mother said, "You should be ashamed of yourself," and hauled me rapidly away. To this day, I think of Mom as an angel, but for the rest of that day, she was an avenging angel. This was the tenth plague of Egypt, and I was the eldest son. She threatened to tell Dad, the death angel, to visit me. Whether she did or not, nothing further happened. But knowing that Mom had a bad opinion of me was punishment enough. I never forgot what I did that day, and what happened shortly thereafter seared this into my memory forever. By this time, I was playing in the front yard again and had reconnected with the neighborhood kids. One day, I was with a group of about four other boys, when my hat got knocked off. It was on the ground, and all of them were pointing at my head and laughing. "Look at him. He's bald!" I immediately felt the justice of what had happened. My ears turned red. I took this as a message from God Himself: "Bread cast on the water returns . . . " (Ecclesiastes 11:1). I resolved never to mock or make fun of anyone again. This lesson is always with me, and has permanently changed the way I interact with people. After that day, the connection with the kids in the neighborhood was broken again. They didn't miss a chance to make fun of me. Even Charlie, who hadn't joined in their laughter, avoided me until my hair grew back. I recovered my hat and accepted their mockery as punishment. Dad hadn't punished me, but this was worse. I had to accept a lot of things about myself and about my world.

And then, there was the hospital! When Mom and Dad checked me back into the hospital, they had to reassure me that this hospital stay wasn't for more brain surgery. I wrongly concluded it was only for tests. That afternoon, two men came into my hospital room and taped my right arm to a board. I was unsuspecting because nobody had told me what was about to happen. I knew nothing. My vision loss was severe enough that I didn't see the needle in the nurse's hand. So, when he plunged it into my arm, I jerked violently and tore my vein open. Blood gushed in a spout about a foot high. I was angry that no one had warned me. Maybe they thought I could see what they were preparing to do. Someone should have asked me, but nobody did. I understand why Mom didn't tell me about the brain surgery, but this was different. I should have been told. As a result, they had to strap down my left arm and redo the procedure. But first, they had to get the bleeding stopped, and I was very upset. I'm sure it hurt Mom to watch, and she was indeed present. I couldn't see her, but at the moment, my focus was on what was happening to me. This time, I didn't jerk. I held my breath and didn't move. The IV bottle held 500 cc of fluid. Within a minute, I got a migraine, and the nurse crimped the IV tube with a little metal rectangle with a wedge cut into it. The nurse moved the tube into the narrow end of the wedge. The migraine subsided as the drip slowed down. The drip started at 3:00 p.m. and ended five hours later. This was repeated every day for the eleven days I was in the hospital. For a while, the vein in the crook of my right arm was not available. Instead, the nurse used veins in my hands and feet.

After my release from the hospital, the IV bottles were smaller, containing 100 cc. For a while, Mom and I caught a bus to the hospital three times a week. One trip in particular stands out in my memory. It was winter and very cold. At the hospital, all the nurses were busy, so a doctor administered the IV. He plunged the needle into my arms, hands, legs, and feet—a total of eleven times. He never did hit a vein. That day, I rode the bus home all taped up, wondering if this was going to be a frequent experience. Fortunately, it was not. Two nurses at Methodist Hospital were magic. They talked to you while slipping the needle into a vein.

I remember saying, "Tell me when to be ready."

And she would say, "Oh, it's already done." I never felt the needle at all. They would have made great assassins!

From that day, when I got to the hospital, I started asking for Miss Love. And if she wasn't available, I asked for Miss Beard. Miss Love was a petite brunette, and Miss Beard was a pretty redhead. I confess to having had a crush on Miss Love, but I would have married either one of these ladies for their sewing skills alone. But aside from their skills with a needle, they were both very pretty. Though I was only eight, I did notice, and the distraction was a bit of normalcy in a world I had no control over.

To put it mildly, that Christmas of 1955 was on the bleak side. There was further bad news. Mom pointed out to our dentist, Dr. Glen, that Tracy's teeth were blue. He sent one of them to a lab to be tested. The results were very discouraging. Tracy had OI, osteogenesis imperfecta, the most common genetic bone disorder. In this disease, the connective tissue is weak. Tracy would always be in danger of breaking bones. Later in life, he would have heart problems and curvature of the spine. Two nicknames for OI are "chalk bones" and "glass bones." The only bright spot in the report was that Tracy had the mildest form, called "blue china." In the most severe cases, children are born crushed to death, having upwards of two hundred and fifty fractures. (So the doctors no longer suspected Mom and Dad of child abuse. If Mom and Dad had lost custody of their kids, Tracy would have moved through foster care, putting other homes in jeopardy of that accusation. Then, that family would have lost its kids too. And how would it have affected me? I would not have been taken to Dr. Herndon, and I would not be alive to write this book. And Kay would not have done well, either.)

So this was a very Blue Christmas. Because of all the medical expenses, money was scarce. If there was any gift-giving in the immediate family, I don't remember it. I did receive something that I valued above any toy I had ever gotten. Grandma Richards gave me a foam rubber pillow for the back of my head. Lying on that pillow was miraculous. The missing chunk of my skull was extremely slow to be filled in. Three months after surgery, it hurt to lay the back of my head on a regular pillow. But when I lay on that foam pillow without hurting, I became obsessed with it. Nothing *else* I got for Christmas could have compared with it.

Tracy in homemade traction, 1960. Author's collection.

Chapter 3

Facing Reality

It takes three months to form a single new habit, and I had lots of new habits to develop. The old ones didn't work anymore. Almost everything was going to be different—the way I walked, the way I brushed my teeth, the way I dressed, the way I read a book, even the way I signed my name. I would do all of these things differently from now on, and what's more, I would get no help to learn techniques for doing any of them. I was strictly on my own. As my vision faded, I could no longer look in the mirror while I brushed my teeth or combed my hair. And I couldn't see my feet while walking around or kneeling to tie a shoestring. At first, I simply leaned closer to the mirror. I didn't know I was spattering toothpaste on the mirror. I continued using my declining vision to do other things. In these instances, I didn't make a mess; they were just not done well. (Mom said I did, too, make a mess.)

Another problem with attempting to use vision you don't actually have is that you slow down because you are trying to compensate. Predictably, I struggled not to change. People resist change, especially when change means they're admitting they're no longer who they want to be. At last, I gave up and did many things by touch. Using vision was too slow, and it was ineffective anyway. My mental processes were changing without my realizing it. Vision is such a powerful tool for gathering large amounts of information. You can take in an entire scene at a glance. In contrast, how long would it take you to touch everything in the room? People use their vision to monitor and direct all their daily routines—chasing a green bean around a plate, or deciding where next to put their foot. I stabbed my plate at random, hoping my fork would spear something. Highly frustrating! I walked, not knowing what my foot would encounter. Sometimes, I stepped on something, other times, off something, or worst of all, in something. A Bible verse sums it up nicely: "We walk by faith, not by sight" (2 Corinthians 5:7). These two tasks (eating and walking) are still a problem. It helps if a person tells me where on my plate certain items are. You do this by using hand positions on a rotary clock face. Green beans are at twelve o'clock. This by no means solves all problems. You can still end up poking at nothing. It's hard to look dignified while you're doing that.

I have severe balance problems as a result of the surgery. So when, without intending to do so, I step on something or off something, I may lose my balance and fall. This has altered the way I walk. I am always braced for a fall, because I can't predict one. It is subconscious. And I seldom fall down. I fall, but I almost always recover before hitting the ground. A cousin once observed me fall and recover. I stumbled around kicking and dancing, doing a couple of 360-degree turns, but I stayed on my feet.

His comment was, "You're the only person I ever met that could lean over at a forty-five-degree angle and recover." Well, you know! I tried it, and I can. Another embarrassing situation is when I reach the top of a set of stairs without realizing it. I take a step that isn't there. Not even Miss Manners could do that and maintain her dignity. Seriously, I'm always aware of how ridiculous I look. To recover some dignity in embarrassing moments like this, I usually say I'm practicing my Charlie Chaplin routine. It helps to find a reason to laugh.

I fought my new reality at every step. Reluctant to admit I wasn't who I wanted to be, I resisted using a white cane for the next forty-seven years. I eventually accepted reality and got one. Using a cane tells me when I've reached the top step. I don't take a step that isn't there, and nowadays, I don't say anything about Charlie Chaplin. It is hard to stop using vision, because using it makes everything quicker and easier. I had less vision, so my task was finding the right mix of vision and touch to accomplish any given job. Finding it means trying different techniques and failing until you find a way that works. This involves identifying all the steps in a process that no longer work. The answer is usually discovering how to perform those steps without using vision. If it's slower, so be it. Many times, I had to revisit a problem. I discovered that the first workable method might not be and usually wasn't the best one. Even when the method I settled on was slow, it got faster with practice. There are obviously good and bad times for trying new techniques. I performed my experiments when the situation wasn't critical. During a final exam at school was bad timing.

I wasn't the only one in the family making adjustments—everyone was. It was absolutely essential that we took each other's problems into account. One of Mom's concerns was to make Tracy understand how vulnerable he was; a hopeless task, as she saw it. He finally realized it, but it was far too late. A few times my blindness hurt Tracy. I once tripped and fell on him, breaking his collarbone. This led to a rule: No clutter in halls or areas where someone might be expected to walk. As we came to realize how fragile Tracy was, Mom and Dad insisted on another rule: No one hit anyone else. We actually succeeded in following that rule. I don't remember anyone hitting anyone. This included spanking, especially where Tracy was concerned. Dad spanked me only once. It didn't hurt, but it let me know he was not happy with me. When Mom raised the specter of punishment, we always backed off and nothing happened. But she was very good at raising images that altered our behavior. Hey, practice makes perfect! Punishments weren't physical. Instead, we lost a privilege, such as not being allowed to watch TV or having to watch others eat ice cream while being deprived of it. Treats were so infrequent that being denied one was a major disappointment. Our parents' approval was so important to us that we tried really hard to keep it.

One night, when Tracy was about four years old, Dad had to do something at the Port of Houston. Mom was busy, so Dad took him along. The port at night was scary to Tracy. Cargo ships hooted, and the yard was full of railroad engines and box cars, all massive and spooky in the dark. Tracy was afraid they would start moving and run over them. After that night, he worried about Dad working at the port, seeing him surrounded by danger. Mom didn't express her worries about Dad, but Tracy—because of that night at the port—sensed her concern.

Our circumstances impressed on all of us how dependent we were on each other. This caused us to worry about each other more than in other families that had smoother lives. But above all, Mom and Dad's faith in a loving God made our family bond very solid.

Chapter 4
Evicted (Gloomy Days and Facing New Challenges)

One cold February night, Dad's mother knocked on the back door, and Kay let her in. It was clear from her face that something was troubling her. She didn't look directly at Mom or Dad. They arranged themselves around the dining room table. Meanwhile, seated in chairs in the living room, Kay and I watched Walt Disney on TV, while Tracy watched it from a wooden pallet on the floor. We kids, being completely absorbed in Walt Disney on TV, were unaware of what happened behind us until decades later. Mom and Dad faced Grandma across the table. Unknown to Dad, someone had told Grandma that Dad couldn't pay his rent and had volunteered to replace him as a renter. She finally looked at her son and explained that she was losing money. Rent money was her only income. "I'm sorry. You need to find somewhere else to live. I've found a new renter." There was dead silence at that table. Dad turned white as a sheet. I was starting my intravenous glucose treatments, and Tracy was in a full-body cast after breaking his leg for the second time. Insurance had canceled both of us. My medication was running seventy dollars a month—the equivalent of a house payment—and we were still in debt from my brain surgery.

Dad finally spoke. "Okay. Are you sure about this move, Momma?"

Mom was going to let Dad do all the talking; she was too upset to speak. Tracy was on the floor and couldn't fall and hurt himself. She knew I was listening to Mickey Mouse on TV. She didn't think the kids were hearing any of their conversation. We had just finished supper, so the dirty dishes were still in the sink.

"Well, Momma, if you'll watch the kids, we'll go look at houses."

Emma Cross had a pained look on her face, and Mom wondered how she could evict her youngest son. Mom couldn't look at her, so she got up to go through new home ads in the *Houston Chronicle*. As it happened, there were two new housing developments in nearby Pasadena, Texas. Mom told us kids that we couldn't leave the house and to mind Grandma until she and Dad got back.

In the car, Mom exclaimed, "Oh, Ray! What else can happen?"

"I don't know, Regena," Dad said. The family finances were a mess. Mom had to choke down her emotion.

Turning onto Empress Street in Pasadena, they stopped at a house for sale by owner. It was a very nice house with a double garage, three large bedrooms, and two baths. Mom liked it very much, but they wanted $18,000 for it. Dad couldn't afford their asking price. They then drove into the Tanglebriar subdivision where, as it turned out, we would spend the next thirty-three years. The house they bought was on Longwood Drive. It was a three-bedroom, one-bath red brick home. The electricity hadn't been turned on, so they went to the car for flashlights. That's how Mom and Dad first saw their new home, walking from room to room with their flashlights, trailed by the agent. It wasn't the house Mom preferred, but it was nice. There were hardwood floors in every room except the kitchen, which had linoleum. That room ran along the back of the house over to the dining area. There was no partition between kitchen and dining areas. A door off the dining room led into the one-car garage. Mom told Dad this was acceptable. They were asking $11,650. Dad qualified under the GI Bill, and left after having put down earnest money. As they drove away from the agent's office, they felt overwhelmed by the new debt they had just taken on, but they had no choice. This house-hunting expedition was so abrupt and so successful—after only a one-hour search. Was that house there waiting for us? Was it coincidence or providence? Mom and Dad never doubted that it was providence and that God was still watching over us all, but they were uncomfortably close to financial disaster. With the commitment behind them, they both felt a real sense of urgency. Mom said she wanted to leave the house in Houston, preferably the next day, or the day after.

When they finally came home after a long absence, they found us still watching TV. Behind us in the kitchen, Dad told his mother they had found a house in Pasadena and had bought it. Grandma said nothing, and we wondered why she left in such a hurry. Mom and Dad were pleased about something, and I found out the next day we were moving. When Charlie came to play, this was my big news. Our new house was in a city named Pasadena, not too far away. Even though I could come back and see Charlie, I wasn't at all happy with this move. I only had one friend left, and I was losing him. Dad came home from work that night, and they tied our mattresses to the roof of the car and took them to the new house. The next few days were rushed as Mom and Dad started boxing things up and taking them out to the car.

That evening Dad's mother walked into the house in front of her garage apartment looking dejected. Her prospective renter had backed out, leaving her with no income.

"Ray, I don't want you to move."

"I'm sorry, Momma, it's too late. I'll lose my earnest money if I back out now. And if I don't use the GI Bill now, I'll lose that too."

We were all in a trap caused by the rumor that Dad wouldn't be able to pay the rent to Grandma. On the other hand, maybe we needed to be prodded into taking advantage of the GI Bill. Mom didn't for a minute think God approved of the trap they were in, but she did have faith that He provided a way of escape.

Dad ran a few errands. He first went by the phone company and arranged to have phone service started; he next went to the offices of the *Pasadena Citizen* and subscribed to the newspaper. Moving day came, and Mom filled jugs from the tap, because the water wasn't connected yet in our Pasadena home. Then we got in the car and left Houston. All the houses in the new neighborhood were brand new, and they were all empty. We had three mattresses on the floor, but no other furniture—not even a table. We ate oranges, apples, and bananas because we didn't have a refrigerator. That, plus three bed frames and a clothes washer, were five more expenses we would have to manage somehow. There was so much to do. Kay and I wandered around the empty rooms followed by Tracy. Dad had built him a wooden pallet mounted on rollers, and Tracy propelled himself turtle-fashion with two arms and one leg. We had nothing to do except read the *Citizen*, which Dad bought a copy of because it hadn't started being delivered yet. Mom read the funny papers to us kids and caught up on local events. A new elementary school, one mile away, J. D. Parks, would open this coming autumn. And when she read that the Pasadena Independent School District was supposed to have the best special education program in Texas, she was absolutely certain this move was God's providence. Pasadena allowed blind children to attend public school, something other cities in Texas didn't permit. This move to Pasadena was, without doubt, even more providential than Mom realized. It gave me the chance for a brighter future. That weekend Dad rented a U-Haul and moved everything, while Mom stayed in Pasadena with us kids. She didn't dare leave Tracy alone; he had already broken two legs.

Before moving on, let me say a word about Grandma Cross. She was reluctant to babysit Tracy for fear he would break a leg while in her care. It had happened once, and it left her extremely guilt-ridden. Tracy could even have a fatal accident! Afraid of being put into a situation she couldn't cope with emotionally, she took the most direct way out. We all ultimately benefited from the adjustments we were forced to make. She found new renters soon after our move to Pasadena. Although Dad would never have stopped paying rent, no matter how heavy his debts became, it was good for Emma Cross to know that she could rent to people other than family. The circumstance under which we moved could have broken our family, but it didn't. This showed my dad to be the great man he was. My father was the son every mother should have. He continued to be a protective, loving son until her death. But more than that, Dad was the father every son should have and the husband that every woman would be fortunate to have. Dad was a man of peace. I never witnessed an argument between Mom and Dad. If they ever had a disagreement, it was behind closed doors—never in front of us. Grandma Cross frequently spent weekends in our Pasadena home. Being around her was a real treat. Born in 1882 to immigrants from Stockholm, Sweden, she represented a vanished, exotic world. Her cookie jar was a bright-red pottery apple. Spiced cookies from that jar always sent my mind back to an earlier time, making me imagine a world where Grandma was young. Sunday lunch at Grandma's house was a pot roast seasoned with rosemary, a dish which to this day brings me fond memories. Grandma was a pleasure to talk to because she talked to kids on an adult level. In my teenage years, she saved Mom and Dad the trouble of telling me about the birds and the bees. Whenever Grandma Cross was in our home, I never sensed anything but friendly relations. I am thankful that this grand lady was part of my life.

Our first Sunday in Pasadena, we went back into Houston to church for the last time. Brother Sawyer preached about forgiveness, saying that God demanded that His children should be a forgiving people. Mom told me much later, "Ray and I certainly needed to hear that sermon in view of what had just happened." That afternoon, gathered around our dining room table, our lunch came out of cans—English peas, cream style corn, pinto beans, and roast beef from Argentina, recovered from a damaged crate at the Port of Houston.

We all waited for Dad to give thanks. "Heavenly Father, you have walked with us through the valley of the shadow of death. Thank you for preserving us all and bringing us here to this house and to this city. We thank you for your providence. We pray this prayer in the name of Jesus. Amen!" We all said "Amen," and then Mom filled our plates.

Our first few days were spent in an almost empty house in a ghost town. The neighborhood was silent—no traffic noise, no bird songs, and no human voices. The wind howled, reminding us how alone we were. The *Citizen* delivered the paper, although it was hardly worth their time. The other houses on the street were empty. Gradually, the houses started to be filled. As the neighborhood grew, the Larkins moved in, a family with seven kids. The two eldest girls, Rose and Kathleen, matched me and Kay in age. Two of the youngest were a few years older than Tracy. The oldest boy, Michael, came down often and visited as Tracy scooted around on his pallet. There being no other kids in the neighborhood, Kay and I were attracted to Rose and Kathleen. Later that spring we went to Rose's birthday party, where we played bingo, pin the tail on the donkey, and other games for prizes. Then, we ate cake with ice cream and went home.

Chapter 5

Between Worlds

Shortly after moving to Pasadena in 1956, my vision was failing fast, and the ophthalmologist, Louis Gerard, set up treatments for three times a week. I was about to turn nine, and my optic nerve was dying. There wasn't much time to stop it. Mom had been taking me on a bus to Methodist Hospital for IV glucose feedings once a week. She told Dr. Gerard about Tracy, saying that she needed to be with him instead of on a bus for hours. Sympathetic to our plight, he arranged for me to get the IV treatments from our new Pasadena family doctor.

"What is that scratch on Mike's face?"

"He has a kitten," Mom said.

Dr. Gerard said in a stern voice, "Get rid of the cat. Now!" The kitten disappeared.

Since Mom didn't drive, Dad always picked us up after 5:00 p.m. and took us to the doctor's office. My first eleven treatments, for which I had been hospitalized, were large, 500 cc, but now they were only 100 cc. For each session, we were in one of the office's back rooms for ninety minutes while the glucose mixture dripped into my vein. Mom read to me and rubbed my forehead to soothe the headaches that never failed to occur. If the flow into my arm was too fast, the headache accelerated into a migraine. The nurse put the needle in my arm and left for the day. Because the treatment wouldn't finish until after office hours, she showed Mom the steps to end the IV drip. Mom had to remove the needle, clean the puncture with alcohol, and tape gauze to the bend of my arm. The janitor let us out, and Dad drove us home. This happened Mondays, Wednesdays, and Fridays. I usually told jokes and otherwise tried to distract myself when the nurse was ready to insert the needle. Only then did I calm down. Those nights I slept well, but the night before one of these treatments I never did. I dreaded five o' clock all day long and was distracted and forgetful. Mom often held my free hand until the needle was in. My grip was hard, but relaxed when the drip started. This nurse was clumsy compared to Miss Love. I definitely didn't want her to jab me twice, so I tried to be very still. I thought of it as posing for a firing squad.

The only one of us kids going to school, Kay started at Golden Acres Elementary on Valentine's Day. On that day, having no Valentine for anyone, she felt that everyone was looking at her. Mrs. Allbritton, her teacher, understanding how her newest pupil would feel on this day of all days, made sure Kay got a Valentine. Mrs Allbritton had been our neighbor in Tyler. Kay remembers her fondly to this day.

I had lost so much time that Mom thought it best to keep me home. I was coping with too many things to be in a classroom. My vision hadn't settled yet. Meanwhile, Mom investigated Pasadena's "sight-saving" program at the new elementary school that would be opening in the fall. But, until I started school again, I needed something to occupy my empty days. She signed me up for the Talking Books program through the Library of Congress. Thus began a lifelong love affair with literature. Read by volunteers, many of whom had careers on the stage, the talking books arrived in belted cartons containing long-playing vinyl records. A record player came through the mail with three books. One of these, *Pirate of the North*, which I read in the dead of winter, drew me into the action, as the boy tramped the Alaskan snows hunting the bear that had been terrorizing the forest. The novel ended with the boy shooting the bear, thus saving his family from starvation and marking his entry into manhood. I was hooked and began to look forward to mail delivery. I had been given a way to see a world I could no longer see. Listening to great books was an escape from a world I didn't especially like.

Life continued to be hard. As if Tracy's days weren't miserable enough, he had cast sores that sometimes got infected. We didn't have the money to keep taking him to the doctor. Instead, Mom punctured the sores with a hot needle and drained them while Tracy screamed. At these times, my tenderhearted sister took me down the street to escape the crying. It upset both of us terribly. Escape for Mom wasn't possible; Mom had to overcome her squeamishness and do what was needed, even when it hurt. She told me in an interview fifty years later, "My life was torture, but it was much worse for my kids." The day finally came when Tracy got out of the cast. This was a big event, because there would be no more cast sores.

Everyone in the family was deeply affected by what was happening to me and to Tracy. There is mental anguish in seeing things you don't want to see.

We didn't realize it at the time, but our family was getting stronger. Tracy and I were isolated, so I talked to Mom more than sons usually do. Tracy less so.

In our interview, Mom said, "The strength in our family was a gift. Through it all, Ray was a tower. He didn't walk out on us. What would have crushed another man didn't crush Ray. I don't say it didn't faze him. How could it not? Ray was hurt too. He was a compassionate, loving father."

This new year saw our new lives start to take shape. Kay finished first grade with a straight-A report card, Tracy started walking again, and I was bearing up under the IV treatments much better than expected. And yet, we all needed a break. Our summer vacation in Corpus Christi proved to be a salve to all our spirits at a low moment.

Speaking of those times, Mom said, "My sister Betty was doing well at Del Mar Junior College, it was good to see Mom, and I saw a crack in my father's gruff exterior when he talked to Tracy. It was good for Ray too, because A.P. got him interested in ham radio, even if we couldn't afford a hobby right then." We went back to Pasadena refreshed, ready to face the world again.

...

In the autumn of 1956, I entered third grade at J. D. Parks Elementary. A special-education bus picked me up in the mornings, delivered me to school, and brought me back home in the afternoons. For the next four years, my school day followed a pattern. I was in a sight-saving class until lunch, at which time I was mainstreamed. I ate with the regular class, and then finished the day in it. Sight-saving classes covered reading, spelling, and math. These were the areas where, supposedly, low-vision students would be at the most disadvantaged. There was a special environment set up for reading. In the corner, a desk had a projection magnifier on its top. The whole thing was enclosed by a tall portable partition. This shut out light, minimizing glare. The projection magnifier was very strange. After placing an open book on a sliding pallet, you reached up and pulled the screen down to the book. It looked like a television, but with a much smaller viewing area. A light illuminated the page, whose image was magnified to four times its normal size, then projected onto the screen. For the next several years at least, 4X magnification was adequate to let me read.

In that class, students wrote on heavy paper ruled with thick green lines. We were expected to write with large letters, making it necessary to have the sheets of paper wide rather than tall. This wasn't at all like the paper in a Big Chief tablet, which I could still write on as long as I put my face close to the paper.

Mom worried about sight-saving classes having kids of different ages and with different levels of vision in one room. Her concern was justified in the end. Since the school was only a mile away, Mom arranged for a neighbor to watch Tracy while she made the journey on foot to see for herself. Not reassured by her first visit, she made several more. My classmates were two older boys and three younger girls. Mom saw how the students behaved in the sight-saving class. There was not much discipline. The fifth grader had a crush on the teacher, Miss G, which she did nothing to discourage. The sixth grader kept to himself, and the girls behaved like you would expect little girls to behave. My discipline lagged too, being right in line with the general breakdown. Punishment was uneven. I was singled out for the biggest share. And once the girls realized I was out of favor, it was easy to make accusations that the teacher believed. I was spanked and humiliated while the class sat and watched. Mom talked to Miss G about it several times but was ignored. Finally, Mom told me I would just have to accept punishment, even if it were unfair. "But be sure you don't deserve it." So, I tried really hard to behave. Miss G sent notes home saying how inconsistent I was. My classwork was okay one day but not the next. Mom told her about my three-times-a-week IV treatments and how much torment I was in. Miss G dismissed it all.

That spring, Tracy broke his right leg. He averaged breaking a leg every eighteen months. After that, Mom was reluctant to let Tracy out of her sight, and once he had recovered, "Don't run" became her mantra. Mom started reading all she could about OI, osteogenesis imperfecta. Strange bottles began appearing, both in the refrigerator and on the dresser in the master bedroom.

Mom often stood over Tracy, an eyedropper in her hand. "Open up! It's time for vitamin X, Y, or Z." I could smell it from across the room.

"No, Momma, please!"

"Yes, Tracy, it's good for you. You can have some chocolate milk afterwards."

This inducement usually won him over, but the same dialogue happened every day. Chocolate milk was the magic bribe. Those drops smelled nasty to me, and I retreated to the other room, in case she thought they were good for me too. I needn't have worried, since the money wouldn't stretch far enough to dose me and Kay too, much less bribe us. There weren't many extras, maybe a toy for Tracy, once in a great while. Yet, Kay and I weren't jealous; we saw how miserable his life was. The few times Mom explained why we couldn't have new shoes or a toy, she would say, "We're poorer than Job's turkey." We, of course, knew who Job in the Old Testament was, and after he lost everything, he didn't even have a turkey.

Kay asked once, "When would a turkey think he was rich?"

Mom had an answer for everything. "Never! A peacock might think he is rich, but never a turkey, certainly not Job's turkey."

Outside chocolate milk, our diet was plain. We lived on rice, beans, and oatmeal—lots of oatmeal. Treats were Spam, Vienna sausages, and an occasional can of Argentine beef Dad brought home from a damaged crate at the Port of Houston.

After a year of treatments, my veins were in trouble. Dr. Gerard gave Mom pills to keep my veins healthy and niacin to increase my circulation. I did a little better but still dreaded Mondays, Wednesdays, and Fridays—60 percent of the school week. Those happened to be the days when my work was bad. The only happy times in my life were when I was listening to a talking book. The worse my life became, the more books I requested. I became Toad in *Wind in the Willows*, Jim in *Treasure Island*, and Ivanhoe in *The Talisman*. When unpleasant things were being done to me, I had a rich dream world that I retreated into.

The summer of my ninth year rolled around, and I went off to Texas Lions Camp (for children with disabilities) in Kerrville. Dad got me up early and took me to Hobby Airport. A little man ran up and introduced himself as the man who would fly me and one other kid to Kerrville on his Piper Cub aircraft. He was only little compared to my father, who was six feet, two inches tall. He stowed our luggage and strapped us in. There was no conversation during the flight; the noise was too great. Finally, the pilot yelled over his shoulder that we had arrived. Then he did something I'll never forget; he switched off the engine, and we dropped a hundred and fifty feet. I thought my stomach would leave my body through my mouth. But he switched on the engine in time, and my stomach stayed where nature put it. Once on the ground, a car drove us to the camp. All arrivals assembled in the main recreation hall, where counselors called out names of campers who would spend the next two weeks in their bunkhouses. I was in unit 4, Fox Tribe. Because of my balance problem, I got a lower bunk. My days were filled with swimming, painting, leatherwork, hiking, shuffleboard, and learning camp skills. Despite Mom's worries, those two weeks swimming, doing arts and crafts, eating good food, and most importantly, meeting kids with a variety of handicaps revived me at a low point in my life.

Mom worried but knew it was good for me to meet kids with other disabilities. She said she knew I would handle it well because I already knew one, Tracy. I came home from Lions Camp, uplifted in spirit by the experience. Those two weeks were wonderful for another reason—there were no needles ripping the joy out of my life.

More good news! Although Dad couldn't leave because he had used up his vacation, he put Mom and us kids on a train bound for Corpus and Grandma's house. There were no needles there, either. My veins needed a respite from all the punishment of the last year. Trips to Padre Island, the T-Head, fresh fish, and indulgent grandparents can restore anyone's spirits.

There were days when we fished on the T-Head and fried our catch right on the beach. The winds kept blowing sand into the food, but we all had a good time. Other times, Mom packed a lunch, and we all went to the beach. We kids all loved it. Mom kept telling Tracy not to run. He had already broken his legs three times, so she was nervous when he got wild. Grandma Richards was a warm and friendly woman, especially tender with us kids. All of us were crazy about her. Mom was able to relax, knowing that Grandma was watching Tracy too. This wasn't hard, because Tracy was glued to Grandma. When the time came for Dad to drive us back to Pasadena, Tracy tried convincing us to leave him there until Christmas. The adults all laughed. Tracy came home with us.

Mom and Dad tried not to overlook Kay, who seemed to be doing well. She was still an A student and never in trouble.

...

One day a boy came around the corner, and after seeing me, he introduced himself. Gerald's family had just moved into a house one block over from us. As soon as school was out, Gerald came over to visit. He preferred coming to my house, there being too many kids at his house. He had four brothers and sisters all crammed into two bedrooms. Tracy followed us around, but we considered him a pest. Mom kept a close watch on me and especially on Tracy. Gradually, she let me and Gerald go farther away from the house. He became my guide to places around our housing addition. We even went to the very edge of the neighborhood, where we found a ditch about seven feet deep. Usually, it had no water in it, and there were interesting things there like blackberry bushes. Mom gave us baskets for the berries, not realizing that we were going into a ditch to pick them. We were smart enough not to tell her, too. Kay came with us on these berry-picking expeditions. With Gerald to encourage me, I pushed my limits back. It will always be amazing to me how I ever persuaded Mom and Dad to let me have a bicycle. Mom was very protective with me, and extremely paranoid about Tracy. And with good reason. Tracy was extremely fragile. As if that weren't enough, she worried about my walking into danger completely unaware. Again, she had good reason to worry. If I held my arm extended in front of me, I could see a little farther than my fingertips. Sitting on the bike, I could see within a small semicircle with me at its center. I was afraid to peddle very fast, since the faster the bike moved, the less time I would have to avoid a collision. If I couldn't see a car approaching, at least I could hear it. Mom probably thought I could see cars coming. It never occurred to me to tell her otherwise. This was the most dangerous thing I did.

Gerald accepted my limitations, and we became fast friends. The neighborhood was in flux, people moving in and out. Kids disappeared and were replaced by new ones. The newest kid was trouble. Is there a neighborhood anywhere without a bully? Ours was Jed, a chunky boy who smelled like urine. He was always playing tricks and starting fights. I'm sure Jed had a stressful home life. From our backyard, we often heard yelling three doors down at his house. The mother's voice screamed curses at her kids. The adults in the neighborhood laughingly referred to Gerald and me as Mutt and Jeff; I was tall and skinny, whereas Gerald was short. I was five feet tall, but weighed only sixty pounds. So, it wasn't very hard to push me around. In fact, Jed beat me up whenever he wanted. If he knew the names Mutt and Jeff, he didn't use them; he had other names for his favorite targets. Mine was "cross-eyes." He seemed to be focused on us, me especially, as the easier to catch. One day, I heard several objects falling around me. Then, something hit my face. Tracy, sitting unobserved behind a bush, witnessed everything. Jed was throwing rocks and grinning at my puzzled expression.

Like the prophet Jonah marching down to deliver God's ultimatum to the wicked city of Nineveh, Mom stomped three houses down our street to the new wicked city, Jed's house, to confront his mother. "You gave all your kids Biblical names. Why don't you teach them some ethics?"

But, the Ninevites were having none of it. This didn't go over too well, and nothing at all changed. To be fair, Jed's brothers and sisters weren't a problem.

They were victims too. One day Jed's little brother showed Tracy a burn on his stomach. Jed had held him down and burned him with a cigarette lighter. When Mom heard about it, she refused to allow any of them in our yard.

My Dad was involved in our lives in a quiet, supportive way. An excellent car mechanic and carpenter, he constructed simple machines—some solved problems, others were toys. When we couldn't afford a traction device for Tracy, he built one. When Tracy was in a body cast, Dad constructed the pallet Tracy scooted around on. He now built something that made me an instant star. Since Gerald and I were always playing soldier, Dad built us a military-style jeep. He cut the lumber using hand tools, and assembled wheels, axles, bicycle peddles, and a steering mechanism. It wasn't small either, seating four kids—two in front and two in back. The headlights and dashboard instruments were of course fake, but the effect was very nice. And, it maneuvered really well. I couldn't have asked for anything nicer. This didn't surprise me; I already thought my calm, resourceful father could do anything. All the kids in the neighborhood wanted a turn riding in it. Everyone envied Gerald and me riding around with army hats and rifles. I let Jed have a turn, and he repaid me by trying to wreck it.

My IV treatments were cut to twice a week. Otherwise, my school life continued to be gloomy. Mom never received notes from the teacher in my mainstream class, only the sight-saving class teacher. Even on the treatment days, I didn't get into trouble in the regular class. Math was the only subject affected on those bad days. The simplest explanation is that the other subjects don't require as much concentration as math, and therefore, I was able to do them even on a bad day. There was a change in the sight-saving class, but it was only temporary. One day a new student, Paul, showed up in class. He had dared a kid to shoot him in the eye with a bow and arrow. Paul lost the dare. But by the end of that year, Paul's eye healed, and he reentered regular classes. Christmas arrived, and the sight-saving kids all stood on stage at Kruse Elementary. We all wore huge white cardboard bells suspended from our necks. I still remember saying "bing, bong" and feeling ridiculous. Nothing else memorable happened the rest of that school year. Spankings were so numerous that they weren't memorable events. Still, my life was better. I only had a hundred IV treatments.

At last, the school year ended. After our summer trip to Corpus, I went to Texas Lions Camp for the second time. There were some familiar faces, but mostly new ones. Again, I came home much refreshed. I spent all my time with Gerald, and Kay found a new circle of friends. We lost the Larkins as neighbors, but two other families moved onto the street. Jerry Jean was four houses to the left on the corner, and Diane was two houses to our right. When Mom could spare her, Kay was with one or both of them. The three of them were frequently together in each other's homes—talking, watching TV, and listening to LPs and 78s. The summer drew to an end, and we all braced for another school year.

Around the beginning of the school year, the IV treatments were cut to once a week on Fridays, making my days more bearable. I needed relief from those treatments because nurses were sticking me more than once per treatment. I was a skinny boy with needle tracks all over my arms. Not all scars are visible. I was so ashamed of my arms that I didn't want anyone to see them. That psychological scar is with me still, over sixty years later. Mom stopped buying me short-sleeved shirts, because I refused to wear them. I had to hide my arms at all costs. Mom said years later that it hurt her to see what was happening to me, but there wasn't much she could do to change it. I needed to feel like I had some control left in my life, so I wore long sleeves even when no one around me did.

Mom wasn't looking forward to the next school year, because she knew all the old battles with the sight-saving teacher, Miss G, would be fought again and again, with no resolution. The summer of 1958 ended, and I entered the fifth grade. I anticipated more abuse at the hands of that teacher, and she more than lived up to my worst expectations. In addition to what was happening at school, Jed, who lived three houses down, enjoyed beating me up. He stalked me at home, and Miss G made my mornings miserable. I never knew from one day to the next how I would be treated in her class. She belittled me in class, which destroyed my confidence in myself, especially in math. Although I only had IVs once a week, my performance still suffered the day I went in for treatment. I made D's in math, yet, as we were told years later, my IQ was between 140 and 150.

Things weren't as bad as they could have been, because there was a new face in sight-saving class. Jack, who was one grade behind me, had vision much better than mine. He had a lively sense of humor, and I liked him immediately. We mostly talked on the phone, but our mothers did arrange for us to visit each other a few times. On Jack's first visit, I could tell that he and Tracy liked each other a lot. Their senses of humor meshed perfectly, and they stimulated each other to be sillier and sillier. Jack had that effect on me too, and he more than succeeded in entertaining both me and Tracy.

Back at school, Miss G now had two targets. Jack and I encouraged each other to be silly in class. This got us both spanked pretty often. Mom gave me another lecture and also talked to Jack's mother. He was the only bright spot in an otherwise gloomy year. Now that I had a friend in that class, it didn't bother me so much that the teacher hated me. Miss G went far out of her way to punish and humiliate me. Because Jack dared to be my friend, he was a new target for her wrath. She was now spanking two boys several times a week.

The contrast between the mainstream and sight-saving classes could not have been greater. I was a good student in Mr. Lowe's class, a marked contrast to my lack of success in sight-saving class. The IV treatments wouldn't explain my failure in the morning and success in the afternoon, especially since the afternoons were closer in time to those dreaded IV treatments. Well, what would? I was sure the explanation was that Mr. Lowe liked me and Miss G didn't. In his class, I was never in trouble and my grades were good. I loved history and always made an A in it. My grasp of grammar was good, and I consistently brought home the highest or second-highest grade in class in English. I was good at diagramming sentences. It was actually fun. One day, Mr. Lowe gave an English test on which I made a high B and a girl made an A. Everyone else failed. This was my first taste of real academic success. The students all liked Mr. Lowe. After lunch, he would regularly read a chapter of a book to us, like *The Swiss Family Robinson*. He made subjects come alive. In his class, I could almost forget that an IV treatment was waiting for me at 5 p.m. Almost! But, not quite. Mr. Lowe played touch football with the boys. He was always the quarterback, no matter which team had the football. I had fun in his class, and I didn't want anything to mess it up for me. This explains my response to what happened next.

In the mornings, Miss G insulted and belittled me in front of everyone. Two instances stand out in my mind. In one, I may have contributed to my problems, but in the other, I was in no way culpable. For years, she had seen me as disruptive and wanted to send me to the Texas School for the Blind in Austin. My chance for a brighter future was in jeopardy. I didn't want to go, and Mom didn't want me to go. That would be banishment from the sighted world, and I would feel defeated.

In the first incident, I rebelled openly. I said I didn't want anything to mess up Mr. Lowe's class. The revolt came when I thought my relations with the kids in his class were threatened. The school building was in the shape of a horseshoe, and the special education class was on the opposite leg of the horseshoe from Mr. Lowe's class but level with it. You could look from the windows in one classroom to the windows in the other. One day Miss G decided that the class would play cat and mouse. The game went as follows: The kids formed a circle around whoever was the mouse; the cat was outside. Mr. Cat tried to break into the circle and catch the mouse. When the cat managed to get inside the circle, the mouse would leave. Then the kids forming the circle with hands locked tried to keep the cat inside. If the cat ever caught the mouse, new people were chosen to be cat and mouse, and the game resumed. It was bound to happen that I would be the cat, and Suzy, the first-grade girl, would be the mouse. So there I was, chasing this little girl. Mr. Lowe's class must have taken a break and started to watch the game being played out across the way. This gave Jed a new opportunity to torment me, because he was one of the kids watching. That afternoon, the kids in Mr. Lowe's class teased me unmercifully. The next day when Miss G wanted the class to play ring-around-a-rosy, I refused and got spanked. I didn't want my other class watching me play what they called "baby games." I again refused and got another spanking. I didn't offer a reason for my refusal. This was a contest of wills, which the teacher couldn't win. I would have let her rip out my fingernails before I would play ring-around-a-rosy. If Miss G had listened to Mom, she would have realized, as punishments, her spankings were nothing compared to an IV treatment. I didn't enjoy being spanked, but it fell far short of the punishment that would alter my behavior. And, I had long ago given up trying to please that teacher. Miss G sent notes home saying that I refused to play with the other kids in her class. After several of these notes, Mom finally wormed the truth out of me. Mom made a special trip to school to tell the teacher why I was rebellious. Miss G's response was that I should be adult enough to ignore the kids in Mr. Lowe's class. Mom tried to make her understand that she was grossly underestimating peer pressure. That teacher didn't listen. Instead, she spanked me repeatedly, sure that I would give in. She told me in front of the class that I ought to be mature enough to play with the younger kids. I wasn't impressed. Well, what did she expect? I was a ten-year-old boy, after all.

The second incident was simply emotional cruelty. One morning I walked into her class to find everyone staring at me without saying a word. Finally, Miss G said, "Don't you think you need to apologize to someone in here?"

This took me by surprise. I couldn't think of anything I had done or said to apologize for, and I said as much. Nobody there could accuse me of doing anything to them physically. My accuser must be a third party not present in that classroom. This person must have told someone there that I had insulted them, or said something nasty about them. I kept asking what I had done or said to hurt anyone. "You know what you did" was the response. I got no closer to an explanation than that. They sat there waiting, an angry teacher and five silent accusers. Forget the lessons for the day; Miss G wasn't going to end this until I apologized. So, I walked over to Jack and apologized.

"No! It's not Jack. You know who you need to apologize to." But, I didn't know. Completely cowed, I apologized to every person in the room, one at a time.

Miss G said, "Your apology wasn't sincere, because you apologized to all the wrong people." I shouldn't have apologized to anyone, since I wasn't guilty of anything. She obviously thought I was mocking her and the entire class. Exasperated, she spanked me with a board. Miss G was a large woman, about five foot eleven. I was ten years old and might have weighed seventy pounds. Justice was out of reach in her class; I just wanted to get it over with. Before she whipped me, I returned to my original claim that I didn't owe anyone an apology. It would have been much better if I had stuck to it. I never understood what caused this confrontation, but I suspected Jed was behind it. This was America, but I never had the chance to face my accuser.

That Christmas was another in a string of sad Christmases because Tracy broke another leg. Mom and Dad had known for two years that he had osteogenesis imperfecta, or brittle bones. A.P. and Grandma Richards drove up for the holiday, and we opened gifts in Tracy's hospital room. Grandpa was overcome when he first saw Tracy in traction. As Mom told me later, "This is a man who I'm sure never cried more than twice in his life, and my sons were the culprits both times." We were cheery for Tracy's sake, and for ours, too. Unfortunately, there would be more Christmases in the hospital. After the holidays, everyone got back to the daily grind. Hope, at last, entered the classroom. Miss G announced her engagement to be married at the end of the school year, and better yet, she was going to quit teaching. Needless to say, I was very happy. It was almost as good as having Christmas not in a hospital.

There was better news. A new special education teacher, Mrs. O, would be in the classroom observing and would be the new teacher next year. Toward the end of the year, Mrs. O clashed with Miss G over her treatment of me and Jack, but of me in particular. The turning point came when Miss G ridiculed me in front of the new teacher. Mrs. O objected, but not in front of the class. There was a sharp airing of opinions. All I knew was that everything suddenly improved. Jack and I weren't punished as often, and there was no more public ridicule. Mom didn't hear about their disagreement until the next year, when Mrs. O took over. The school year finally ended on what I considered an optimistic note.

A further ending was that Jed the neighborhood bully failed fifth grade. Over the summer, he approached me. "You are the only one that didn't make fun of me." I don't remember exactly how I responded, but I didn't take this as my cue to do what everyone else was doing, make fun of him.

Cross family (*left to right*): Ray, Mike, Tracy, Kay, and Regena, 1956. Author's collection.

Chapter 6

A World Lost

That summer of 1959, I went for my third and final time to the Texas Lions Camp. I met and talked to other kids enduring hardships. I befriended kids who had palsy, who couldn't walk, who couldn't see, who had lost arms and legs, and who had hemophilia. I saw these kids thriving, and I think it helped me have the courage to take on hard tasks later in life. A hundred and twenty boys and girls were divided up into units, each having the name of an Indigenous tribe. Mine was Fox Tribe. Is there a Native American tribe anywhere named Fox Tribe? Maybe, but I have my doubts. Some of the other units did have authentic Native American tribal names. Counselors called names and kids stepped forward to their units. My name was called, and I joined the other Foxes. Our counselor called the last name, and the little group followed him to our quarters. We turned onto a path that sloped down toward a bunk house with two wings meeting in a central lobby. Two rows of bunk beds ran the entire length of each wing. Audley Blackburn and I shared one of the two bunk beds nearest the door into the lobby. I had the bottom bunk because of my balance. Audley was the first totally blind person I had ever met. He said he went to the state school for the blind in Austin. I was interested in how he traveled and how he wrote. He was eager to show me how to punch out Braille characters using his slate and stylus. We immediately formed a team. I moved around a little faster than he did, so when we had to move quickly with the rest of the unit, he held my elbow, and we followed the others. He was perhaps in more danger doing this than if he went places on his own. But, we were kids, and we weren't as careful as we should have been. Knowing Audley did not change my mind about going to the blind school in Austin. I didn't want to live in Audley's world.

Every kid in camp had a physical disability. Some problems were obvious, while others weren't. As we looked at each other, we tried to guess each other's disability. Butch finally told us he was a hemophiliac. Others, like Alex, tried to hide it. But when you live in such close proximity with twenty boys, there's no hiding. One night after we were all in bed and the lights were out, someone switched the lights back on and caught Alex taking off his pants. One of his legs was missing. It is healing to be with a group of people from whom you don't have to hide your weaknesses. All our limitations were on display. If any of us were depressed, his outlook brightened when he saw the disabled kids around him smiling and having fun. Alex came out of his shell and told us that he lost his right leg at a gas station. His father's car was being worked on. He shouldn't have touched the jack, but he did; and the car fell on him, crushing his leg. We were sympathetic listeners. Several boys were on crutches. Their upper body strength was envied by the rest of us. They could do push-ups from a handstand. We were really impressed and careful not to make any of these boys angry.

Our days were taken up with swimming, arts and crafts, camping skills, organized games, and free time. Novice swimmers learned the basics in a pool three feet deep and several hundred feet across. When the basics were mastered, a camper moved into the second pool, which was seven feet deep. Alex quickly moved into the deep end where he proved to be the best diver. His remaining leg was so strong, he could leap higher off the diving board than anyone else in camp. As for me, I graduated from the shallow end to the deep end, the two ends being separated by a fence. You couldn't swim from one pool to the other. My new swim instructor on the deep end was an extraordinarily good-looking brunette. All the male counselors competed for her attention. She had me start with some exercises to help get comfortable with the deep end. Getting into the water while grasping the edge of the pool, I released my hold and sank to the bottom in a squatting posture. A thrust upward with my legs sent me quickly to the surface. After swimming, we returned to the bunkhouse for free time, which lasted right up to lunch. Unlike at home, the food in the lunch hall was plentiful. Pitchers of milk traveled up and down the table. Buttered cornbread was popular and disappeared quickly. It was crowded, so cafeteria staff made frequent rounds to replenish platters of meat and vegetables. Until then, I was a picky eater, but the vegetables were well seasoned and buttered. We were so active, we burned off all the calories we consumed. The campers observed a few budding romances. Some of the counselors from female units were extremely popular. We ten- and eleven-year-old campers considered this behavior very icky. After lunch was nap time. We were told not to swim on a full stomach. Even though our tribe had already been swimming, we were still forced to take a nap. After lunch, we spent two hours learning various arts and crafts. Then, it was back to the bunkhouse for free time. And then, it was dinner, 5 p.m. After a week of sizing each other up, the two wings met in the lobby in a massive pillow fight. It raged back and forth up and down through both wings, not ending till everyone was too tired to swing his pillow. Alex lost his prosthetic leg but proved even with one leg to be too elusive to catch. He leaped like Superman through the small opening between the top and bottom bunks to escape. A gang of boys chased him with pillows ready to smash him. Who would have believed that Alex could easily outrun his pursuers?

On the first Saturday night, all 120 campers sat in a building that had a stage. The counselors displayed their talents, whatever they might be. The sidewalks after the show were crowded. I was guiding Audley, but I couldn't use sound to help me navigate, because people stood around talking and making too much noise. I couldn't listen to my environment. Frustrated, I said to Audley, "Hang on. We're going to leave the sidewalk." If I couldn't use my ears, I'd use my feet to feel my way along a known path. So we went down into a ditch and followed it all the way back to the bunkhouse. Yes, the blind were leading the blind, but we arrived to an empty bunkhouse, and we took showers while there was still hot water.

The campers also had a talent show. Fox Tribe formed a chorus and sang the theme songs from the four branches of the military. As we practiced, the counselor directing us was walking back and forth listening.

Suddenly, he stopped and pointed straight at me. "You! Stop singing!"

Well, I was insulted. And, to add insult to injury, the military theme was my idea. However, I said nothing; that is, I sang nothing, just moved my lips.

During the second and final week, Fox Tribe went on an overnight campout at a place called Suddenly. I think the name referred to how abrupt the view was when you topped the hill. Well, Audley and I felt cheated. That night sitting around the campfire, we sang songs about "greasy, grimy gopher guts," and other equally romantic topics. We enthusiastically cooked on the campfire and then consumed hot dogs and hamburgers. The last event of the evening at Suddenly was a round of ghost stories. The counselors had prepared a grand finale. At the end of a particularly long and suspense-building story, the narrator said, "And he saw it!" At that instant, a spotlight illuminated a figure in a sheet screaming bloody murder. It was a heart-stopping moment.

Our day was at an end, and we set up cots and lay down in sleeping bags. Even though the month was July, I was cold. Next morning, we ate bacon and eggs cooked over a campfire, broke camp, and returned to the Fox Tribe bunkhouse. We arrived too late for swimming and too early for lunch.

Free time was scheduled every day, allowing ample opportunity to play games. The back porch ran the entire width of the bunkhouse, allowing plenty of space for shuffleboard and table tennis. Quite a few of us played chess, and a lively chess rivalry developed and thrived. I wasn't one of the better players but enjoyed it just the same. Audley brailled a deck of cards and taught several boys in our wing to read enough braille to play in the dark. For a while, a midnight poker game flourished. We were supposed to be asleep, but we were playing cards in the dark, having learned grade 1 braille from Audley. He brailled two corners of each card so that we could read them. But herein lay the problem. When it came time to lay down your cards, we each announced what kind of hand we held. Of course, everyone had to feel everyone else's cards. This led to lots of grabbing and yanking of cards, resulting in a certain amount of noise. Occasionally, we lost interest in the game and decided to play a prank. We purposely shuffled the deck, making the maximum noise. The point was to bring the counselors storming out of their quarters. They didn't sleep in the wings but directly behind the lobby. We wanted them to try to catch us, which they never did. They did try, but never succeeded.

One night the Foxes were ushered into the lobby for "we didn't know what." All wearing angry faces, the counselors proceeded to tell us how rotten and generally disobedient we all were; they had decided to punish us all for our own good. I think I've heard that line somewhere before. One by one our names were called. The offender went through a door, which closed behind him. A few minutes passed in dead silence. Then a terrible screaming and crying, interspersed with sounds of heavy blows on flesh, erupted from the room directly behind the lobby. The boy back there at the moment would beg for mercy in a pitiful voice, while the counselors shouted. Each boy went crying into one of the wings of the bunkhouse before the next boy was called forth from the lobby full of waiting, frightened boys. A counselor periodically stepped into one of the wings and threatened to whip the boys there again if they didn't stop whimpering. When I heard my name called, I limped through the door terrified and thoroughly cowed. Instead of a beating, a counselor told me it was a prank, and that I should yell and scream while he pounded the bed with a belt. My vocal cords were paralyzed with fright, and I couldn't manage more than a subdued grunt. My apparent bravery during a beating raised my reputation out there in the lobby, at least temporarily. The campers in Fox Tribe had been paid back in spades for those midnight poker games.

The day came to earn my swimming badge. The task was to swim the length of the pool twice. In preparation for my test, my instructor ordered everybody out of the pool. As I swam, she walked alongside me with a long metal pole, ready to extend it to me should I get into trouble. Although perfectly reasonable, this undermined my confidence. Was she and everyone expecting a disaster? So, I panicked and grabbed the pole that she was extending. The test was over; I failed. I lived down to what I thought her expectations were of me. My courage failed, not my skill. I was very disappointed in myself.

The two-week period was now drawing to a close. I said goodbye to Audley, and I wouldn't meet him again until forty-five years had passed. On the final night, we each received a Lions Club bandanna and a T-shirt with an emblem on it. We sat and watched campers receive awards for different camping skills and other accomplishments. Then Mom and Dad drove me, Kay, and Tracy to a hotel in Austin. We swam in the pool and generally had a good time. After checking out, we drove through San Antonio. By this time, the calendar flipped into August, and San Antonio was toasty to say the least. Mom opened a can of chocolate milk with a can opener. The temperature was above 100 degrees, so the milk bubbled out of the slit as Mom worked the opener. It was unbelievably hot; we were all happy to leave San Antonio and get home.

Summer couldn't end without a trip to Corpus Christi. Grandma Ruth was my favorite person in the whole world. Next was Aunt Betty. Seeing them was medicine. But, no matter where we were, the magic woman was Mom. Always reading medical books, she made some suggestions that our family doctor accepted. She gave us the best medicine, love in abundance. She thought about us and our welfare, both physical and spiritual, all day. It showed, especially when one of us kids was sick in bed. In addition to dosing us with pills and drops, she did small things to put smiles on our faces. I was once in bed with strep throat, and everyone else in the family had it too. As I lay there, she put a plate of steak smothered in onions on my desk, despite the fact that she was sick too. It wasn't everyday fare, and I knew it. This reminded me how important we were to Mom, because she did the same for everyone. She showered her love equally among her kids. And, Dad wasn't left out.

The next school year was an eventful one. Tracy started first grade. He was homebound because of his brittle bones. Kay, one year behind me, entered the fifth grade and seemed to be doing okay. However, this tenderhearted girl was being affected; she just didn't voice her feelings.

To paraphrase Charles Dickens, the sixth grade was the best of times; it was the worst of times. When I saw Dr. Gerard for a vision check, I pleaded for the IV glucose treatments to end. To my surprise and relief, he reluctantly agreed, saying that the treatments had ceased to be effective. I was eleven years old. Dr. Gerard's only worry was that stopping them might cause my vision to plummet. Considering my emotional state, now was the time to take that risk. I told Dr. Gerard I'd rather be blind than continue the IV treatments. I did, however, continue to take niacin tablets. The side effects from niacin were hot flashes that lasted about thirty minutes. During one of these episodes, I lit up like a Christmas tree; my nose and all of my joints flamed a bright red. However, I considered this trivial. Terminating the IV treatments, on the other hand, was major. It also really helped the family finances. As the doctor feared, I gradually lost more vision over the next year. It finally stabilized at around 20/800. Even so, halting the IV treatments made this the best of times. These were the best of times for another reason. Mrs. O, the new sight-saving teacher, agreed that I should stay in public school rather than go to the school for the blind in Austin. That was a relief to us all. Without the IV treatments my classroom consistency improved. I wasn't exactly studious, but my grades were average. I was no longer a D student in math. Mrs. O had progressive ideas about educating the blind. She introduced me to the Cranmer abacus, over which I was enthusiastic. Its beads were threaded on ten wires that lay on a red velvet bed. Each of the ten wires had two sections, with two beads in the upper section and four in the lower. This allowed you to represent a ten-digit number. You had to remember where the decimal point was; nothing on the abacus indicated where it was. It helped my ego to think I knew something the sighted kids didn't know. Mrs. O also taught us all touch typing, a skill that, in view of the emergence of the personal computer decades later, gave me an advantage in three different careers. This year I was in Mrs. Keller's class the second half of the day. For the first time, I enjoyed both halves of my school day.

These also were the worst of times. The physical pain was behind me, but the emotional pain lay ahead of me. The IVs had kept my vision from slipping away. When they stopped, my sight went into a severe decline. This was the background for what happened next. Three incidents came together to shape my life for the next six years and beyond. The first of these incidents was encouraging. One day in Mrs. Keller's class, there was a drill in math. Two kids at a time were sent to the board. I stood waiting, chalk in hand. She read out a long division problem. I didn't know where my knowledge of math ranked against the kids in Mrs. Keller's class, and I was grateful this was something I knew how to do. I solved the problem in my head and hurriedly wrote down the problem, showing all the steps like the teacher instructed us to do. I wrote it down, but not in the order she wanted. I wrote it in reverse order, starting with the answer. Since I already had the answer, I wrote it first and then showed the steps. Anxious not to be embarrassed, I wrote furiously, like I was demon possessed, and I wondered why everyone started to laugh. The other guy had barely touched the board. When they continued to laugh, I checked my answer to see if I had made a silly mistake, but I hadn't. My nose was almost on the board as I wrote, and I thought maybe that's why they were laughing. Or, maybe it was what they saw. Maybe my standing there, face against the blackboard, flailing arms, writing at top speed, was pure slapstick. Mrs. Keller said, "Well, Mike definitely won!" So, they weren't laughing at me; they were laughing with me. I returned to my seat, relaxed and smiling.

The second incident reinforced the first, and it started me thinking in a new direction. The competition that grew between me and Andy Reece set my life on a new path. Andy, who sat in the seat behind me, always told me his score on the previous day's test papers. Andy was studious, and so his grades were consistently better than mine. The girl I had a crush on was there listening. Tired of being embarrassed, I started to study at home, and one day I had the better score. Wow! This is better than candy! I knew Andy made straight A's. I thought, "I would like to do that! I wonder if I could."

The first two incidents seemed to open a door, but the third one slammed another in my face. It completely shattered my illusions. My vision suddenly went into free fall. I pretended the decline wasn't happening, but my denial ended on the playground. That afternoon Mrs. Keller's class played kickball, the boys against the girls. When it came my turn to kick the ball and run bases, the girl pitcher rolled the ball; I ran forward and kicked it solidly. I then turned and ran toward first base. When I couldn't find it, I dropped to hands and knees and crawled around looking for it. I pleaded with that base to come to me, but it kept its distance. It wasn't that base I looked for; I was looking for the door back into my world. A girl walked slowly up to me, and hesitated. We were on different ends of the same pain. I knew she didn't want to be the one to tag me out. That reluctant touch shattered my last illusion of belonging. Surrounded by sympathetic classmates, deeply ashamed, and profoundly alone, the gulf between them and me was too vast; I couldn't reach across it. I turned away, unable to hold back the tears. In that moment, I saw everything differently. The darkness in this new world wasn't a lack of light; it was a lack of hope. Isolation is much harder to bear than blindness. I didn't lose more vision that day, I lost an entire world. I remember thinking, "Whatever I do after today, I do alone." (I forgot about my mother. She wasn't going to let me face the world alone.)

I don't know the girl who tagged me out. My vision was so bad that even if I had looked up at her, I wouldn't have recognized her. Across all these years, I offer her my hand and say, "It's okay. You helped me. It had to happen."

My classmates were blameless. Any problem was mine, not theirs. The kickball incident was preceded by another, less painful moment, but nevertheless a forerunner of things to come. When the boys started playing softball, I was picked for a team. My vision hadn't yet fallen into the pit. I hit a home run my first at-bat. I stopped at every base, not knowing how far away the ball was. But my team yelled, "Keep running," and I did. My next at-bat was a triple. This time, I stopped too often to make it to home. Andy Reece brought me the bat my next at-bat. My previous hits were pure luck, because I never again hit the ball. My vision was failing even then, and shortly thereafter, the kickball game happened. Andy and the others were pulling for me, but I fell out of their world anyway. After these events, I made myself an untouchable; Andy didn't, and the other kids didn't. For the next six years and beyond, I was a recluse, despite being surrounded by people. When John Donne said, "No man is an island," he never met me.

That summer I didn't go to Lions Camp. This left me with plenty of time to consider what I wanted to do, and what my limits would allow me to do. I stopped trying to fit into the old, familiar world. I was looking for a new one. Meanwhile, I had to live in one that seemed to have rejected me. I put a barrier between me and everyone else, with the exception of Gerald. However, within another year, even Gerald was gone. I turned inward toward my immediate family. I had to decide who I was, who I could be, and who I wanted to be. I came to consider people outside my family as distractions. I substituted listening to talking books from the Library of Congress for social interaction. Did this or any world have a place for someone like me? Could I force it to make a place? I doubted it. My mind was full of dark thoughts. Unaware that there were any famous, successful blind people, I got only negative images of blind people from TV and radio. Selling pencils and light bulbs wasn't a life I wanted. The idea that ultimately solidified in my mind was that I couldn't be anything without an exceptional education. I didn't realize how far that thought was going to carry me.

At the end of that year, I announced to Mom and Dad that I would make straight A's in junior high. Mom later confessed to me that she didn't know whether I could accomplish that or not, but any parent is glad to hear their child say something like that.

Mom didn't spend a lot of time reading to me, but that would change drastically in junior high. We didn't know it, but the future was already being shaped. Mrs. Keller started telling her husband about me. Lonnie Keller would be the principal at the new junior high school I would attend in the fall.

Chapter 7
A World Discovered

The year 1960 brought changes to the Cross household on many fronts. Needing a hobby, Dad bought a short-wave radio and took the test for a General Class license. He passed and was given call letters K5UHF, a moniker that everyone envied. (UHF is an abbreviation for "ultrahigh frequency.") Through his ham radio, we kept in regular communication with Mom's family, because Grandpa A.P., Uncle Wilton, and Uncle Joe were all ham radio operators. No one except Dad, on his side of the family, had a license. On Saturday nights, we all joined a broadcast on forty meters. In ham talk such a confab is called a QSO. This gave us the privilege of talking to A.P., Grandma Richards, and Mom's brothers without running up a long-distance phone bill. All the cousins even got their turns to visit. We didn't know any other kids that got to talk to all their relatives all at once. It was almost as good as meeting face-to-face in a family reunion. Its novelty never failed to tempt us away from the television. When you spoke into the microphone, you couldn't hear a broadcast from anyone else. So, when you were finished speaking, etiquette demanded that you say the word "over" into the microphone. This habit was easy to pick up, allowing the conversation to flow smoothly. As much as we enjoyed these meetings in space, none of the kids ever got the ham radio bug, meaning that none of us ever took a test for a ham license. I studied the Morse code but didn't take the test on it for a Novice license. You didn't get to talk until you got a General Class license.

The bond between Mom and each of her kids was different. Mom was helping Kay advance in home economics skills. Rightly or wrongly, Mom saw herself as a nurse with Tracy as her patient. And, she helped me by reading to me and preparing me for tests. By 1960, Kay quietly supported Mom—cooking, sewing, and doing various other household chores. Without this pearl of a daughter and sister, Mom, indeed the whole family, would have been overwhelmed. Mom was determined that Tracy also should have some home economics skills. She found a pattern for cutting out a shirt; she also found a frayed bed sheet with a nice design in it. Under Mom's supervision,

Tracy cut out the pattern. Next, she sat him down in front of an old Singer sewing machine. He did everything, even sewing on the buttons. The shirt was good enough to become a regular part of his wardrobe.

All the kids were in school, and life in general was more demanding, more complicated, and faster paced. There was an important change in the grading system: 92 was a B, 84 a C, 75 a D, and anything below 75 an F. The family doctor signed papers allowing Tracy to be homebound. He started first grade; Kay was in sixth grade, her last year of elementary school; and I entered San Jacinto Junior High School, which housed grades seven through nine.

The day before classes started, Mom went with me to the open house. I met the seventh-grade counselor, Dean Cherry, who seemed genuinely concerned that my year go smoothly. He wanted to understand my physical limitations and how he could accommodate my needs. In 1960, blind students were exempted from physical education. I couldn't bring myself to mention the kickball episode from the year before; I was certainly relieved not to have to play sports with sighted kids. At last, he handed me a copy of my class schedule. Instead of PE, I had a study hall. I couldn't read it, so I passed the schedule over to Mom. Without her, I would have been totally lost. The only teacher I met that day was the special education teacher, Jane Brown, who would teach me math. It was a given that blind students never took math in other than a special education setting. I couldn't see the numbers above the classroom doors; instead, I counted doors. This was easier when the halls weren't full of people. Today gave me the chance to do this in a relaxed atmosphere. For each class on my schedule, I first found an obvious landmark, then counted doors until Mom told me we had reached the right one. We went through my entire schedule this way, more than once, hunting and counting doors. We were ready to go home when I could lead Mom through my schedule and stop at all the correct doorways. This would be a lot harder when the halls were full of noisy kids. Tomorrow, I would learn that navigating through a crowd is beyond inconvenient; for me, it is impossible. I move between landmarks, which are hard to find in a jostling crowd. I stop often to get my bearings while people flow around me. At these times, I'm aware of being an obstacle to traffic. I don't like the feeling of being in everyone's way.

The first day went okay; I didn't get lost, not once. But the second day didn't go well. On the way to my reading class on the second floor, I lost count because of the crowd. I took a seat in what turned out to be an eighth-grade

English class. Not yet having the reading teacher's voice clearly fixed in my memory, my ears didn't tip me off that I was in the wrong class. I wondered why I didn't hear my name at roll call, but because I felt inferior to everyone, I was too timid to raise my hand and ask why. The teacher collected papers after giving us a spelling test. Of course, my test paper had a name not on her roll. Seeing me in the hall, the seventh-grade reading teacher asked me why I hadn't been in class. I said I hadn't skipped class, and that she should have my test paper. During math class, Mr. Cherry called me to his office where we straightened everything out. The reading teacher figured out whose class I had gone to and retrieved my test paper. I was more concerned than the adults. I felt like a criminal.

We then discussed the problems I had moving between classes. Listening to Mr. Cherry, I realized how many people were watching out for me, helping me face my difficulties. The stairs were a cause for worry; I might be jostled away from the rail, which—because of my balance problem—I clung to for dear life. I slowed down the people on the stairs, because I moved so cautiously. I wouldn't climb the stairs unless I had a hand firmly on the rail. Another thing that really slowed me down was dealing with a locker. Its combination required me to twist the knob left, right, and left again. Unless I got all three numbers correct, the locker wouldn't open, and I had to clear it by spinning the dial through several revolutions. I had so little time that I couldn't afford to mess up. The problem was that I couldn't see any of the markings on the dial. I had read O. Henry's story, "A Retrieved Reformation," about Jimmy Valentine, giving me the idea to try my luck as a safecracker. So, I tried it. I turned the knob very slowly and heard faint clicks as the dial moved through the numbers. Each time the dial hit the correct digit, the click was a little different. Oh wow! It worked! I could have opened anybody's locker, but I needed absolute quiet. I couldn't do it with a hall full of noisy kids. This was a much bigger crime than just going to the wrong class. Needless to say, I never mentioned to anyone my ability to pick a lock. To solve these three problems—getting lost, being late to class, and managing stairs—I kept quiet about the locker issue. Mr. Cherry arranged for me to leave each class a few minutes early for the next class. After this accommodation was made, I never again got lost or was late. Without the mass of humanity in the halls, I counted doors correctly and used my locker. I moved around quietly and was always waiting outside my next class when the bell rang. Even with the extra time, using my locker slowed me down. One day, something happened to make me stop using lockers altogether. I found my locker the same way I found my classes. I counted lockers. On this day, I got the locker open only to discover that it wasn't my locker. I hurriedly closed it, found the right locker, and got my books for the next class. I never again opened a locker; instead, I carried everything around with me in a book satchel. Aside from these few hardships, on the whole, I was so grateful to my counselor and my teachers for their accommodations that I felt an obligation to be the best student I could be.

Reading was a struggle. My eye glasses were so strong that to bring the print into focus, I put my face so close to the book that my nose touched the page. The magnification was in a little bubble at the bottom of the lens for the right eye. I have no vision in my left eye. Looking through that little bubble only allowed me to see five characters. To read a line of print, I had to move my head back and forth across the page. I couldn't write with these glasses, because my nose got in the way. Pencil and nose needed to occupy the same space. The solution was to have a weaker, second pair of glasses that would allow me to move my face away from the page enough for my pencil to be where my nose used to be. During tests, I constantly switched between these two pairs of glasses. Not only did I read slowly, but the repeated switching was a further slowdown. I didn't have time to ponder a question, so I had to be ready to write the answer as soon as I finished reading. How was I to compensate for all the time I couldn't avoid wasting? My test preparation had to take wasted time into account.

Convinced that, without an exceptional education, I would have a dismal future, I let Mom and Dad know my fears. They both agreed to help me achieve all my education goals. Those goals weren't clear to me yet. At first, Mom only read books to me, but at my request, she soon got more involved. When I came home in the evenings, I ate supper prepared by either Mom or Kay, and then I allowed myself to watch, or rather listen, to thirty minutes of TV. Afterward, I sought Mom out and asked her to read. She never refused. Although Mom was glad to see me take such an interest in homework, I owe a lot to her for her support and dedication. This year marked a turning point in my life. New routines hardened into a discipline. In Mrs. Tally's seventh-grade English class, I learned to outline, a skill I applied in all current and future classes. I recognized that knowing how to outline was invaluable.

Semesters were broken into two nine-week periods. When the first nine-week report cards came out, I had made an A in everything. This was my goal, but I didn't know if I could achieve it. Reinforced by this success, my study habits became entrenched. Mom didn't have enough time to go around. She couldn't devote all her time to reading my books, taking care of a second disabled son, taking care of a daughter, being a wife, and running a house too. In addition to all that, the strain on her voice was terrific. Dad bought a tape recorder to minimize the time she spent reading. Mom was relieved to be able to read a chapter only once. I listened to these tapes over and over. While I listened, I made a detailed outline, stopping the recorder occasionally to put a thought in its proper place in the outline. The night before a test, I challenged Mom to stump me. I handed her the textbook and my outline of it, which I had memorized. I told her to ask me anything. Everything was fair game, even asking me to quote a caption under a picture in the text. My instructions were, "Don't ask a question you think I can answer. Ask me the questions you think I can't." When thirty minutes passed without my missing an answer, I declared that I was ready. Not only do I owe Mom a debt of gratitude, but I owe the same debt to the rest of the family.

Dad saw me becoming more studious and intellectually inquisitive. One night, he invited me to accompany him to a lecture in downtown Houston. We picked up two of his friends from the Port of Houston, Hank Mahallic and Zack Davis. Zack and Hank made me feel as if it were natural for me to be in their company. I felt privileged to be with these men. We walked into the large auditorium and took our seats. The news was full of people claiming to have sighted a UFO, unidentified flying object. Our speaker was George Van Tassel. For the next two hours, he told us how he had been kidnapped by extraterrestrials and reeducated. Most members of the large audience were pretty skeptical, including the four of us. He claimed to have received wisdom from a group of aliens called the council of seven lights, and he had written a book about the experience. A student from Rice University asked him a long, involved question that I didn't understand. But, I was impressed and wanted to understand. Dad said, "Well, study hard, and someday you will." On the way home, my mind was opened to new possibilities. The fact that I was here in adult company being treated as one of them, the fact that they asked me what I thought, made me see myself in a new light. Dad was recognizing that I was moving into manhood. He was no longer perceiving me as a child. I had lost one world. Was Dad showing me that there are others? He let me come into his world that night, and I was accepted. After this, our relationship changed. Dad didn't read to me, or coach me like Mom did, but he became the encourager, like Barnabas in the book of Acts. He made an effort to praise me at meaningful times.

Listening to talking books also developed and encouraged me. I received books like *Twenty Thousand Leagues Under the Sea*, *David Copperfield*, and the *Hornblower* novels about the British Royal Navy. Talking books had many benefits—listening expanded my vocabulary, corrected my pronunciation, and moderated my Texas accent.

A few days before summer break, Mr. Cherry called me to his office. "At the assembly tomorrow, you will be called to the stage to receive the Academic Excellence Award. Will you have any trouble climbing the steps to the stage?"

His announcement was altogether unexpected, but I recovered quickly. "No, sir. If I walk slowly, I can get on stage with no problem."

"Good," he said. "This award is given to students who have made straight-A report cards all year."

Needless to say, I left school that day on cloud nine. I think Mom was just as gratified as I was. And, my cloud was even higher because 92 was a B. All the work that Mom and I had put into my schoolwork had paid dividends. Instantly, repeating this became my yearly goal. Holding myself to this standard drove my thinking and helped me focus on the future. After that day, I never doubted the value of intensive study. In fact, my appetite for it came to dominate my life. Many times over the next several years, I pressured Mom to devote hours prepping me for one exam or another.

The summer following seventh grade, Dad drove us to Dallas to visit Mom's Aunt Hazel and her husband, Horace, an executive at the Nabisco Corporation. Families were larger in the early part of the twentieth century, and so it wasn't unusual that Mom was six months younger than her aunt. As girls, they had hung around together like sisters. Not having seen each other in fifteen years, they had lots to talk about. Hazel showed Mom and Dad around her beautiful home. It was very nice, since Horace was an executive. While they were catching up and laughing over fond memories, we kids played with cards, but mostly with Trouble, their spaniel.

The next day, we drove to Fort Worth to visit Dad's brother Wesley and his wife, Lilly. She was in and out of the hospital until her death, because a surgeon had removed a large portion of her stomach. Despite this, Uncle Wes was the jolliest man I've ever met. He would be a perfect Santa Claus. He always listened to children and answered as if they were adults. This alone endeared him to all us kids. I was impressed when Dad told me that Uncle

Wes worked for General Dynamics and had worked on the line building B-36 bombers. We walked through one at Carswell Air Force Base. It was an immense red and blue airplane. I was overawed by its range and bomb load. Built after 1949, it played no part in World War II. These bombers were capable of flying to Europe and back without refueling. But being still a kid, the job I really wanted was Uncle Wesley's previous job in an ice cream factory. He still always had some in the house, and he liked to put a spoonful of vanilla ice cream in his coffee. The memory that lingers in my mind is Uncle Wes drinking a cup of coffee, listening to us kids, and saying, "Why, sure. Tracy, you're a little chatterbox. You must-a been vaccinated with a Victrola needle." Except for Mom and Dad, we had him to ourselves because Uncle Wes's son and daughter were both married and living elsewhere.

Next, we went on to Cooper, Texas, where Dad's Aunt Alice lived. She was a widow, her husband having been gassed in World War I. He came home a broken man and died not long afterward. Everyone was attracted to Aunt Alice, probably because she made whomever she was talking to feel special. She called everybody kid or kiddo. Her conversation was never about herself, and her questions showed genuine interest. While you were answering, she was putting delicacies in front of you. I can still hear her saying "Well, kid, would ya like another piece-a pie?" When everyone was busy gorging themselves on apple pie, she sat down at the kitchen table across from Dad. "Well, kid, what do ya think?" Aunt Alice was eager to hear news about Dad's brothers Calvin and Wesley, and sister Helen, who lived far away in California. Dad said nothing memorable: No one got shot, or went to jail, or even got in a fight. Eventually, Mom noticed that we were restless. After a decent interval of time, Mom and Dad said goodbye, and we all trooped out to the car.

It was on to Greenville to meet another platoon of aunts, uncles, and cousins, this time on Mom's side of the family. Grandpa A.P. had eleven brothers and sisters, all of whom begat generously. Every time I turned around, there was another cousin, or two, or three. I couldn't keep them straight. Finally, we had seen almost everyone. So ended our restful summer. This period came after several unrelenting years of disaster. Mom and Dad needed this peaceful time to recharge emotionally and to see faces they hadn't seen since before life got bogged down with all the problems.

Back home, one of Kay's friends offered us a beautiful black puppy. We had recently fenced in the backyard, and so Mom and Dad agreed to let her have it. Part cocker spaniel and part walking hound, the dog went without a name until a salesman knocked at the door one day soon after we got her. This so scared the dog that she yelped in fright and peed on the floor. Kay immediately named her Sissy, and it stuck. Sissy was so gentle that Mom thought Tracy could play with her and not get hurt. There was no question whose dog she was, but since Kay played a lot with Tracy, Sissy seemed like the perfect dog for the pair of them.

Tracy, who rarely left the house because of his body cast, was starved for companionship. Kay and I were at school all day, leaving Tracy without any kids to talk to. One afternoon, as he lay in the corner on his pallet, Mom saw a mouse in her kitchen. She snatched up a broom and started pounding the floor as the mouse jumped around.

Tracy raised himself as much as he could and pleaded, "Stop! Don't kill it! It likes me." Mom continued beating the floor, but it got away. Although the mouse was spared, Tracy was upset that Mom didn't let it visit him.

Academically, eighth grade went very much like seventh grade, except that one of the courses was American History, not Texas History. I enjoyed every subject, especially history, English, and science. Mom continued preparing me for tests. If I had any doubts about the value of her coaching, they vanished in my battle with American History. One day the teacher divided the class into two teams. She went around the room in seating order asking questions about the American Civil War. When anyone answered incorrectly, a person on the other team across the aisle was asked the same question. This continued until someone answered correctly. Several times, a question circuited the room and came to my seat, and because of my thorough preparation, I was ready with the answer.

In science, we had divine help learning about the weather. Mother Nature arranged a spectacular demonstration of her power. That year, Hurricane Carla disrupted life all up and down the Texas coast. Covering much of the Gulf of Mexico, it came ashore at Port O'Connor, about 150 miles south of Houston. Its winds were strongest at Port O'Connor, 145 miles per hour, but they weren't weak in Houston either, close to a mere 100 miles per hour. Our streets flooded, and we sheltered in place for days. Gradually, all the houses on our block lost power except ours. Dad relayed messages over his ham radio and later received an Amateur Radio Relay League award for service during an emergency.

A medium-sized, heavy-set black dog sought shelter from the hurricane on our front porch. No one knows how he got into the garage with Sissy, but he did. The storm ended, and the dog's owner showed up to claim him. We weren't surprised when Sissy had a litter of puppies. We kept one, a black-and-white male with wavy hair. All through my teenage years, whenever I needed a break from study, I enjoyed tossing a ball for Sam to fetch, which he did, or else I would have never found it. But, most of the time, I was too busy to go outside and play with a dog.

I wrote my first term paper in Mrs. De Graphenreed's eighth-grade English class on the topic of hummingbirds. Its title was "The Littlest Acrobat." When Dad bought me the *Plain English Handbook*, I memorized a long list of conjunctions and their meanings. That book cemented my knowledge of grammar. I discovered that I liked composition and playing with words.

I barely had a life outside of studying, but what there was involved Gerald. Jed, the neighborhood bully, had two favorite targets, Gerald and me. He lay in wait for us, making it hazardous for us to visit each other. He focused on me because I was such an easy victim. But he was about to disappear from the landscape of my life. By the time I was thirteen, Jed had been stalking me for five years. Suddenly, I hit a growth spurt, changing the balance of power. Standing five feet, eight inches tall and lifting weights, I was no longer an easy target. Now unafraid of Jed, I wrestled him one day at Gerald's. To me it was a wrestling match, but to Jed it was a fight. I didn't realize it was anything more until Jed left crying. This was the end of our encounters. But he still ambushed Gerald on the way to my house. Since Gerald came less often to my house, I went to his instead. With my newly acquired power, I didn't bully Jed, but someone else did. Jed's world was suddenly turned on its head. A bigger bully arrived in the neighborhood. The new guy ignored me and Gerald but targeted Jed. Now Jed left us alone, because he was hiding from the other bully.

On a hot Friday afternoon, Dad stood watching me do what he referred to as the "telephone book exercise." In this exercise, your heels rest on the floor while the balls of your feet are on the telephone book. The exercise was to stand on tiptoes and then lower your heels back down to the floor. I did three hundred repetitions, never having done that many and not suspecting the price I was going to pay. I took my barbells to Gerald's and spent the night. Next morning, I awoke realizing something was wrong. My legs were as hard as a brick and extremely sore. Not remembering that I had gotten the Salk vaccine, my moan was pitiful. "Gerald! I've got polio!" In a calmer moment, I would have realized what the problem was. That morning Gerald walked down the sidewalk, telling me where to turn, while I crawled behind him a block and a half home. That journey was agony because I carried the barbells across my shoulders. Of course, my hands weren't free. I wasn't crawling on all fours, but walking, squatted low to the ground. I was unable to straighten my legs; they would only open about 45 degrees. So, I groaned at every painful step. The ordeal seemed to last hours. When I finally struggled up onto our front porch and put the barbells down, Dad helped me into the house. He reassured me that I didn't have polio; I had just exercised too much. Good! But, my relief didn't make it stop hurting.

My grades were so important to me that I dropped almost everything else. As I became more studious, Gerald and I seldom saw each other. I also seldom saw Jack after that year. I began telling my few friends that I couldn't play. Instead of spending time with friends, I stayed home and studied—effectively ending any social life I had left. Most kids' lives bloom in their teen years, but mine started to pass without anything happening.

My only other meaningful social contacts were in my extended family, and most of those were infrequent. The cousins that lived close to us were both at least ten years my senior. We did enjoy visiting Grandma Cross. Her movements were ponderous, and her speech was slow and thoughtful. We kids watched and listened carefully to this lady from an earlier, Nordic world. Dad often on his way to the Port of Houston dropped me or Kay off at Grandma's house for the day, and picked us up on his way home that night. Grandma Cross still didn't trust herself to watch Tracy well enough to keep him from getting hurt. My family used to tease me unmercifully, saying that my sense of taste and smell needed a drastic recalibration. One day on the way to visit Grandma, I suddenly sat bolt upright in the back seat and said, "I smell hamburgers." This was an unfortunate thing for me to say, because we were passing a sewage treatment plant. There was disbelief in that car, then raucous laughter. We never again passed that plant without someone saying "Yum, I smell hamburgers."

It was becoming apparent to everyone how truly advanced Kay's homemaking skills were. When Grandma's renter asked for pointers on cleaning and cooking, Grandma recommended Kay as a helper. Although Kay was only eleven years old, she spent the day ironing, cleaning, and cooking. The renter's young wife boiled beans without having first washed out the dirt and rocks. As you would expect, the result was nothing you would want to eat. Kay demonstrated how to make Southern cornbread and cook a big pot of pinto beans, which the renters both thought were marvelous.

At the end of my eighth-grade year, Mr. Cherry didn't let me know that I would receive an award. So, on the next to last day, when sixth period was over, I went to the bus instead of to the auditorium. At the assembly, Mr. Keller called my name to present me with the Academic Excellence Award, but I wasn't there to receive it. I had missed the announcement about the assembly. There was one more day of school. Mr. Cherry called me to his office. He was puzzled because he knew I had been at school the previous day. I was surprised when he presented the award to me. This restored my confidence. I stopped doubting that I could earn awards. From then on, my expectations of myself were high.

Another summer was upon us. Mother wanted to visit her college roommate, Anna Francis in Bartlesville, Oklahoma. Tracy set up a squawk when Dad said he had to leave his pet rooster at home. "Who's going to take care of him? He will die!" This was unlikely, since once before in our absence, that chicken had traveled freely around the neighborhood, even going in and out of stores in the nearby shopping center. Maybe Mom remembered this and was afraid of what trouble it would get into this time. For whatever reason, she gave in. "Okay, okay! We'll take the chicken, but I don't like it!" We headed north into stormy weather. We ran into a thunderstorm about fifty miles from the Oklahoma border. Lightning split the night, and a tremendous thunderclap deafened us all. The rooster jumped straight up and had a brief but furious attack of the squirts. It literally scared the crap out of that bird.

Mom exclaimed, "Pee-yoo! What is that smell?"

Tracy came to the defense immediately. "It's not my rooster's fault. He was scared."

Thankfully, I sat on the far side of the back seat from the bird. Kay, who wasn't so lucky, giggled.

Dad said, "A new fragrance is born, Fowl #5." This was, of course, a reference to a perfume on the market.

The bird was not the only one scared. The storm wasn't finished with us. A ball of lightning hit the ground and started rolling toward the car. Dad was already thinking the Red River would be too swollen to cross because it had been raining hard for hours. That ball of fire made his mind up for him. He turned the car around, and we left in a hurry. Dad didn't want to disappoint Mom, but he decided we didn't need to see Oklahoma.

That was a smelly trip. The rain was coming down in sheets, so rolling down the windows to air out the car was a bad idea. I don't know what the others did, but I held my nose for hours, breathing through my mouth. We drove by Aunt Alice's house about midnight. It was raining so hard that we drove straight through Cooper without stopping. That night was a real toad strangler. Good thing we didn't stop! Aunt Alice's roof had collapsed; she was cursing and mopping. Dad called her later, and she said if we had stopped, she would have handed each of us a mop and said, "Now work." But, we drove on through, not stopping till we got to Great-Grandma Richards's farm in Campbell, Texas. Dad got out and knocked on the front door. Great-Grandma's two elderly unmarried daughters were surprised, but welcomed Dad, who signaled us to get out of the car, which we did. I was relieved to get out of the car. Not only were my legs cramped, but my nose was sore from holding it pinched shut for hours. The rain was coming down hard, making it necessary to run across to the porch steps. The rooster stayed in the car, at least for the moment, although I think Dad eventually put its oversized cage on Great-Grandma's back porch. It paid for its sins by being thoroughly soaked.

Next morning, there was little evidence of the previous night's storm. While one daughter cooked, the rest of us assembled in the living room full of mismatched couches and chairs. Great-Grandma was the oldest woman Kay had ever seen. The daughter not occupied in the kitchen stood behind Great-Grandma's rocker, combing out her long white hair until it touched the floor. While waiting for breakfast, the daughter entertained us with two stories about Mom and Dad. Here are those stories in my words.

In 1945, Mom lived in San Diego working for the Navy department. When the Merchant Marines discharged Ray Cross, he set about looking for a car so that he and Regena could move back to Texas. He finally found a Studebaker, but it hadn't been driven in four years. War rationing made gasoline and rubber tires hard to get. Covered with four years' accumulation of leaves, the only visible parts of the car were its windows. Ray bought it even though it had no tires and its gas tank was rusted out. He put on tires, mounted a gallon milk jug on the trunk, filled it with gas, and ran a rubber tube from the jug over to the engine. He did nothing else to the car; and that's the way Regena Cross saw her new car. That night being warm, the neighbors were all relaxing on their front porches. The appearance of this pile of leaves moving slowly down the street caused universal howls of laughter. Ray got out of the car, unhooked the milk jug, and emptied it into a gasoline can. Regena was dismayed. Over the next few days, Ray replaced the gas tank, and together they cleaned off the leaves to find a gleaming maroon car. The upholstery and rugs needed to be replaced because the car had been used as a dog house. After all the improvements, no one was laughing any more. They packed up their belongings and drove back to Cooper, Texas.

Ray entered East Texas State Teachers College on the GI Bill, majoring in engineering. He switched to education because, as he said later, "at the end of World War II engineers were a dime a dozen." In 1949, Ray Cross was teaching sixth grade in Tyler, Texas. Regena was a twenty-eight-year-old young mother. She had just witnessed a big black dog trounce the family pet. During that time, everyone was leery of strange animals, fearing they might have hydrophobia. Afraid for her two young children, Regena retrieved Ray's rifle from the closet and stepped to the back door. She whistled to the dog, who was about to enter the woods. When he turned his head, she put a bullet just forward of his left ear. When Ray came home, he found the body behind the house in the woods. "He never knew what hit him," Dad always said when telling the story. Regena had never fired a gun in her life. Ray Cross married a kitten; that evening, he glimpsed a tiger.

We looked at our parents with new eyes. Our mom, what a woman! Our faith in Mom and Dad, who never let us down, was now ironclad. Our confidence in both of them was unshakable.

Suddenly, smells from the kitchen captured everyone's attention, and the cook called us to table. After a hardy country breakfast of toast, bacon, and farm-fresh eggs, we walked through fields full of hundreds of chirping baby chicks. Seeing her chance to dump the rooster, Mom finally convinced Tracy, after some fast talking, that his pet would love it there with all those girl chickens. Tracy cried a little but gave in to her arguments. We never had another opportunity to visit Mom's roommate in Oklahoma, but we left the farm minus one rooster. (That rooster never crowed when he was with us, but started crowing at the farm.)

Until I started the ninth grade, there had been no friction with students, teachers, or the school administration. Again, the day before classes started, Mom found my classrooms and helped me count doorways, telling me if I missed one. My special education class was Algebra 1. I was worried that I was behind in my knowledge of math, but I needn't have worried. I would find that out in one of my other courses, science, which made extensive use of algebra. (This would give me the confidence to make a decision that confronted me at the end of the tenth grade.) The first time I went to this class (the period before lunch) I got a surprise—it was an advanced science class. The teacher, Mr. Skarda, met me at the door and told me there was no room in his advanced class for a blind student. He said this was a mistake, and I needed to take something else. I told him I had made straight A's for the last two years, and I intended to stay. My timidity was gone. Afraid he would try to flunk me out of his class, I studied the book intently. Mom read the material, but I could tell she wasn't grasping it. In class, I wasn't mistreated. I was always prepared, and at the end of the first nine-week reporting period, my average test score was 98. After that, Mr. Skarda wasn't worried. He took an interest in how I was doing in my other classes. On one occasion, he even talked to another teacher about a question I had in her class. It was about pigmentation versus wavelength, not my behavior. I was a strict rule keeper. I tried very hard not to give my teachers any cause for complaint.

One October afternoon, Kay and I came home from school to find Mom sitting on the couch watching the television intently. Because this was so unusual, Kay asked, "Mom, what's wrong?"

Without taking her eyes from the screen, she replied in a frightened voice, "We're on the brink of World War III."

The US Navy was blockading Cuba, and the Soviet Union was making threats. The world was on the edge of nuclear war. When Dad arrived home, he and Mom went into the bedroom, shutting the door behind them. We listened to the news, yet we could hear voices from the bedroom. I don't remember what Tracy was doing, but Kay and I walked into the backyard to have our own discussion.

"What do you think, Mike?"

"Kay, do you remember when my Sunday school class went on a progressive dinner?"

She nodded, forgetting that I couldn't see her body language. Finally, she said, "Yes, I do."

I responded, "Well, one of the houses we visited for one of the dinner courses had a bomb shelter in the backyard. I went down into it. It was tiny. There was food and water for a few weeks, but what then! When you come out after a nuclear exchange, what would be left? Nothing! The infrastructure would be rubble and there would be dead people and animals everywhere. I don't want to survive a nuclear war."

Kay listened. When she spoke, she didn't sound afraid. "If it happens, we might as well stand here in the yard and watch the missiles come in."

I'll never forget that conversation. I was absolutely sure there wouldn't be a place in such a world for any of us, but especially for me or Tracy. Next day, Dad drove a new Chevy home and started packing it with food, water, and clothes. Kay and I thought there was nowhere to go to get away from a nuclear disaster. Dad said, "We'll go to East Texas, out in the sticks." A day or two later the crisis had passed, and life resumed its usual pace. But, it did leave its mark on our family. We had a new car. And, a second outcome of the Cuban Missile Crisis was that Dad installed a mobile short-wave radio in the car. His thinking was that if we had to become refugees, we needed a way to communicate with the rest of the world. Grandpa A.P. bought a new mobile rig for his car and gave his old Swan rig to Dad. After that day, every ham operator in the family had a ham radio in his car.

Later that year, Tracy broke his leg again. Mom and Dad took him to the emergency room and demanded that no one touch him except Dr. Harrington, his bone specialist. The call was placed, but Dr. Harrington was in a car wreck on the way to Pasadena. They wondered why he didn't come; unknown to them, he was in the hospital being treated. Time crawled by slowly as Mom and Dad held Tracy, passing him back and forth to keep up their strength. Tracy had been there nine hours when Dr. Harrington's partner showed up. This being broken leg number five, Kay and I were used to seeing Mom and Dad under pressure. Though not directly involved, we were under stress too, not being aware of what was happening. We weren't afraid that Tracy would die, but we should have been, because he came close more than once.

Heretofore, all my English teachers had been women, so Mr. Terry was a new experience. A big man, he walked around the classroom quoting poetry or from a play. We read Charles Dickens's *Great Expectations*. I think he read to us, fearing that we wouldn't get the flavor of the work otherwise. I certainly remember how he sounded. Once during the year, he allowed himself to be diverted, something that the students never quit trying to do. He had been a weather observer in the US Army. That day, he gave us a short lecture on cloud formations. The class's attempts to divert him never again worked.

World Geography class, even more than the science class, stands out in my memory. Mrs. Eversmeyer finished tapping the map on the wall with her long pointer.

She turned and addressed the class. "Do you understand me, people?" We said we did.

An air raid alarm sounded, and Mr. Keller's voice came over the public address (PA) system. "Students, whenever you hear this alarm, you are to file into the hall, sit down, and cover your heads. Your teachers will have more instructions at this time. Listen carefully." And the PA went silent.

Mrs. Eversmeyer talked for a few minutes about civil defense and said we should not panic. This was another "Do you understand me, people?" moment.

I raised my hand and asked innocently, "Do we go to our next class after the crisis is over?" I may as well have asked what to do after a thunderstorm. That was the only time I ever heard Mrs. Eversmeyer laugh. There was a moment of silence followed by a universal roar.

World Geography was memorable for another quite disturbing reason. Students must adjust to the way a teacher gives tests. It is especially true in my case. Mrs. Eversmeyer's World Geography class pushed my study habits to the limit. The first time she gave an open-book test, something I had never encountered, I felt that my weak point was being exploited. Open-book tests were supposed to be easier because you could look in the book for answers to questions on the test. And, since they were easier, open-books were unannounced. My reading speed was below a snail's pace. By the time I could have looked up anything, the class period would have long ago ended. Even though this put me at a further competitive disadvantage, I didn't question a teacher's right to give an open-book test. I didn't do well on the first one. The teachers at San Jacinto had always given me every chance to succeed, but this was war! I had to prepare every day for an unannounced open-book test. Well, I was used to overcoming disadvantages. Every challenge was a contest I had to win. Demanding perfection from myself, I was determined to make 100 percent on every test no matter how hard it was. The problem was that my reading speed was too slow for me to use the book during a test. My only resource then was my memory. That would have to be adequate. I had been making outlines of my textbooks since seventh grade. Mere familiarity with the outline in here wasn't going to be enough. I would have to memorize the text. But, I was almost doing that anyway. In fact, I really had studied that way for American History last year. The hardship would be to prepare that way every day. Otherwise, it was nothing new. In my study of American History, I naturally resorted to this strategy since it was so full of important dates and names. I listened to the tapes carefully, over and over. As a result, I seldom had a history test paper that wasn't perfect. I'm not brilliant; I'm just very determined not to be defeated by any challenge. I was willing to make any effort to succeed. Because of this experience, I started to overprepare for everything. I relied more and more on my memory, and it was getting stronger. This would prove very important in Algebra 2. Memory is like a muscle; the more you use it, the better it gets. Conversely, the less you use it, the worse it will be.

Just when I thought my life couldn't get more complicated, I dropped and broke my reading glasses, and there was no money to replace them. The left lens was completely gone, and all that remained on the right side was the lower third of that lens. Fortunately, it contained the bubble I looked through. Unfortunately, it sat at the bottom of a shard of glass in the shape of a sawtooth. Putting the glasses on brought my eye in close proximity to broken glass. Mom covered the top two thirds with tape. In order not to block light, she used Scotch tape. Classmates and teachers never said a word about my weird glasses. Of course, I was cautious when switching glasses. During the next open-book, I wrote down the answers while everyone around me was flipping pages. As the years passed, I began to believe that every hardship I had to cope with equipped me to deal with a later challenge. Everything that happened seemed to prepare me for future successes. My religious upbringing made me think that there was a hand in my life, bringing me challenges to overcome and opportunities that forced me to make choices. So, as hardships came along, I started to wonder what new challenges I was now prepared to face.

With all the pressure in our lives, we needed time to relax and unwind. We found it in front of the TV. Of course, we had to endure the commercials, which we considered propaganda. All of us were confirmed skeptics. We began quoting passages out of not only good movies, but more often bad ones. That went doubly for commercials. These sales spots were wasted on the Cross household; we didn't believe a word of it, no matter what the message was. In fact, the better the promise, the more we disbelieved it. If we could parody a sales pitch, the more memorable it was. Our favorites were those whose message could be misquoted, or even distorted. One commercial, in particular, contributed to Mom's extensive arsenal of threats. In that commercial, John Goodman is slapped, and says, "Thanks, I needed that." His response meant "thanks for bringing me to my senses." That commercial had its roots in scenes from both literature and movies. In a movie—I forget which one—the leading man and his leading lady ended a dispute by slapping each other. The very next scene showed them exchanging wedding vows. We were supposed to understand that the slaps woke them to the realization that they were in love. At first, we simply quoted John Goodman. "Thanks, I needed that." But, more humorous to us was imagining what the person doing the slapping was thinking. Mom speculated that the person thought "I ought to slap a slat out of you." Since Mom never struck anyone, she replaced it with a question. "Would you like me to slap a slat out of you?" This became Mom's standard way of saying, to usually me or Tracy, "You need to come to your senses and not be so ridiculous." Other people might say, "Get outta here," or "I've never heard anything so stupid in my life!" This turned Mom into the perfect drill sergeant—or so she thought. She did issue threats to keep Tracy from doing something she perceived as dangerous. All her threats were empty. Eventually, Mom realized that we didn't take any of them seriously. They got to be a joke. One of us, usually Tracy, would do something just to hear her issue a threat. Knowing that she was being teased, Mom would ask that "slap a slat out of you" question in an amused voice. A more serious and very effective warning was "I guess you don't like chocolate milk, do you!" That stopped Tracy in his tracks every time.

The summer after I finished ninth grade was especially memorable, because it was my first trip outside Texas. One June day, we packed up the Chevy and headed north to visit Mom's older brother, Wilton, and family in Brigham City, Utah. He had moved his family up there to work for a company producing rocket fuel for the space program. The mobile short-wave radio made that trip much more bearable. Our first night on the road, we listened to sailors on an aircraft carrier somewhere in the Pacific. They called home via a telephone patch to different American cities. These conversations were boring, but the fact that we were listening to an aircraft carrier excited all us kids. At several stages of our journey, Dad was able to tell Wilton where we were. We also talked to Mom's brother Joe and his family, who were traveling through the Grand Tetons.

The second day, we drove into southern Utah, visiting Zion National Park. Four hours out of Brigham City, everyone needed a potty break, so we stopped at a roadside geyser. Dad was carrying Tracy, Mom was guiding me, and Kay was trailing along behind Dad. We came to a wide ditch, and Mom said, "Take a big step." I interpreted big to mean high. Wrong! She should have told me to take a "broad step," but she didn't elaborate. So, I lifted my leg high in the air, thinking I needed to step over a tall barrier. I planted my foot in the ditch, dead center, drenching myself with stagnant water from the pool around the geyser. This pulled Mom off balance, and she almost fell in the ditch beside me. But hardly any water splashed her. Needless to say, we didn't stay there long.

"Well, isn't this just great! Now you smell worse than an outhouse! Ray, can you take Mike to the public restroom?"

"Yes. I'll take Tracy, too."

Kay and Mom went to the lady's room. Meanwhile, in the men's room, I scraped mud and went over my blue jeans with wet paper towels, to no effect. I was so wet that I needed to remove my jeans and ring them out, but I wasn't about to do that surrounded by strangers. I was grateful for the silence. No one said anything. But I was afraid they were thinking, "Yeah, we see teenagers frolicking in stagnant pools every day." At that moment, I fervently wished to be the invisible man. It was a relief to hide in the car, but we all had to smell me for the rest of the trip. Traveling at speeds above fifty-five blew away the odor, but whenever we drove slowly through a town, the stench overwhelmed us. Four hours in a sixty-mile-per-hour breeze left me still more than damp, but not sopping wet. Finally, Dad said, "What's that perfume again, Fowl #5? I don't think it'll ever sell." If we hadn't been close to our destination, nobody would have laughed at this. But deliverance was at hand. Once again, the short-wave radio helped. It occupied our minds, even when our noses were punishing us. Tuning around the dial, listening to the BBC, Radio South Africa, Radio Ireland, and Radio Moscow, we could almost ignore the stench in the car. We arrived at midnight, and I immediately stripped and took a bath.

I was amazed by three things in Brigham City, Utah—how dry the climate was, how late the sun shone in the sky, and how soft the grass was. It was Kentucky bluegrass, and it totally captivated me. It was so, so soft! Like our family, Uncle Wilton and Aunt Christine had two boys and a girl. Tracy, Kay, and I each had a playmate of the same gender, but a few years younger than we were. I paired with Randy, Kay with Martha, and Tracy with Larry. Full of pent-up energy from having been pinned down for countless hours in a car, we all went wild. Mom kept yelling at Tracy to slow down, which he did until her back was turned. I spent the days playing the organ by number, eating Bing cherries off a huge bush in the front yard, and listening to cousin Randy practice the oboe. Tracy and Kay were similarly occupied with Martha and Larry, although they didn't torture their parents with the oboe.

Several days after our arrival, most of the family drove to Bear Lake. I stayed behind with Randy and Aunt Christine because he had oboe lessons. Although I wasn't along on the trip, I heard about it. They stopped about a hundred yards below Ricks Spring. Tracy couldn't resist taking a drink from this cold, crystal-clear stream. Always on the watch for danger, Mom let him know she didn't like it. She was always saying, "Don't you have any sense?"

She was skeptical of me but absolutely positive that Tracy didn't have any at all. "That stream is full of germs and parasites. Bears do their business in that water. Would you like to die of dysentery?"

Tracy started to cry. He didn't know what dysentery was, but he was sure he had it and now life was over.

Dad cleared his throat and said, "Oh, I think it'll be fine."

Mom's younger brother, Joe, who had been hauling a Mobile Scout travel trailer through the Grand Tetons, joined us in Brigham City. Now that we were all together, Aunt Christine took us all to see the Mormon Tabernacle. We parked several blocks away and started walking. Kay said, "There sure are a lot of drinking fountains here." We passed one or two, when I realized how thirsty I was. We halted to take a drink. Amazingly, we were all thirsty at the same time. We quickly dispersed to different fountains and took long drinks. All satisfied, we continued. It was so dry, nobody perspired. Within fifty yards, we were all thirsty again. We had passed more fountains, and now I knew why they were all there. I was dying of thirst! At last, we arrived at the tabernacle and found a large crowd there.

Tracy asked, "Where's the choir? I thought they were always there."

"Yes, Tracy, they're chained to the benches. They're just gone for a potty break," Kay said.

The tour guide said, "If you would all be seated and silent, I'm going to drop a pin." (Normally, you wouldn't hear a safety pin hit the floor. But the acoustics here were really good.)

And he did. It sounded like someone had dropped a handgun. I was impressed. The demonstration over, it was time to go back to the cars. On the sidewalk again, the fountains slowed our progress, not because they were in the way. We couldn't resist their siren call. We didn't pass many without taking a drink. Even drinking so much, I felt dehydrated. It was a relief to get back to the cars and go back to Brigham City. Once there, Joe's wife, Aunt Jean, volunteered to get hamburgers. She returned saying that Yankees didn't know what a hamburger was. "Hamburgers don't have catsup on them. They have mustard."

Next day, we all trooped out to the Great Salt Lake. It was thirsty fun for everyone except me; not able to see any of it, I was bored. At the end of ten days, we left Uncle Joe's family in Brigham City and started the journey back to Texas. We were in no rush, because Uncle Wilton was supposed to meet us in Mesa Verde and go on to Fort Stockton, where Uncle Joe would join us. So, allowing them time for their own excursions, we relaxed, stopping at Indian reservations and other interesting spots. At Carlsbad Caverns in New Mexico, we paid our money and joined a group picking its way along rough, narrow tunnels down into the cavern. The tour guide pointed out various rock formations, such as one that resembled a cluster of grapes. We trudged past a small lake full of crystal-clear water. Although it appeared to be a few inches deep, its bottom was actually ten feet down. A short time later, we entered a cavern the size of the Astrodome. The guide announced that he was going to extinguish the lights, but before doing so, we should all be seated.

He said, "After the lights are out, don't move. We don't want anyone to have an accident. It would be dangerous to move around in the pitch dark."

As the lights went out, Mom's voice addressed Tracy. "Are you listening, Tracy? If you get lost in here, you'll starve to death before anyone finds you. Your body will become a tourist attraction. They'll say, 'Here lies a little boy who didn't listen. He moved after we told him not to.'"

Tracy responded, "Oh, let's play hide-and-seek in the dark," but he didn't move a muscle.

I think Mom suspected she was being teased, but she still leaned over and growled in his ear, "Would you like chocolate ice cream anytime this decade!" I started to laugh but stopped when the lights went out.

Sitting down here at this moment, everyone got a glimpse into my world. I didn't hear anyone breathing, just the drip, drip of water on stone. Plop, echo, a long silence, plop, echo. It was as loud as that pin at the Mormon Tabernacle. The lights back on, we followed the guide into a smaller cavern. The backlighting around its perimeter didn't provide much illumination, and Kay said the Coke machine in the corner stood out brilliantly like a neon sign. Tourists stood at a long counter buying hamburgers, hot dogs, and beer.

When we drove through the many campsites in Mesa Verde in Colorado, there was Uncle Wilton with a trailer the twin of Uncle Joe's. He had caught the bug. When he and Aunt Christine saw all the portable conveniences, they were enthusiastic to get a trailer. After everyone was settled, we spent a hot, tiring day climbing into cliff dwellings and looking at caves whose ceilings were heavily stained with smoke from cooking fires. Tracy wanted to go everywhere we went, but Mom wasn't about to let him risk breaking a leg this far away from medical help. If he were to get hurt high up in one of those cliff dwellings, the ambulance attendants would have a hard time getting him out on a stretcher. The museum, on the other hand, Mom thought, was a much safer place for a fragile little boy. "He does the wildest things and never thinks about getting hurt. I have to put the fear of God in that little boy, or he'll kill himself." Anyway, that's what Mom thought.

Not only could we read Mom's mind, but our thinking had been thoroughly infected by her paranoia about Tracy. Several of her warnings to Tracy are burned deeply into my memory. "Don't do that! Don't run! You're gonna get hurt now! Be careful! Put that down! You don't need to be touching that! Slow down! Don't get hurt now! I wouldn't do that if I were you!"

As Mom decided how much freedom to give Tracy in this museum, she had all of these warnings on the tip of her tongue, ready for immediate use. He didn't get the run of the museum; he got something less, the walk of it. I had my own ears, but Mom was my eyes. Her word pictures were poetic. The mummy and the men and women in the paintings stared mournfully back at us like the people in Dante's Inferno. They looked like someone's attempt to make dolls out of leather. I have no fond memories of Mesa Verde, probably because I was so miserable from the heat; I was very happy when we left after a single night.

At the end of a long, hot day, we stopped in Fort Stockton, Texas, for the night. Our family was in a tent, but Uncle Joe and Uncle Wilton were pulling Mobile Scout trailers. We were envious because you just hopped out of the car pulling one, unlocked the trailer door, and you had instant comfort, without any setup. All three families had a hot meal that night courtesy of the trailer stoves. Dad pitched our tent a short walk from a launderette, so Mom used water from there to make Kool-Aid. After supper, three families' worth of cousins ran around the park teasing tarantulas, searching for treasure, and generally making noise. Cousins Larry and Allen found a five-dollar bill. Dad was telling jokes to Mom's brothers; I could hear them choking and gasping for breath from their laughter. The hour was late and things got quiet. Taking advantage of the inactivity, Mom filled two jugs with water from the launderette. While putting a few quarters in the washing machine, she looked up and saw a sign she had previously overlooked. It read, "Warning: this water should be used for irrigation purposes only." The water hadn't affected her, but merely reading that sign made her sick.

She rushed back to our tent. Tracy, Kay, and I were just settling down to sleep, when Mom rushed in. "Well, I guess we're all gonna get sick," she announced to everyone.

So, we worried about that all night long, but we never felt bad.

The next day was Sunday. Our three families had a small informal church service, after which we broke camp and left. The Cross family drove back to Pasadena, and everyone else went to Corpus Christi to visit Grandma and Grandpa Richards.

Kay, Mom, and Tracy at Rick's Springs, Utah, 1964. Provided by Kay Cross Hayter.

Pop-up trailer built by Ray Cross and a coworker, 1968. Author's collection.

Chapter 8

Triumph and Tragedy

In the fall of 1963, I entered Pasadena High School as a sophomore. The school had been constructed in 1938. America hadn't yet emerged from the Great Depression, giving the architecture of that era a drab, inelegant appearance. The buildings were cramped, as if the construction crews discovered they were missing a lot of bricks and other materials too.

On the day before classes started, when Mom walked through my schedule with me, we came across Mr. Keller, PHS's new assistant principal. I was glad to have a familiar face in the administration. I say familiar because he had been the principal at San Jacinto Junior High School throughout my years there. The link was even stronger, because his wife had been my sixth-grade teacher at J. D. Parks Elementary. I felt that Mr. Keller, like his wife, took an interest in my progress. I didn't want any privileges, but I wanted an ally when facing unreasonable barriers.

"Hello, Mrs. Cross. Have you found all Mike's classes?"

"Yes, but this is a big campus."

"Mike, have you found any obstacles you can't deal with? We can move a class from the second floor to the first, if you need us to do that."

"No, sir, but the place is so big, I'm worried about getting to my classes on time."

"We'll let you leave class early to get across campus. That seemed to work well at San Jacinto, and the distances are so much greater here. I'll set that up with your teachers. We want everyone to be safe and have a good year." He turned to Mom. "If there are any problems at all, let me know." With that, he strode off, and Mom and I continued our walk.

I was struck again by how sprawling the campus was. When I thought we had been everywhere, there was another building. The school must not have been built all at one time. Some buildings sat where you wouldn't expect a building to be. Two of them crowded each other, leaving only a gloomy little alley between. Special education teachers, such as Mrs. Ellis, held their classes in a corner of the library, which lay along that alley. There were separate buildings for the administration offices, science, art, the core subjects, the band hall, the gymnasium, and the cafeteria. Since most buildings weren't close together, there were covered walkways between them. No two of my classes were in the same building, which alone would keep me hopping. And the not-so-insignificant distance between buildings would keep me moving around in a dangerous rush. But the part of the architecture that most concerned me was the layout of the stairwells. The stairs at San Jacinto Junior High had been inside. Here, they were all outside. They tended to be at the very end of a building, and as such there were fewer of them. As I would find out, the stairwells would always be crowded, intensifying my discomfort. It was as if the whole building were trying to go down a fire escape in a hurry. To my mind, that is what these stairwells resembled.

Mrs. Ellis's other students were in junior high school, thus complicating her days in two ways. Not only did her class preparations span different subject matters and different grade levels, but her days were full of travel between San Jacinto Junior High School and Pasadena High. As usual, my one special education class was math. In tenth grade it was Plane Geometry. Solid Geometry was offered in the eleventh and twelfth grades. In addition to teaching me geometry, Mrs. Ellis also consulted with my other teachers about any problems I encountered in their classes. She offered to type the tests they gave me into a large font. But most of the teachers didn't request it.

While I was beginning high school, Tracy was starting fourth grade. He had been taught in a homebound program for the first two years of school. But last year, when Mom asked the family physician for the paperwork permitting Tracy to continue to be homebound, he refused, saying that Tracy needed to be in public school. This made Mom angry. "My son is too vulnerable. This is not in his best interest." She pleaded with the doctor to change his mind, but he was obstinate. He should have listened, as it turned out. Third grade passed uneventfully for Tracy, but this year would justify Mom's fears. The second week of school it happened. During a ball game on the playground at J. D. Parks Elementary, Tracy dropped the bat and started his limping gait toward first base. He never made it. He stumbled and fell backward, sitting on his foot. Tracy heard his femur snap. He knew immediately that it was broken and that he shouldn't move. The kids in his class knew that he was fragile, having already suffered five broken legs. Tracy calmly said, "Somebody, get the teacher. I just broke my leg." No one doubted his statement. Not only did the teacher rush over, but the principal—Mr. Sitton—accompanied by the school nurse, quickly arrived. As word spread, faces appeared at all the classroom windows, and a group of classmates gathered around to shade Tracy from the sun.

"Are you sure your leg is broken?"

"Yes, I heard the bone snap, and it really hurts. Please don't touch me until my mom gets here."

Then Mom got the phone call she dreaded but had expected sooner or later. She phoned Dad and then Aunt Betty to let them know where she would be. Mr. Sitton picked Mom up and sped back to J. D. Parks, where they drove onto the playground, stopping beside Tracy. Mom immediately took charge. She and Tracy were each relieved to see one another—Tracy because she was there, and Mom to see how calm he was.

Mom looked at Mr. Sitton. "We need to lay Tracy in the back seat of your car and drive to Bayshore Hospital."

Sounding anxious for the first time, Tracy said, "Oh please, be careful."

Mom said, "Tracy, we're going to be as gentle as we can." Turning to Mr. Sitton she said, "Here's how we're going to do this: I want you to lift him up under his arms, straight up, and slowly. I will straighten his knee and support his leg. Lift slowly, and then slide him into the back seat. Someone open the back door. You get into the back seat and pull him in after you." And that is what they did, while everyone watched. Tracy cried out when Mom put her two hands around the break. Getting into the car was awkward. Tracy's face was now white. Mom sat in the back with him while the principal drove. "Drive slow. We don't want to be in a wreck." A stretcher was waiting when they arrived. The hospital people slid the stretcher in under Tracy from behind him. This jostled the leg as little as possible, and they carted him away.

Mr. Sitton handed Mom a piece of paper with his home phone number and said, "Please let me know what happens." With that, he went back to school.

In the hospital, they laid Tracy on the X-ray table and pulled the stretcher out from under him. The doctor said, "Let's see what we're dealing with here." He returned, carrying the developed X-ray. "It's a clean break. That's good. Tracy, this is going to hurt. We're going to set your leg now, so get ready." The X-ray tech held Tracy under his arms while the doctor pulled hard on his foot. Tracy gasped. The doctor stopped pulling when the leg looked straight. A second X-ray showed that it wasn't lined up right, so they repeated the tug-of-war. The third X-ray looked good, and they put a cast on the leg.

That day, I was called out of class. Dad picked me up and drove me home. You never get used to being traumatized, even when it happens repeatedly. You learn to cope, but it still upsets everyone and disrupts everything.

During Tracy's weeklong stay in the hospital, he was never alone for more than thirty minutes. After Kay and I went to the school bus stop in the morning, Dad—who had slept on a cot in Tracy's room—picked Mom up and drove her to the hospital. When he got off work, he brought her home. Kay had supper waiting, including a sack lunch for Dad. He said hello to us, then returned to Tracy's side.

When a day nurse came to check on Tracy, she saw his new guitar. She said, "Hi, do you play the guitar?" Tracy told her no, but that he was wanting to take lessons. He and Mom were surprised when the nurse said, "My son plays. You may have heard of him—Roy Orbison." Her name tag read "Nadine Orbison." This providential meeting came at a time when Tracy was badly in need of encouragement.

When I remember these times, I realize what superior parents we had. They absorbed the extra burdens without ignoring everyday responsibilities. Mom still read and coached me as always. Dad was a real rock for all of us. They both remained calm under stress.

I was still reading with the broken glasses, then switching to a weaker pair to write responses. I tried to minimize the amount of reading I did in class and thus maximize my writing time. During tests, I didn't have time to reread anything. The last four years had made it plain to me that, given enough thought, weaknesses could be converted into strengths. Even further, accepting hardships and coping with them can lead to unexpected advantages.

Is there an English teacher anywhere who doesn't begin a school year by asking the class to write a paper describing their summer vacation? I doubt it. As far back as the third grade, I had been writing about vacations where nothing happened. They were boring to read because they were certainly boring to write. So, when I got that assignment yet again, from my tenth-grade English teacher, Mrs. Kern, it was time to do something different. That night, I became Walter Mitty, although I didn't know who he was. I only knew that I couldn't bring myself to write another dull vacation article. So, I embellished, just a little bit. What I wrote was largely fiction. In reality, we had made an uneventful trip to Brigham City, Utah, to visit Mom's brother and three of my cousins. Sight-seeing at a roadside geyser, Mom, as usual, guided me, while Dad looked after Kay and Tracy. Now, ambiguous language is dangerous. She said, "Take a big step." Did big mean high, or broad? I didn't have time to ask. I chose to interpret big to mean high. Well, I was wrong! I think I must have looked like a baseball pitcher winding up. The result was that my foot didn't make it across the ditch. Instead, I planted it smack dab in the middle. Off balance, I fell to my knees in the ditch, almost pulling Mom in after me. So, rather than touring the park, I went to the public restroom and tried to wash away some of the mud and stagnant smell from the pool around the geyser. This is where the narrative becomes fiction. In my story, a group of guys got splashed with stagnant water. The culprit couldn't be the kid wallowing in the ditch! Nor could it be the frustrated lady trying to pull him out! Therefore, thinking this other group of guys did it, they charged in swinging. During the scuffle, someone threw a rock, hitting a buffalo. The buffalo then crashed into a pump house that was powering the fake geyser. Naturally, the geyser fizzled. When the police arrived and sorted through the accounts of what happened, they arrested the park's owner. Mrs. Kern was not fooled. After reading it to the class, she suggested that I consider becoming a playwright. I did try to write short stories; however, my future would lie in a different direction, one that I never could have foreseen.

Mrs. Kern did, however, put a lasting mark on my life. It happened this way. Once a week, she gave a spelling test over a list of words. For extra credit, she also had us spell a word she hadn't told us to be familiar with. The words, usually of foreign extraction, represented a hole in my class preparation. She would pronounce the word and say, for instance, that it was from German, Italian, Middle French, Greek, or Latin, whereupon someone in class would gasp excitedly at the hint. We got a further hint when she pronounced the foreign word from which it derived. Her hints also mentioned Greek and Latin roots, suffixes, and prefixes. I wasn't catching any of her hints, so I went to a bookstore and bought dictionaries in French, German, and Italian. I studied pronunciation rules for each language, confident that next time she gave hints about an extra credit word and pronounced its foreign root, my chances of spelling the word would improve. It did help, but not as much as I thought it would. However, it awakened in me a taste for comparative linguistics. I found another book that was more helpful on the spelling tests, even more than the dictionaries. Dad took me to Sears to look at books. I found a small black book about Greek and Latin roots, prefixes, and suffixes. The loss of this book is the only grudge I have ever held against my dad. Mom complained about the mess in my closet, so Dad scooped up everything on the floor of the closet and put it in the attic. Of course, my Greek and Latin roots book was now in the attic, and as much as I protested its loss, Dad wouldn't bring it back down out of the attic. He probably had no idea where in the attic he had put it. I'm still mad, some fifty-plus years later.

Before leaving English literature, let me relate a second important incident. Important because it let me know that my approach to study was effective. The class was reading a good bit of poetry, both British and American. One day Mrs. Kern announced that our test the next day would consist of a series of poetry fragments. Our task would be to identify the poem from which each fragment came. Because of Mrs. Eversmeyer's ninth-grade World Geography class, the preparation for this type of test was nothing new for me. That night Mom drilled me for hours until I was satisfied. The day after the exam, Mrs. Kern addressed the room. "I was afraid I had made this test too hard, but it wasn't because Mike made a hundred on it. I am disappointed nobody else passed. So, tomorrow you get to take it again." Far from enjoying remarks like these, I wanted to hide. I didn't want my peers to start hating me. I sympathized with the class, yet I felt obligated to do the best I could. If the teacher felt vindicated in the way she designed tests, I felt vindicated in the way I prepared for them. I was safe as long as I kept preparing the way I did. I worried about alienating my classmates, but I didn't know how to express these concerns to a teacher. Someone like Mr. Cherry back at San Jacinto would have been the right person to talk to about it, but I would have felt awkward even mentioning it to him. Plus, I would have sounded arrogant, so I said nothing. Fortunately, embarrassing moments like this didn't happen very often. Next day, I studied while the class retook the poetry test.

I was so driven that I would never ever sit idle. Furthermore, I felt my disadvantages too keenly to think I could afford to waste time. So, when others were visiting before the bell rang, I was taking a last-minute look at an outline or at a homework paper prior to turning it in. This probably made me seem unapproachable, so while I was on speaking terms with everyone, I didn't get close to anyone. I was too embarrassed to ask people, whom I probably knew, "Who are you?" My vision was too poor to recognize anyone by sight, and unless a person spoke, I had no way to recognize him or her. For that reason, I didn't speak unless spoken to. It never occurred to me to explain this to anyone. And, if I started that explanation, I would be talking to an unknown face, but likely not a stranger. In the noisy halls, voices weren't distinct. I never knew who stood in front of me unless he or she said something.

The Pasadena Independent School District demanded that each student take two years of foreign language. I chose Spanish. Mom was not much help with it. Progress in the class was slow, and thus the reading assignments weren't large. Even with my reading speed, it wasn't difficult to stay abreast. This afforded Mom some needed relief. Most of her time helping me was spent on English literature and World History. She didn't do much, if any, reading in geometry or Spanish.

Despite my vision loss, I retained an interest in art, so I signed up for an art course to let my creative juices flow. It was my attempt to hang on to the world even as my ability to see and appreciate it continued to fade. This class literally rubbed my nose in my limitations. I'm certain I often walked around with paint on the tip of my nose. Though I liked painting and drawing, I had more success with three-dimensional art, such as clay sculpture and papier-mâché.

I said earlier that I never wasted time. I decided long before the academic year ended that I was wasting quite a bit of time. In view of my visual limitations, even being in an art class was a mistake. It wasn't a big mistake, but a mistake none the less. And yet, everyone absolutely needs to find his own limits; no one should let others tell him what they are. This means that mistakes and wasted time are inevitable. So far, my mistakes hadn't hurt my grade point average.

...

The year 1963 was one of those years that everyone who lived it will always remember. On November 22, I was standing outside my World History classroom waiting for the bell to ring. Two boys passed, and one said something about the president being shot. I took this to be a reference to Lincoln. After the bell had rung and the students were seated, the principal, Mr. White, made a public address announcement that stained our day. John F. Kennedy had been shot and was even then near death in Parkland Hospital in Dallas. After the announcement, there was an intense silence broken occasionally by muffled crying. For the rest of the day, we changed classes, but nothing happened. No one said or did anything. At home, Mom was watching the soap opera *As the World Turns* on TV, with CBS occasionally breaking in with news bulletins. Still in a cast, Tracy lay on a pallet in the corner.

"Mom, do we have to watch this! Can't you turn the channel to something else?"

"No, we can't. This is my house, and we'll watch what I want to watch."

Suddenly, Walter Cronkite broke in with a bulletin announcing the death of John F. Kennedy. Mom immediately picked up the phone to call her sister Betty, but Betty was already on the line. Mom must have picked up just before the phone rang.

"Are you watching TV, Regena?" They both watched in shock.

Back at school, people moved silently through their classes. Everyone on the bus that afternoon was subdued. That weekend, we all watched our president's funeral procession.

The Christmas holidays were approaching, and I was cold in my red cardigan. I sat in the library across a table from Mrs. Ellis. My breathing was ragged.

"Mrs. Ellis, I am having an asthma attack."

"Oh, Mike, do you need to go see the nurse?"

"Yes, I can't keep my mind on what you're saying. I'm sorry. I feel like somebody kicked me in the back."

"That's all right. Let me put my coat on, and I'll walk down there with you."

I grasped my book satchel and rose. It slipped from my grasp onto the floor.

"I'm sorry, I didn't realize how weak I am."

"I'll take your books. You should have said something sooner. Did you feel like this when you came in here?"

"Yes, I did."

"Well, let's go now."

The nurse had me lie on a heating pad, and I immediately started feeling better but continued to be weak. The heat broke up the phlegm in my lungs, and my chest rattled with every breath. The nurse notified the office that I should be sent home. The secretary called Mom, who in turn had Dad pick me up. Mrs. Ellis stood with me until Dad's car pulled up beside us. She had to help me into the car when Dad opened the door. Thankfully, the ride home was short. Once there, I stayed on a heating pad, coughing and wheezing. Mom covered the floor near my bed with newspapers, knowing that I would get into an upside-down position to cough. For the next three hours, I alternately lay on the heating pad and leaned over the side of the bed, my face almost touching the newspaper, and heaved to try to clear my lungs. Gravity helped me cough up ribbons of thick phlegm. Violent spasms jerked me bolt upright. I needed desperately to heave, but I didn't have the breath to do it. I was a puppet being yanked in and out of twisted positions. This left me shaken and gasping for air. About five o'clock, my spasms had subsided somewhat, and Mom came into my room and said that Aunt Betty had invited us for dinner, which was cornbread dressing and turkey. I would have risen from my death bed for Aunt Betty's dressing. Despite this miraculous recovery, I was careful not to leave the heating pad behind. Now, Aunt Betty was always cheerful and encouraging. When she set a plate of dressing in front of me, I was almost cured. And when she followed it up with a wedge of pecan pie, I agreed with Robert Browning: "God's in His Heaven—All's right with the world!" But heaven and hell were jousting over my almost dead body. Eating during these bouts of asthma could be dangerous. If I felt my lungs being sucked into a bone-jarring, racking, cough spasm, I had to spit, or else choke on food. I think I pioneered the art of eating while being tortured. Ultimately, things went from bad to worse, and I had to return home to stand on my head while heaving and coughing up phlegm. The next day my chest was so sore that I tried not to cough, but I couldn't stop myself. I didn't control my body; it controlled me. The end of the day left me completely spent. Luckily, I got sick on a Friday. That was a really rough weekend, but due mainly to that heating pad, I was able to go to school Monday.

Tracy spent three weeks at Bayshore Hospital, when his new bone specialist put a pin in his leg. On Christmas day he was still at Bayshore, and we opened gifts in his hospital room. Tracy smiled and pressed keys on a toy organ, which made enough noise to be festive. I saw Grandpa A.P. cry for the first and last time. Tracy, on the other hand, was pretty cheerful; this was broken leg number six. My brother was nothing if not resilient.

Spring semester 1964 began with a school-wide assembly. I never knew what happened at that gathering because the principal, Mr. White, said that anyone attending the new high school next year should leave. A third of the auditorium rose and left. Starting that day, the student body divided itself into "us" and "them." As someone headed to Sam Rayburn High School, I was part of "them." We were referred to as "Rayburns" and excluded from events. I was completely unaffected by the ostracism, since I never attended dances, parties, or any extracurricular activities. A person can't be deprived of a possession he's never had. I had no sense of being excluded, because I hadn't felt included since the sixth grade. All attempts to make me feel disloyal fell on deaf ears. I wasn't loyal or disloyal; I was disconnected. Outside academics, student life meant nothing to me.

The fall semester had been so eventful, not to say painful, that by comparison, nothing memorable happened that spring. Time flew by, and the school year drew to an end. With just the two of us in the library classroom, Mrs. Ellis shut the geometry book and looked up.

"Well, I think we've covered everything. You've done well. Do you have any plans beyond geometry?"

"Yes, I would like to take Algebra 2."

"I won't be your teacher next year."

I didn't say anything. She had my full attention. Jane Brown had been my math teacher prior to Mrs. Ellis. I wondered if she too was leaving.

"I don't know enough to teach Algebra 2. You will have to take it in a mainstream class." This was not good news. I was shocked. The idea of sitting in a math class with sighted kids terrified me.

"Isn't there anyone else in special education who could teach it?"

"No, there isn't. I can teach you another subject, but not math. How would you feel about being in a regular class?" I made my decision on the spot.

"It's scary, but I want to try it. Could you let me have a copy of the Algebra 2 textbook to read over the summer?"

"Yes, I can do that. And I'm sure your teacher will let me type your tests in a large font, so I will still be around to help."

I left class with nagging self-doubt but determined to face the challenge. Maybe I would even fail, but I had to find out about myself. Next day, Mrs. Ellis gave me an Algebra 2 textbook.

"This is checked out in my name, so be extra careful with it."

"Thank you, Mrs. Ellis. I won't waste your gift."

So ended math instruction in special education.

I found the courage to accept the new challenge because I had been studying math on my own, outside of class. At the time I bought the Greek and Latin roots book, I had found a much more valuable book, *Basic Mathematics: A Survey Course*, by Walter W. Hart, published in 1942 by D. C. Heath & Co. It covered basic arithmetic, geometry, algebra, logarithms, and trigonometry. The book was developed especially for high school students, both girls and boys, who were not going to college or technical school but were preparing for service in the armed forces and in industry. It was based on Hart's interpretations of current needs as found in Bulletin TM 1-900 of the War Department, Leaflet #62 of the Office of Education, and Bulletins 24 & 26 of the Civil Aeronautics Administration. The cover of this slim book showed an aircraft and beams of light shining up from search lights below. As the cover suggested, the problems stated in its pages were full of references to military hardware. The book didn't waste space. A chapter ended on a page, and if there was room, the next chapter began on that same page.

Every student in a math class asks the question, "What good is any of this stuff, anyway? Its only purpose seems to be to torture kids!" That book, *Basic Mathematics*, started to answer that question with a resounding "Yes, it has gifts for anyone with an open mind." The first gift I recognized is an application of the distributive law. The last property of the number system talked about in high school algebra is distributivity of multiplication over addition. It can be used to multiply one two-digit integer by a second two-digit integer in your head, without using pencil and paper.

And then I found a bigger gift. Can multiplying very large numbers together be made easier than wasting an entire afternoon grinding it out with pencil and paper? The chapter in *Basic Mathematics* that gave me that bigger gift and let me see that mathematics could be exciting was the chapter on exponents and common logarithms. It was a revelation to me that multiplication and division could be reduced to addition and subtraction through the use of common logarithms. And once I grasped the idea, I felt like a new person. The ability of mathematics to give me that feeling has never deserted me.

I found common logarithm tables magical. Is mathematics magic? I had begun to think it really was. (In 1964, using common logarithm tables made sense, but when scientific calculators became available, this was no longer a reasonable use of time. Today, anyone who uses common logarithm tables must be very curious about history and extremely bored.) Everything I learned about common logarithms was done on my own time, with no teacher involvement.

Sitting there facing Mrs. Ellis, I had all this experience with logarithms behind me. So, when she told me I would have to take math in a more demanding setting, I thought I could be ready. At my request, she agreed to check the Algebra 2 text out of the library over the summer. My intent was to read it cover to cover, working the problems. Since I would be at a disadvantage in the algebra class, I was determined to get a head start. Everyone should take ownership of his or her education. We should all become self-motivated learners. When roadblocks in the future are certain, this is only wise.

On the last day of the school year, my attendance at an assembly was required. I went up on stage to receive the Academic Excellence Award for making straight A's all year long. In keeping with my status as a Rayburn, I got an empty envelope, instead of one containing a gold pen inscribed with the word "Scholarship." By mistake, some of the pens had been sent to Pasadena, California, not Pasadena, Texas. I never found out how many envelopes were empty. So ended the tenth grade.

That summer I worked through the Algebra 2 book. I had never read a textbook over the summer, but fear is a great motivating force. Since reading for long stretches of time make my problems more intense, I am always looking for better techniques to handle my reading load. I had discarded several methods because they were too time-consuming or were physically painful. I needed to find better methods before September because as I alternate between reading and writing, I have to switch between two pairs of glasses. This costs me time and effort. There are obviously good and bad times for trying new techniques. During a mathematics final is the wrong time to experiment with the placement of a movable light source, like a flashlight. In my case, I was able to read large print books into my adulthood. If I had put my face any closer to the book, I would have had to cut my nose off. The biggest problem with having my face that close to the book I'm trying to read is that my head is usually blocking the light. The illumination needs to come in at a slant. Its source should be off to the side, or perhaps in front of me. Beyond this, my advice may be wrong for someone else with vision problems. Everyone with a vision loss is unique. A healthy optic nerve is pink, whereas mine is almost white. So, most of the image collected by my eye gets lost on the way through the optic nerve to the brain. This includes how bright the image is. When it reaches my brain, the image is dim. To rectify this, the image needs to be brighter when it starts the journey. The final image not only has to be bright enough, it can't contain any glare. To solve both problems, the light source must be the right distance away and at the correct angle. The light in the room may be bright enough, and if so, it may be that moving my seat to another spot in the room puts the light source at a better angle. To find a solution can be frustrating and requires that you not give up. Aside from using a portable light, my relation to a window or overhead light is extremely important.

An inescapable fact is that I can only see about five characters at a time. This requires me to move my face back and forth across the page. Not only does this strain my neck, but it also makes it difficult to breathe because my nose frequently caves in when I'm looking at characters along the book's spine. At that moment, two of those characters are out of focus since the part of the page they're on is on a steep slope down into the binding. Another factor is heat. There's no problem if the room is cold, but if the room is warm, my glasses or magnifying glass keep fogging up, forcing me to keep wiping the lens on my shirt sleeve. Sometimes I had to hold my breath to read, because when I exhaled, my warm breath was trapped close to my eyeglasses, thus fogging them up. The cool breeze from the air conditioner didn't reach my room at home. I had to wipe off my glasses at least once a minute. Under such conditions, a person really has to be obsessed with a book. If there is a good way to use bad vision, I have never found it.

Sam Rayburn's first graduating class began September 1964. As Mom and I walked the halls to go through my schedule, I was relieved that I only had to navigate one building, and the stairs were all inside. Classes were much closer together, unlike at Pasadena High. I only had to worry about the halls being crowded. The air conditioning kept us cool as we roamed around counting doors. Sam Rayburn High School was the first school in Pasadena to have air conditioning.

That year, Mrs. Ellis had two students in her sight-saving group at Sam Rayburn, me and my best friend, Jack. A year behind me in the tenth grade, his particular interest was radio and TV. Jack, who had always exhibited a great sense of humor, was taking speech classes, and he began to have a reputation for comedy. The year before, being at different schools, we never saw each other. Although we were both now on the same campus, the situation was similar; we were so busy we saw one another rarely. He had a new set of friends who shared an interest in mass communication and comedy. Our interests diverged, and we slowly drifted apart. Relations were still warm, but we moved in separate circles. Jack's grew, while mine shrank till it contained only me and my immediate family.

The honor society provided me a new circle of acquaintances, but again, I failed to take advantage of a social context in which it should have been easy to start friendships. Meetings were brief, and I was passive. Its members may have gotten together after school, but I went straight home and stayed there studying. I made no friends, and there was no one I talked to regularly. Mea culpa; I was very hard to get to know. For one thing, I didn't eat lunch in the cafeteria with everyone else. Instead, I sat on a patio bench, studying and eating a hamburger or chili burger from the fast-food window. The patio people kept to themselves. Thinking I would slow down the serving line and annoy those in line behind me, I avoided eating in the cafeteria.

I was achieving what I wanted, but with all of my disadvantages, real or perceived, I kept myself balancing on a tightrope. My mind was always on business, all day, every day. Mike, the ultimate dull boy! I have no regrets though; if I had had a social life, I would have fallen off the tightrope, and my future would have been lost.

I didn't realize how bad my vision was until one day, I stopped at a water cooler near the school office. I bent forward to take a drink and got a mouthful of hair. A girl was already there. Boy, were we surprised! I, of course, jumped backward in embarrassment. She popped up and sped off down the hall toward the office. She said nothing at all, so I have no idea who she was. But my guess is she was a student who worked in the office. Anyway, I thought that her lack of reaction probably meant that she knew who I was, and that I might not be aware of her. At least, that's what I hoped she thought. In the future, I would be slower to approach a fountain.

Usually, I knew by the roughness of the ride in our neighborhood, when the school bus was approaching my stop. I guess I wasn't paying close attention because I missed it. The driver finally looked around and saw that I was still on the bus. "You need to get off and go back about three stops." I got off, completely lost. I started walking in the direction that the bus had come from. Not able to see far enough to recognize anything, I listened for a familiar sound, like a voice or a dog barking. No good! I kept walking in the direction indicated by the driver and listened very intently. Ten minutes passed. Did I hear something? Yes, it was Kay calling me from a great distance. I stopped, and she came up to me crying. My sister, the tenderest of tender hearts! I took her hand, and we walked home.

I was somewhat apprehensive about sitting in Algebra 2 classes with a room full of kids who could all see the blackboard. How would they react? Indeed, how would the teacher, Mr. Knuple, react to having a blind student in his class? The first day, I approached him as the other students left the class. I walked promptly up to his desk before he could leave; I had a slight case of nerves, having worried about this moment all during class. The principal, Mr. Lomax, had surely informed him he would have a blind student in his class. Now, the way to begin an acquaintance with any teacher is to let him or her know that you are serious about the subject matter. In my case, this was not an exaggeration; I wouldn't be there risking myself in this experiment otherwise. He asked me how much I could see and what he could do to help. I told him I couldn't see the board, and it would help if he would read what he wrote on the blackboard as he was writing it. I needed to know, character for character, what he wrote or pointed to. Mr. Knuple asked how I wanted to hear equations read. I gave him a few examples. The way he read an equation was exactly the way I needed to hear it. Being more knowledgeable than I, since, after all, he was the teacher, he had a few suggestions. All his suggestions eased my effort. I was greatly relieved. I didn't have much time to get to my next class, so we continued this conversation over several days. During the first weeks of class, I occasionally suggested a slight refinement, such as saying "open parenthesis" or "close parenthesis" rather than simply saying "parenthesis." I kept my requests to a minimum, not wanting to become annoying to him, or to the class.

This was a new and more demanding challenge. I was used to memorizing facts the night before a test for the purpose of recalling them the next day. However, holding equations in memory after only a single reading would be the most taxing thing I had ever done. I couldn't allow myself to be distracted by whisperings around me. Mr. Knuple ran a no-nonsense class, so there wasn't much of that anyway. Rather than remembering entire equations until he was finished discussing a topic, I tried writing them down as he read. I discovered I couldn't keep up, and I had to ask him to repeat what he had just read. I couldn't be in position to write soon enough to be responsive to his voice. Finally, I quit trying. Instead, I relaxed, sat back, and visualized the equation being written in chalk on the blackboard. To my surprise, it went much better. Handling the paper and the pencil and positioning my head to focus on the paper while not blocking the light was altogether too much work. Imagining a moving piece of chalk minus these distractions was easier. Yet it was an intense struggle not to lose the image. I needn't have worried about being disruptive to the class; more than one classmate told me that the teacher's reading aloud slowed him down, giving them more time to absorb what they were seeing. I hope they weren't just being nice. It is appropriate for me to say at this point that my classmates were extremely nice.

The special education community was watching my math experiment. This had never been done before. A sight-saving student's math education had always both begun and ended in a special education setting. I was the lab monkey. And Mrs. Ellis didn't throw me to the wolves and walk away. Mr. Knuple allowed her to type my algebra tests in large font. He then proofed her typing before giving me the test. It worked really well. Only once did an error in typing cause me to get the wrong answer. On that occasion, I verified my answer, and showed him the test paper. He graciously gave me full credit. I poured a lot of energy into Mr. Knuple's algebra class, feeling that

I was an imposition on teachers and classmates alike. At some point during the struggle, I discovered a love of mathematics. I hadn't yet thought about majoring in math, but thanks in large part to Mr. Knuple and the teacher I would have the following year, the day was coming when I would make that choice. There were 160 students in all of Mr. Knuple's classes. He gave three A's, and I got one of them.

My English teacher was Mr. Terry, whom I had had in the ninth grade. As always, we pounded away at grammar. His delivery to the class was somewhat dry, but I could tell he loved his subject. That year we read classics such as Shakespeare's *Julius Caesar*, Thornton Wilder's *Our Town*, O. Henry's "The Ransom of Red Chief," Samuel Taylor Coleridge's "The Rime of the Ancient Mariner," Henry Wadsworth Longfellow's "The Wreck of the Hesperus," Edgar Allan Poe's "The Cask of Amontillado," and Washington Irving's "The Legend of Sleepy Hollow."

In Chemistry 1, I had two lab partners. I don't have much to say about that class, except I enjoyed memorizing elements in the periodic table and balancing chemical equations. One lab session stands out in my mind. We were running short on time, and it looked like we wouldn't finish the experiment. I suggested to my partners getting out the Bunsen burner and raising the temperature of the test tube by 10 degrees centigrade. I had read somewhere that it would cut the reaction time in half. It did, and we finished the lab early. After that, we started every experiment by getting out the Bunsen burner. Of course, the teacher watched to make sure we never did anything dangerous.

Not every lab would be as smooth as this one. I benefited from being in a high school with 3,000 students, 500 of them in my graduating class. No one doubted my ability. I had received the Academic Excellence Award four times. My suggestions were listened to. The day was coming, in a college electronics lab for physics majors, when this wouldn't be the case. My college lab partners would know only that I was blind. I would have to prove that my presence didn't cripple the three-man lab team. But this lay far in the future.

At the end of my junior year (eleventh grade), I received the Academic Excellence Award for the fifth time. For this achievement, I received a white letter sweater. On its left breast, the word "Scholarship" was written, descending down the vertical leg of a blue letter *R*.

America was under siege! The Beatles appeared in concert in Houston on August 19, 1965. Kay and two of her friends—Jerry Jean and Diane—hopped a ride with a classmate, whom they barely knew. In route, the driver announced,

"This is my first time driving on the highway." Kay's stomach sank through the floor, and she started praying silently. The car full of girls arrived safely, and they found themselves fighting for seats, since there were no seat numbers stamped on the tickets. They procured good seats, twelve rows back. So, did they see or hear anything? No! Everyone was standing on her seat, screaming and practicing her latest trampoline jumps. If there had been a baboon on stage, the girls from the second row back would have been none the wiser. Standing on a seat, jumping up and down—or watching others do it—must be addictive, because a few months later, Kay and her girlfriends went to a Dave Clark Five concert. After watching more female mob hysteria, Kay had had enough of concerts.

I looked forward to our yearly summer trip to Grandma Richards's house on Highway 9 outside Corpus Christi. One of the nice things about being in Corpus is the availability of fresh seafood. Trucks drove up and down the highways and through the neighborhoods selling shrimp and flounder. There's nothing better than hush puppies and a fish fry of fresh flounder. Kay and I thought it was funny that a flounder has both eyes on the same side of its head. One time, Tracy came tootling into the room—not making motor noises, but instead swishing the spit in his mouth back and forth in time to his steps. He stopped and looked around for something to do. He saw me and Kay standing over a fish on ice. When Tracy asked why its eyes were like that, Kay saw her chance for a little payback.

"The better to put the evil eye on people! Tracy, that fish knows about the cherry and the other tricks you played on us. It's puttin' the evil eye on ya, both of 'em!"

"What's the evil eye?" he asked.

She told him, "When both eyes are on the same side of his head, he's puttin' the evil eye on somebody. See! It's looking at you right now."

Tracy backed away, laughing nervously. Could Kay play tricks too?

September rolled around, and I braced for another grinding year. In addition to Jack and myself, Mrs. Ellis had three female students. On the day before classes, we all met and went through our schedules. Five mothers were there helping us count doors and whatever else we needed. We five students had known each other at J. D. Parks Elementary; it seemed to us in a distant past. After that day, I didn't see any of them. Mrs. Ellis, my civics teacher, ran interference for all of her blind students. We also all owe a debt of gratitude to Carter Lomax, our principal, who smoothed the way for all special education students, whether blind, or deaf, or in a wheelchair. (In January 2007, Carter Lomax Middle School opened its doors to students in the Pasadena ISD.)

By the autumn of 1965, I had well-established reading techniques, but I needed something to provide relief when my elbow locked up from leaning on it too much. Playing fetch with either Sissy or Sam on a hot September day was not the break I had in mind. A sudden addition to the family gave me the perfect excuse for a break; beyond that, it cheered everybody's life.

Mom answered the doorbell. It was Penny, a lady from church. A devotee of TV preachers, Penny was on a mission. She came to deliver one of the TV's favorite messages. No one else at church had a good opinion of the TV preaching because it often propounded a prosperity gospel. Related to the divine right of kings, it holds that having wealth and power is a sure sign of God's approval. The reverse is also true—if you are poor and powerless, and especially if you are disabled, God doesn't like you. You brought it all on yourself. This being the thought in Penny's mind, she needed to convict Mom and Dad, too, of sin. The evidence of Mom's guilt was the overwhelming mass of tragedy in our family. Tracy and I were being punished for our parents' sins. Instead of getting angry, Mom opened a Bible to the book of Job and started reasoning with a woman whose friendship she valued. Job lost his wealth and his entire family except for his wife. As he sat in a trash heap, his three friends came to tell him to repent of his sins. Their accusations were essentially what Penny had just said to Mom. Job forcefully refuted all their charges. By the end of the discussion, Penny asked Mom's forgiveness and left. The encounter could have ended a friendship, but because of the way Mom handled it, there was a good outcome, and an additional, unexpected outcome. A few weeks later, Penny again rang our doorbell. This time, with a heart full of Christian compassion, she introduced us to a long-haired Chihuahua puppy. She was so lively, Penny's boys had named her Bounce-A-Lot, which seemed to us very appropriate. She was like a rubber ball, bouncing everywhere. On the third such visit, Penny made Bounce-A-Lot a gift to Tracy. This frisky little playmate was certainly a better companion for him than a mouse or a rooster.

Besides being exactly what Tracy needed, Bounce-A-Lot brightened all our lives. Quickly becoming an important member of the family, Bounce-A-Lot was very attached to Dad. A game of hide-and-seek became a daily routine. When Dad came home from the port, she met him at the door. Dad always picked her up, handed her to one of us, and then hid somewhere in the house. When he called Bounce-A-Lot by name, we put her down, and she then ran all over the house looking for him. One day she couldn't find him. Dad hid in the hall bathroom tub and quietly pulled the plastic sliding shower doors closed. When she wandered into a room far from the bathroom, Dad again called her name, and she got excited. Finally, Bounce-A-Lot walked into the bathroom, but then turned around to leave. Then Dad opened the shower door and scooped her up. She was one happy dog!

Bounce-A-Lot had too much energy and too much curiosity to stay in anyone's lap. The exception was Dad's lap. Nothing held her attention very long. Again, there was an exception—ice cream. When we discovered this, Dad decided to dip a bowl of ice cream and lay prone on the couch to eat it. Bounce-A-Lot hopped up onto his chest and sat there watching him. Her eyes tracked the spoon as he ate. But she sat patiently waiting until Dad gave her the last bite. She finished and sat there shivering from the chill.

Away from school, I usually sat at my desk with Bounce-A-Lot in the bottom desk drawer on a pillow. She was great company for study. When I needed a break, she was ready to play. As usual, I studied every spare minute. Hearing was one of my strengths. I could be engrossed in a book and yet be perfectly aware of my surroundings. One day I heard a faint click, followed by the hiss of escaping gas. I sat up abruptly.

"I heard that, and I want some."

After a short pause, footsteps came down the hall and up to my desk. Mom put a mug in front of me and poured Dr. Pepper.

"Darn! You can't get away with anything in this house." She walked out, laughing.

I smiled and took a swallow of foam. Trying to sneak a soft drink past me got to be a game. Kay or Tracy, even Mom and Dad, would go into the garage and close the door. I always heard and would meet the offender as he or she came out of the garage into the kitchen: "How about some of that Coke?"

Alas, there is a disturbing downside to having superior hearing, and it was about to be driven home to me forcefully. September and October are hot in Texas, and I continued leaving my windows open at night. The venetian blinds stirred and banged back into place with the night breeze. It was so peaceful. What was that scratching noise? Something rattled the papers on my desk. There was a plop onto the bed. I froze. It instantly flashed into my mind that a roach was after me. I think I could have been a track star, because in one fluid motion, I executed a broad jump from a prone position on the bed. I turned and started slapping the bed and the papers on the floor, following the noise the bug made in its flight through the room. My life was under attack from bugs, specifically roaches. The thumping went on awhile, before Mom and Dad's door flew open. All six feet, two inches and two hundred pounds of angry father stood in my doorway.

"What's going on in here! Stop that banging and go to sleep!"

"I can't sleep. I keep hearing bugs crawling around."

Mom jumped out from behind Dad with a flyswatter in her hand. Smack! "The roach is gone now," she exclaimed. Mom looked around the room and searched through the bed sheets without finding anything.

"Dad, it was there. I heard it, and it jumped in bed with me!"

He was exasperated. "Well, it's not there now. Mike, it's really late, and I have to work tomorrow. Try to go to sleep. It's just a bug. It ain't gonna hurt ya!"

No one speaks the King's English at two o'clock in the morning. I personally think if you woke the Queen of England up at, say, midnight, she would have a Texas accent. Thoroughly awake, Mom and Dad left and the lights went out. I had reservations about lying down in that bed. Screwing up my courage, I got back in bed but lay there in fear, alert for the faint sounds of bugs crawling. Fatigue overtook me, and I knew no more. I usually slept late Saturday, and because those filthy roaches fractured my night's rest, I really needed some extra sleep. That morning, Mom stopped at my door. "Do you plan to join the living?" No response. She went down the hall. When ten minutes passed and I still hadn't appeared, Mom came back and flipped the light switch. "It's past nine o'clock! Who won the war last night—you or the bugs?" I didn't think it was so funny. I sighed, got up, dressed, and followed Mom to the kitchen, where I ate a leisurely breakfast, after which I returned to my room to go through my previous night's homework looking for errors.

But my worst encounter with bugs came later that day. I reached into the refrigerator and got out the purple metal drinking cup, a present from Grandma Cross. I drained the grape juice, tipping the cup to the ceiling. Something was tickling my lip! I examined the cup with a finger, yelled, and hurled the cup across the kitchen. It was a dead roach. My fear went up a notch. I slept defensively, always ready to rocket out of bed and take the battle to the enemy. The fight was wearing me out. This scenario repeated itself into November, when the first cold front rattled the house. The roach attack was over.

Kay and Tracy were afraid of roaches too. Knowing that gave Tracy an opportunity for mischief. One day Kay and I were in Tracy's room listening to him play an acoustic guitar, when he stopped playing and looked over at Kay. "Oh, Kay! Kay! Roach!" He leaned forward and slid his guitar pick across the floor toward Kay. Even though she was watching him and knew it was only a guitar pick, such is the magic in Tracy's voice that Kay squealed and hopped up on the bed to escape the phantom roach.

One Friday Mom called me to breakfast. I finished reviewing homework and walked into the kitchen, where everyone was eating bowls of oatmeal in silence. Dad put down his coffee cup and straightened the newspaper. "I need to read an article out loud to you all. It is about Mike. He is student of the month for November." He finished reading, laid down the paper, and looked over at me. "Let's hear it for Mike. Hip, hip, hurrah!" Everyone joined in the cheer. I left for school feeling great. At 7:00 a.m., Kay and I walked to the bus stop on the corner.

I was only now taking my second year of Spanish. I needed it to graduate. My first year of Spanish was in the tenth grade, and I took no foreign language at all in the eleventh. I don't remember now why I skipped a year between Spanish 1 and 2, but I did. Now I faced the consequences. The summer before my senior year, I went to the library and checked out two books, a trigonometry book and a Spanish 2 text. These were the very ones used as textbooks in the Pasadena high schools. I spent my summer vacation reading these books diligently and doing the exercises. I also reviewed my homework papers from Spanish 1. This reacquainted me with the Spanish 1 vocabulary and grammar. I saw now that taking a year off from Spanish had been a bad idea. I took these books with me everywhere. On vacation, Dad again had to tell me to put my books away and enjoy myself. In facing my fears and my challenges, I had lost the ability to enjoy myself in what should have been a relaxed setting. I drove myself relentlessly, all the time. I felt guilty when I wasn't studying. This wasn't normal, but it continued to serve me well.

My worries about Spanish vanished the first week of classes. I had to stand before the class and talk about my vacation without speaking any English. In fact, the teacher didn't allow English to be spoken in her Spanish 2 classes. I wrote out a speech about my summer and memorized it. When the teacher said she was pleased with my speech and my accent, my fears vanished.

In the face of everything happening at home, I am amazed that my twelfth-grade academic year ended as well as it did. I had discovered in Algebra 2 that

I could thrive in a mainstream math class with sighted kids. But my anxiety about being the only student in a math class who couldn't see the board would never completely go away. Reading the trigonometry book over the summer helped my confidence. I told myself that I needed to do this to counterbalance my disadvantages. Mr. James Smith was exactly the right teacher for me at this point. He was enthusiastic and very encouraging. I had dealt with my self-doubt in Algebra 2, and now with my newly acquired confidence, I was enjoying myself. Yes, I was enjoying myself! Mr. Smith was a big part of that. The spring semester he taught Elementary Analysis. This was my first glimpse of pure mathematics. Actually, geometry was pure, but it was dry and uninteresting. Elementary analysis, by contrast, seemed creative. I had come to see mathematics as the way to unlock secrets. I liked the feeling of power it gave me. One Saturday in the spring semester, Dad drove me to the Rice University bookstore where I bought the book *Calculus with Analytic Geometry* by Johnson and Kiokemeister. I put it on a shelf for future study and focused on my high school courses.

There was no textbook in my physics class. The book the teacher, Mr. Whitaker, was lecturing from was from the Physical Science Study Committee, an MIT-based group working on designing introductory physics education materials, but none of the students had the book. I recognize now his teaching style as sort of a mild version of the Socratic method. More than once, the class lost the thread of the lecture. For the first time, we saw a derivation of an equation, whereas we were used to the equation being stated without any argument about its legitimacy. Most of us didn't want to see a derivation. "Just show us the equation, and we'll believe it without an argument." I also often wondered where the lectures were headed. One of the questions on the physics final was "How could you know by observation that the Earth is round?" We had never discussed anything remotely about the Earth's shape. I had never read a sailor's account of watching a ship's mast sink below the horizon, which was the answer that other people gave. I wrote that you could look at the moon during an eclipse and notice the Earth's shadow took the form of an arc. I got credit for the answer. However, it was strictly a guess because I certainly couldn't see the moon.

My English class was taught by Mrs. Jo Lyday. She was beloved by everyone who ever had her because she made the material interesting and enjoyable. There's that word again! I guess I did enjoy some things after all. Not confining herself to straight lectures, Mrs. Lyday sometimes brought her guitar and sang a ballad. We read some of Chaucer's *Canterbury Tales*, Dickens's *David Copperfield*, and Shakespeare's *Hamlet*, among others. We prevailed upon her to talk about her doctoral dissertation on J. R. R. Tolkien's *The Lord of the Rings* trilogy. At the end of the year, Mrs. Lyday presented Noam Chomsky's linguistics work on transformational grammar.

A few days before the end of the school year, I was called to the office. I didn't understand why. I racked my brain, trying to think of what I had done to be in trouble. When I got there, I saw Roger Woest and Anne Lacy, and I knew they wouldn't be in trouble. I relaxed. What the principal, Mr. Lomax, said astounded me. Anne Lacy and I were both ranked number one in our class of 530 students. We finished in a dead heat and would both be named as valedictorian. Roger Woest would be the salutatorian. We all three were receiving the Academic Excellence Award, in my case for the sixth time. For the senior year, this award was a plaque with the words "Academic Excellence" emblazoned in bold letters across its top.

About mid-morning on the last day of school, awards were presented. The culminating event was the announcement of the valedictorian and salutatorian. Anne, Roger, and I were called to the stage. I'm sure that everyone wondered why three names were called. Our rankings were announced. The class of 1966 rose as one and applauded. Resplendent in our moment of triumph, we stood there to sustained, loud, enthusiastic cheers. I was embarrassed. A few nights later, Anne and I sat side by side on stage as covaledictorians while Roger stood and addressed the class. He was a great choice for the valedictory address. I wasn't surprised that Roger and Anne were on the stage. I was surprised that Mike Cross was there.

I had made straight-A report cards for six consecutive years, throughout junior and senior high. Of course, I was satisfied with my accomplishments so far, but there was a long road ahead. Outside the single instance in ninth-grade science, my ability was never questioned. But the other legally blind kids I knew did get negative messages about themselves. And even I had one more negative message coming. That sight-saving teacher from J. D. Parks Elementary, Miss G, came to lunch on the last school day at the invitation of Mrs. Ellis. Did Mrs. Ellis know something about my history with that teacher? Jane Brown and Mrs. O had moved away. Thus, all of my special education teachers still in the area were there to see me graduate. I suppose Mrs. Ellis thought having a blind student be valedictorian was surprising. But it wasn't enough. When I told that elementary school teacher, Miss G, that I planned to major in mathematics, she scoffed. Some prejudices die hard. That made me angry and more determined than ever to succeed.

At last, I had the time to study that calculus book from the Rice University bookstore. The day after high school graduation, I got it out and started reading. I had three weeks to finish the book. The summer classes at San Jacinto Junior College didn't start for a few weeks. Although I thought I would probably attend Rice University in the fall, I knew that nothing was certain. By virtue of having graduated at the top of the class, Anne Lacy and I each had received a package offering a scholarship to any of the twenty-eight religious colleges and universities in Texas. The most generous of these was a $2,000-per-semester scholarship to University of St. Thomas in Houston, and the least was a scholarship for $100 per semester to Abilene Christian College. None of these could tempt me away from Rice, or from my backup choice. In case I didn't go to Rice, my plan was to enter the University of Houston with freshman history and English out of the way. If, on the other hand, I attended Rice in the fall, the summer would have been wasted, since those junior college courses wouldn't transfer to Rice. I had a scholarship from Anderson Clayton (a Houston-based company dealing in cotton and other goods), no matter which university I attended.

Once registered for classes at San Jacinto, I started reading the calculus book, working the problems as I went. I did this from sun up to sun down, six days a week, for three weeks. I took time only to eat, sleep, and make pit stops. My reading glass, an Agfa Loupe with eight power magnification, resembled an oversized church communion cup. I put my eye to it, as if I were looking through a microscope. My hot breath kept fogging up the lens. Every few minutes I had to wipe the lens with a cloth. My right arm stayed bent for hours, and it felt as if I had arthritis in my elbow. Ignoring it, I kept reading and working problems. Between problems, I straightened my arm, which helped quite a bit. At the end of those three weeks, I had finished differential and integral calculus and worked through the section on differential equations. As it turned out, those three weeks of studying calculus were invaluable; they prepared me for a crisis I would face that fall. San Jacinto Junior College classes began, engulfing me in course work. I wanted to get English, history, and political science courses done before the advanced math courses were upon me. I took two English and two history courses that summer and two political science/government courses the following summer.

The summer might have been uneventful, except Mom's worst fears for Tracy were realized. He broke his leg for the eighth and final time. The fact that he broke his femur (thigh bone) wasn't the tragedy. The tragedy was that it never healed and, worse than that, why it didn't. His bone specialist put a rod in Tracy's leg. The surgeon's mistake was that its diameter was too large. He hammered it down into the knee joint with a mallet. To the doctor's surprise, the bone disintegrated. The fragments broke down into calcium, which came out through Tracy's kidneys as kidney stones over a three-day period after he had come home from the hospital. Tracy, who was in a body cast and couldn't move, screamed day and night. Kay and I, when we weren't at school, left the house in tears, taking long walks. But Mom couldn't leave. She stayed there helping her younger son deal with his agony as best she could. His urine was both bloody and clouded with milky white patches. This was another one of those times when Tracy could have died. Without Mom's vigilance, he would have.

During that horrible month, the fourteen-inch incision, completely covered by the cast, got infected. Tracy went into shock, and Mom had to get medical attention fast. The surgeon had to cut a window in the cast to expose the incision, and other small cuts were made into the cast here and there to open up spots over pressure sores. Mom and Dad had no money, so they were the ones who treated Tracy's leg daily at home. While Dad held the body cast in position, Mom poured hydrogen peroxide into the wound. The hip-to-foot cast made cleaning Tracy's leg awkward. Dad turned and held him at an angle so Mom could get to the infected areas. While they worked on him, Tracy covered his face with a pillow and screamed into it. Even though Kay and I were in her room with the door shut, the pleading and screaming wrenched our hearts and tore us apart. When we couldn't bear it any longer, I opened the door and, followed by Kay, barged into the master bedroom.

"Stop it, right now!"

They paused. Dad spoke in a calm voice. "Mike, if we don't do this, he'll lose his leg."

Rebuked by Dad's quiet appraisal of reality, I took Kay's hand and led her out of the house. We could do nothing to help the little brother we loved. So, in tears, we escaped to the far corner of the street where we couldn't hear. As Kay and I stood there crying, we talked to God earnestly. After half an hour, we returned home. Tracy's ordeal was over, at least for that day. Kay and I took long walks daily until the infection was cleared up. These were horrible days and nights.

The surgeon ultimately had to replace the rod with a smaller one, but Tracy's leg never recovered. Between hip and knee, there was nothing except a rod and bone marrow. No surgeon would touch Tracy after that. Where the rod connected to the hip, there was a small hook that cut into muscle at every step Tracy took. It was too painful to walk, so Tracy was forever after confined to a wheelchair (or later to a walker). Mom told me, decades later, that Tracy bathed with his trousers on because he didn't want to see his leg or know anything about it. Although he knew they hadn't amputated it, he was afraid of what he might see when he looked. Inevitably, Tracy forgot not to look down. It wasn't as bad as he feared, but it was bad enough.

This was such a horrible time that I don't understand how any of us functioned—especially at the level we did. How Mom and Dad brought us through it, again I can't even imagine. But we had help from above, and I have no doubt that part of it was a little dog named Bounce-A-Lot. Depression could have swamped the family, but our parents kept pressing forward, when it would have been so easy to give up. Kay and I spent long hours at school (and in Dad's case, at work), thus escaping what was going on with Tracy. But Mom couldn't escape. She was dealing with it twenty-four hours a day. For this reason, I consider Dad and Mom to be the two strongest people I have ever known or ever will know. They should have taken the surgeon to court, but they didn't. I have blocked from my memory many of the details of what I witnessed, but some are too strong. Kay, my tenderhearted sister, couldn't talk about any of this until she was in her forties. In August we went to Corpus. Our time there was a necessary relief for all of us. By then, Tracy was no longer in a body cast, but he was in a wheelchair. All twelve of Tracy's years on earth had been stressful.

In late August, I received a letter from the Rice University admissions office. I was still on the waiting list to get into the dorms. Rice freshmen were not allowed to live off campus, so unless I made it into the dorms, I wouldn't be attending Rice. I never heard anything further from that institution. This made my mind up for me. I would attend the University of Houston in September. My junior college gamble paid off; the credits would transfer.

In 1966, registering for classes at the University of Houston was a multi-day process. At the end of two days, I had my classes. I signed up for British Literature (a sophomore course), the first year of French, Differential Calculus (the first in a 3-semester sequence of courses teaching calculus), and the mechanics course for physics majors. I had never heard of a placement test, but if I had, I might have placed out of Calculus 1, 2, and 3. And I would have missed an important step in my mathematical maturity. Dr. Ingram, instead of diving straight into differential calculus, made us prove some basic facts about integers, rationals, and reals (real numbers). This seemed like a waste of time to me, but that only underscored my ignorance. Without this step, I would have had a harder time adjusting my thought processes to upper-level mathematics. The same would have been true if my teacher had been anyone else, because only Dr. Ingram was presenting this material, so I hit the jackpot. Unexpectedly, I found I enjoyed proofs.

I seriously considered a second major, either physics or linguistics, but my chief interest was mathematics. This choice of majors led to an intense confrontation with the Texas State Commission for the Blind. It happened this way. The university library had recordings of some texts. The State Commission for the Blind had offices there in the audio-visual section of the library. So, wondering if it had any recordings of my textbooks, I walked into their offices a little curious and brimming with confidence. Hey, I was the David who slew Goliath! One of the students working there was majoring in math. You would think he would have been an ally, right? No! This student asked my major. When I responded that it was math, he turned and went into one of the inner offices. A few minutes passed, during which time I asked about the tape I needed. The student worker reappeared and challenged me with a math problem calculated to intimidate me. He asked me to solve a differential equation, although he didn't identify it as such. This is a level of math you don't normally encounter until the junior year. Luckily, it was only a simple first order linear homogeneous differential equation. This is the first type presented in the book *Calculus, with Analytic Geometry* by Johnson and Kiokemeister that I had bought at the Rice University bookstore and studied earlier in the summer. I remember thinking that the student worker must be taking differential equations this semester, and since this was just September, I knew more about differential equations than he did. That wasn't even a hard problem. I answered him within seconds. He never said a word. He just turned and left. I never saw him again. I'd like to have been a fly on the wall back in that inner office when he told them what happened. Far from discouraging me, this encounter did the reverse. Nobody at the state commission ever tried to discourage me again. I decided then and there not to ever ask advice from anyone at the commission. They had narrow opinions about what blind people are capable of doing. I was told by other blind students that they were dissuaded from technical majors, especially math. The blind students who ended up majoring in math (about four in number) said they also had been discouraged by the commission. In contrast to the people at the State Commission for the Blind, my family thought I could leap over any barrier, no matter how high. I appreciated their boundless faith in me, but it was as unrealistic as the commission's incredible lack of faith in the blind students in its care. My resolution not to ask advice of anyone at the state commission should have extended to include my own family members, but I would find that out much later, the hard way.

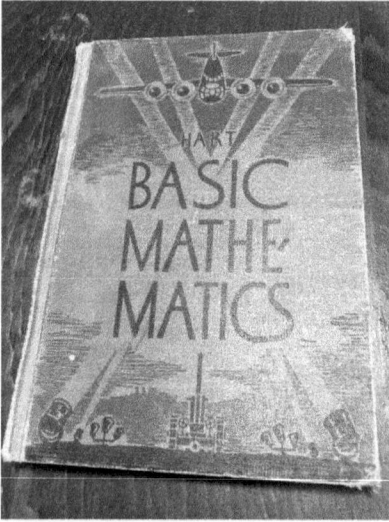

Basic Mathematics book cover, copyright 1942. Author's collection.

Mike Cross senior picture, 1966. Author's collection.

Mike Cross in his letter sweater, 1965. Author's collection.

Chapter 9
University Undergraduate

In the fall of 1966, I took Calculus 1 (Differential Calculus) at the University of Houston, where I spoke to Dr. Ingram on the first day. I asked if he would tell me exactly what he was writing on the blackboard, rather than just pointing and saying "this" or "that," it would be my responsibility to keep up. This was the standard approach that I took in all my classes, not just the math classes. When a professor forgot, I always raised my hand and reminded him to read the board to me. This seldom happened, though. I only had one professor who wasn't willing to work with me. That class didn't end well at all. But, for the most part, teachers respond positively to students who make a sincere effort in their classes. I was asking these professors to do something extra, so I felt obligated to be diligent and grateful.

I realize that the reader is probably not a mathematician, yet I feel compelled to present a few concepts I encountered early on in my first semester of calculus because they were major forces in shaping my identity. The class began the study of calculus with a discussion of some fundamental concepts of logic, and of sets. We were told some things we already knew, such as that 0 is the "additive identity," meaning that adding 0 to a number x results in x. It didn't change the number x. It preserved the number's identity. Also, 1 is the "multiplicative identity," meaning that multiplying a number x by 1 results in x. I thought we were wasting time, until we were asked to prove some basic facts, such as that these two identities are unique, 0 is not 1, and you can't divide by 0. None of this was difficult, but its purpose was to train us to construct arguments and prove theorems. Here's a sample proof:

> Let's assume, for the sake of argument, that 0 has a multiplicative inverse, whose value would be 1/0. That is, you can divide 1 by 0. Such an assumption leads to the contradiction that 1 must equal 0. (But I had previously proven that 1 does not equal 0.) In most classroom presentations, the three letters QED signal the end of the proof. QED is the abbreviation of the Latin *quod erat demonstrandum,* "that which was to be demonstrated."

After a rigorous consideration of number systems, the class finally got to the body proper of two-dimensional calculus (calculus in the X-Y plane). Several concepts needed to be defined: upper and lower bounds, least upper bound, and greatest lower bound. The most important concept that is needed for the development of calculus is that of a limit. Once these concepts were defined, calculus was off and running for the class. (See the appendix at the back of the book for a brief but rigorous discussion.)

My other classes were interesting, although not as interesting and fulfilling as calculus. Having read over the summer the calculus book that I had bought at Rice University's bookstore not only smoothed my way with the State Commission for the Blind, but it also gave me an advantage in physics. The textbook for that course presumed a knowledge of calculus. That particular physics classroom was arranged like a stadium with bleachers, seating three hundred students. Most of the people around me were freshmen taking Calculus 1. So I was one of the few not struggling with the math. In fact, since I understood differential equations, I would have understood shorter, more sophisticated mathematical derivations. Kenneth Hogstrum, whom I knew from Sam Rayburn High School, sat beside me in physics. He was gracious enough to make me a carbon copy of his notes. I made a B, while Kenneth made an A, in that class. Years later, Kenneth got a PhD in nuclear physics, becoming the head of radiation at MD Anderson Cancer Center. Still later, he taught physics at Louisiana State University.

I found French not to my liking. Its grammar was very similar to that of Spanish, and most of the vocabulary had a very familiar look but not sound. Overall, I thought French was inefficient because the terminal letters in words were often silent. But, worse than that, it sounded very pretentious. I didn't enjoy French nearly as much as Spanish. Still, I made an A the fall semester.

British Literature was in another of those monster classrooms. You stepped down into it like a sunken living room. But all the chairs were on ground level. This was a relief because of my balance problem. In the physics classroom, I carefully ascended the steps into the bleachers. Expecting to fall at any moment, I never felt safe until I was seated. In the British Literature classroom, I sat in the front row, hunched over and taking notes in a shorthand of my own devising. The presentation was straight lecture. Dr. Day wrote nothing on the blackboard. He never pointed at anything and said "this" or "that." That was another relief. I had no trouble taking notes. Having always loved history, I listened enthralled to Dr. Day's lectures about the events contemporaneous with the literature being covered. I was a math major, but this British Literature class was fascinating. He even talked about the evolution of the English language. This, and linguistics, made me think about a triple major. But no, that would be too much. Math and physics were more than enough to keep me busy.

In French, I got an A in the fall and a B in the spring. In physics, the opposite happened, B in the fall, and an A that spring. In January, I was inducted into the honor society, Phi Kappa Phi.

My freshman year, I commuted from Pasadena to the University of Houston, riding primarily with three high school acquaintances, Kenneth H., Kenny, and Alan. Never having been in a group of guys that joked and teased, at first I didn't know how to relate. Being in their company finally overcame my reserve, and I even relaxed enough to join in the teasing. I soon found myself looking forward to their company. Teasing me and each other mercilessly, they were continually doing something funny. Sam Rayburn's archrival, Pasadena High School, had kept our football team from winning district the previous year, so the two Kennys were ready to see a revenge match. They drove into the enemy's camp, Eagle Stadium. It had just flooded. (September rains always bring major flood problems to Pasadena, Texas.) When Kenneth parked and got out, the water covered the curb. He looked away just as Kenny leaped over the curb. When Kenneth looked back, he didn't see Kenny anywhere. Suddenly, a head broke the surface of the water, and Kenny swam across to the stadium side of the seven-and-a-half-foot-deep ditch. When this story spread around among the other Rayburn graduates attending the University of Houston, I was no longer the one being teased the most.

In the spring, Kenneth and I were in Dr. Rich's electromagnetism class. This man's credentials were impressive. He had a doctorate in physics, a master's in mathematics, and a license to practice medicine. When he walked into class, he started lecturing immediately. Again, Kenneth was making me a copy of his notes. And what was Dr. Rich writing on the board? He filled it with vector calculus, line and surface integrals. His equations were full of divergence and curl operators. Although I had seen this material in Johnson and Kiokemeister's calculus book, I needed a thorough review, and I needed it right then. How did I respond to this emergency? I went to the Cougar bookstore, bought a *Schaum's Outline of Vector Analysis*, and caught up with where I needed to be. Convinced I would fail the midterm, I studied the *Schaum's Outline* with as much diligence as I had done with the Johnson and Kiokemeister book. I took a further step: for the first time, I attended problem-solving sessions given by Dr. Rich's teaching assistant. These two efforts paid off. The A that I received on the midterm should have calmed my nerves, but it didn't. Still apprehensive about this class with such a brilliant professor, I merely replaced fear of the midterm with dread of the final. Well, a little fear can work wonders. I left the final thinking I had done well, and indeed I had! Kenneth and I both made an A, two of the three given in that class of three hundred students.

The other physics course I took that spring was a lab for one hour of credit. Kenneth was my lab partner. Otherwise, I would have been totally lost in there. The instructor was a Chinese teaching assistant. I never understood a word he said. Kenneth didn't understand either, but he could read the board. The instructor may have thought he was speaking English, but we were all sure he was lecturing in Chinese. Although I got nothing from his lectures, I read Kenneth's notes and all class handouts. I got out of there with a grade of C and, due to the circumstances, was very glad to get it.

The school year closed. I had a 3.5 GPA both semesters and was on the Dean's List. As the reader can tell, I owe much of my success that freshman year to Kenneth's help.

During the summer of 1967, I took at San Jacinto Junior College two courses in political science/government that would be required for graduation, so as not to be bothered with them while I was concentrating on math and physics during the regular school year. That year I discovered a jeweler's magnifying loupe which clipped to the earpiece of regular framed glasses. The loupe had two lenses which were mounted on an arm and could be pulled down and peered through. Each of the lenses was 5X, and pulled down together amounted to a combined magnification of 10X. Provided I could get sufficient light, this worked fairly well. When I was ready to write an answer, I moved the lenses out of my line of sight long enough to write. The lenses were small, and all characters had to slide past the area directly under them, making reading with them a slow process. I didn't have time to read a question twice. And too, doing this over a long period of time gave me a headache. This made finals hard because I was doing this for three hours at a stretch.

In the fall of my sophomore year, I almost had enough hours to be classified a junior. My grade in the third semester of calculus was a B. Not knowing what to expect until the second test, I had lost enough points on the first test to put an A out of reach. The third semester of physics, Physics 296, covered waves and oscillations. Again, my grade was B. It piqued my interest that the teacher was a physicist from the Manned Spacecraft Center of NASA at Clear Lake. (Today it is known as the Johnson Space Center.)

Back in the fall of 1967, I had started to dream of earning a doctorate in mathematics. A check into the requirements told me that I needed two years of foreign language, and not just any foreign language would do. Those most acceptable were languages where there was a backlog of untranslated works in mathematics. My year of French was acceptable even though there wasn't much of a backlog. For a second year, I wanted something different. The math department advised me that the language having the largest backlog was Russian. Enthusiastic about the challenge, I signed up. The teacher, who was from Moscow, must have had one of those names that defied pronunciation, at least by Americans. Whatever it was, he had changed it to Smith. The students in our small class understood him even though his accent was heavy. Class wisdom was that since not many people study Russian, Mr. Smith's flunking any of us would amount to his torpedoing his job. This was probably wrong, but this conjecture remained untested since none of us failed the course.

One of the men in that class had taken Russian in high school. I concluded that if Mr. Smith didn't grade on a curve, it would be hard to make an A, but I needn't have worried. I made an A both semesters, and so did the three other math majors in the class. One of them was a triple major. His second and third majors were German and Russian. The guy that had taken Russian in high school made a B.

The struggles with the language alone guaranteed camaraderie. Learning became a community project. Designed by the Greek Orthodox priest Saint Cyril, the Russian alphabet is called the Cyrillic alphabet. It has thirty-three letters, not all of which are actually pronounced. There are silent letters, which, when standing next to another letter, change the way that other letter is pronounced or even whether it is pronounced at all. Some consonants are spoken very differently. The Russian letter "*L*" is formed deep in the throat, and the tongue may get stuck. It sounds like a car engine trying to turn over. You take a running jump and you don't make it. Being a devoted fan of the Rocky and Bullwinkle cartoon show, I naturally pretended to be Boris Badenov when I spoke—and with some success because even Mr. Smith complimented me on my accent. I never told anyone what I considered the joke behind my accent.

Six weeks after the students had seen the Cyrillic alphabet for the first time, Mr. Smith assigned the class a fifty-page short story by Alexander Pushkin, titled "The Shot." To give an idea of the difficulty we faced, the story was in a Russian fifth-grade reader. Mr. Smith was pushing us hard. I spent an inordinate amount of time in the Russian dictionary to read that story. The sound of the language really appealed to my sense of humor. (The Russian word for "blind" sounds like "sleep-oy.") Those Boris and Natasha cartoons from the Rocky and Bullwinkle show were floating around in my head.

How difficult is Russian? I can think of only four cognates; these were the Russian words for chair, couch, hospital, and newspaper. Of course, there were words, such as "radio," that were borrowed from English or other languages. But overall, I found the vocabulary to be totally alien. Speaking a complete sentence was a real struggle because you were thinking your way through the labyrinth of grammar as you spoke. Russian is inflected, like Greek and German. In addition to the five cases in those languages, Russian has one called the instrumental case. If you were to say "We are going to Moscow by train," the word for train would be in the instrumental case, because it was the instrument used to travel.

One day, the class was trying to find the logic behind a particularly weird point of grammar. I proposed a geometric theorem for navigating the rule. The class being full of math and physics majors, we all had a laugh. Another peculiarity of Russian is inconsistencies. There are some verbs that switch infinitives halfway through the conjugation. But sudden changes and switches are not limited to verbs. Once, I said jokingly that the rule being discussed was only true until three o'clock in the afternoon.

Enthusiastic about the Russian language lab, I perfected my Boris Badenov accent. No one suspected anything unusual. One day, the guy who had taken Russian in high school leaned over to me in the lab and said, "Cross, you have an unfair disadvantage." I was flattered by his joke. This particular guy was a sloppy dresser. I remember one of his outfits especially, because someone else remarked on it when he wore it to a formal event. We, as a group, were singing a Russian folk ballad in front of a gathering of students of other languages, like French and German. I was wearing a suit, as were most of the other men. But this guy wore blue jeans and a short-sleeved bright-yellow shirt with horizontal stripes, each in a different but equally bright color. I know because one of the math majors described it to me in vivid detail. We were surely the motliest group at the party. It probably hurt just to look at us.

The math major who described that shirt to me was Dick, a tall and rangy man who commuted to the University of Houston over a long distance. This made it impractical for him to go home between classes, so on his class days, Dick spent long hours on campus. In the spring, Dick showed up in one of my math classes. This led to our going to the library together, comparing notes about Russian and math, and occasionally eating lunch together. Polite and friendly, he was the first person at the university whom I talked with on a regular basis. Conversations didn't stay on academics. Seven or eight years older than I, Dick seemed to understand that my social life had been pretty limited. As a married man, he gave me some welcomed advice about women in general. Everything he said was laced with a generous helping of humor. I remember Dick fondly.

Not since junior high school had I had any major problems in my journey toward my goals. I had started to think mistakenly that they were all behind me. The challenge from the State Commission for the Blind had been so easily overcome that I failed to see it as a warning. When the state agency supposedly on the side of the blind doesn't have confidence in its clients, blind students suffer. That should have told me that more battles were ahead. In fact, the war would never end. So I should not have been surprised that prejudices were very much alive in the sighted world. Even beyond that, unless people understood your problems, they wouldn't know how to help or give good advice.

In the fall semester of 1967, I did okay in calculus, physics, and Russian, but in another area, I lost the struggle for the first time ever. I should have known that signing up for anything beyond those three courses (four, counting the physics lab) was asking to be overloaded. Maybe sighted students can do it, but I can't—especially when three of the four courses were difficult and demanded a lot of time. It came about this way. Kenneth had suggested taking Engineering 226, a FORTRAN-based computer science course covering numerical analysis techniques. It was a one-hour course, and I was already familiar with some numerical methods. And if I had stayed with that plan, I would have been all right.

I was in the math department offices up on the sixth floor of the liberal arts building being counseled about my fall schedule. "Well, Mr. Cross, the more economical way to take this is Math 190, a four-hour course, rather than this one-hour engineering course followed by a second engineering course." I could tell he didn't want me to take an engineering course. He continued,

"This replaces those two engineering courses, and it's finished in one semester instead of two." I should have asked why this was a math course instead of a computer science course. Unknown to me, the University of Houston computer science department didn't offer courses at an undergraduate level at that time. This should have raised a red flag. I didn't stand my ground, and I paid for it. So, I signed up to do in one semester (in a math course) what other science-oriented people were doing in two semesters (in engineering courses). Also, those engineering courses would have been more in line with my field of interest at the time, which was physics.

I made no inquiry at all about the computing environment for Math 190. I should have at least asked about the course content. I had been in the engineering building and knew that there were lots of keypunches available there. In contrast, the underground pit housing the UNIVAC had one small keypunch area and very few keypunch machines. If I had known this, I never would have signed up for Math 190. Perhaps I would have walked out if only I had asked a few questions. Life gets hard when you don't ask the right questions. John Wooden, the famous UCLA basketball coach, lived by a maxim: "Failing to prepare is preparing to fail." Up to this point, I had lived and breathed this same maxim, although I had never put it into words.

I had allowed myself to be talked out of my own carefully thought-out plan. This was the first domino to fall.

On the first day of computer science class (Math 190), I met my two lab partners. It seemed that there were not enough keypunch machines to go around. So every keypunch card deck was a joint effort by three people. My two partners told me that my input was not needed, but they really meant that it wasn't welcome. This was the second domino to fall.

I approached the professor about not saying "this" or "that," but rather explaining what he was pointing to. He agreed readily enough. Yet, in class, he ignored my attempts to ask for clarification. Doing exactly what I had asked him not to do, he always pointed at the board and said "this" and "that." Outside class, he was always too busy to talk to me. The dominoes were toppling.

The computer programming language used in the course was not FOR-TRAN, but MAD, Michigan Algorithm Decoder. Our text, the "MAD magazine," as I called it, was very slim and worse than worthless. A month passed, and one day I found myself calling home.

"Dad, I need to drop this computer science course. It's not going well at all."

"Mike, I've heard you predict disaster before, and you always make an A. Don't drop this course. You'll do okay." But I did not do okay.

Even as I saw the train wreck coming in Math 190, my grades were good in physics, Russian, and third-semester calculus. What lessons did I take away from this experience? Don't let anyone change your plans unless you have the time to check out those changes. What I would conclude later is that sometimes the path to success goes through failure. For the sake of a career I didn't know I would have, I needed a computer science course with a broader focus than numerical analysis, and the engineering course wasn't it. This was the wrong time for me to take computer science. The situation that would accommodate my needs wouldn't be available for a few more semesters. If I had dropped this course, I would have walked away from computer science and never returned to it. So, this was a necessary failure that would propel me into a rematch.

Christmas 1967 was a dark time for me. The first F I had ever received filled me with self-doubt. I never said a word to Dad about not letting me drop the course I had just failed. I'm sure he felt guilty. But I was the boy who had cried "wolf" once too often. He had confidence in me, and I had let him down. Worse than that, I had disappointed myself. Yes, a lot of things went wrong, but the blame was mine. For two weeks, my mood was dark and brooding. I wasn't ready to retake the course, at least not right away. I had to understand what had just happened and plan how I could keep it from happening again. I couldn't count on fewer obstacles the next time I took the computer science course. I would just have to overcome the situation, no matter how bad it was. It would push me to the limit. How would my other courses fare during such an effort? I decided to isolate it by retaking the course over a summer. I counted on a monumental struggle and didn't want anything else distracting me from the fight. My anger gnawed at me. This marked a change in me. I was skeptical of advice from anyone, and I decided in the future to drop a course if needed, without asking permission. Time for Mike to grow up! I am responsible for my failure—nobody else is.

Taking the two engineering courses would not erase the F. I would have to take Math 190 over again, and I could count on all the same obstacles. But I would wait and take it during a later summer. In the spring of 1968, I took Russian, psychology, advanced calculus, and junior-level mechanics, my final lecture class in physics. I dismissed my self-doubt, and I doubled and tripled up on math courses. I never again failed to make the Dean's List.

That year, in the spring of 1968, I also took my first elective, Introductory Psychology. We read about Pavlov's dogs, positive and negative reinforcements, and other basic facts. One day, on my way into class, I hugged the wall to allow someone to exit as I entered. The result was that I ran into a pencil sharpener mounted on the wall at eye level. Its crank handle caught my right eye and left me dazed and shedding copious tears. I didn't want to miss a lecture. My eye watered all through class, and after class, everyone rushed away. I was too shy to stop a stranger and ask to be assisted to the university clinic. This incident was all the more frightening because my right eye is the one with some sight left. It really hurt, and that eye dripped tears and was inflamed for days. Needless to say, I was unable to take notes, or even concentrate on a lecture. That pencil sharpener bordered a pathway. From my perspective, the layout was thoughtless. Sighted people, on the other hand, would have no trouble avoiding it. Still, I wished it were somewhere else. Anyway, I walked around between classes, and by the time I found a person and decided to ask where the clinic was, the bell rang for the next class. That night Mom looked at it. My eye hurt, but there was no serious damage. After this semester, my courses weren't heavy reading courses. This took a burden off Mom, who had been reading my textbooks into a tape recorder.

From this point forward, my mother was uninvolved in my studies because I was taking mostly math and physics. Over the previous seven years, her assistance had been invaluable. Anne Sullivan's contribution to Helen Keller's future was no greater than Mom's care for me and Tracy. I wasn't as great a challenge as Helen, but Mom had two sons having very different disabilities to deal with. Tracy's frequent medical emergencies added another dimension to her task. Tracy and I always agreed that Mom saved my life once and Tracy's life three times. In addition, she had a household to manage. Anne Sullivan and my mother were superior women, models for all time.

My social life opened up a tiny crack. When I was twenty-one, a girl I had known for years asked me for a date. That was my first date. However, the crack didn't widen very fast. My second date was when I was twenty-four. This time, I asked out that same girl. The third date with that girl came much later. My fault! In between those two dates, I began to take more notice of campus events. At last, I was learning to waste time without feeling so guilty. Plays, movies, and concerts occurred at several spots around the university. I didn't yet have an interest in patronizing any of them, but I knew that they were popular entertainment opportunities.

On campus for fourteen hours at a stretch, I had no opportunity to relax and listen to a talking book. I looked for a place where I could simply sit in a comfortable chair and go to sleep. Without catnaps, my concentration flagged. A dark corner in the library fit the bill nicely. One day, I fell asleep and must have hit the play button because a librarian tapped me on the shoulder. "Please turn off your tape recorder, or you'll have to leave." Too embarrassed to stay, I turned off the recorder, collected my books, and left. I would have to look for a new spot, and be more careful with the recorder. Aware of my problem with long days, Mom phoned the Church of Christ office at the Religion Center on campus. Not wanting to be distracted from my studies, I was reluctant to get involved. However, one day, I found myself sitting on the couch in the Church of Christ suite of rooms. Avoiding the library, I had left class with hours to kill, wondering where I might find a quiet place to study. That day I decided to try the church suite. Adjoining the room where I sat was the Bible Chair Director's office. I have discovered that people will talk to me as long as I don't start discussing math, which I have trouble not doing. There was a voice behind the closed door. He was on the phone. On this already unusual day, when I no longer heard the voice, I knocked on the door and introduced myself. Shaking hands with Steve Smith, I could hear the smile in his voice as he talked.

"What are you studying?"

I explained that I was working toward a BS in mathematics. If he was surprised, I didn't sense it.

"You are welcome to drop by between classes and visit. You might even find a math major to talk to. We always have coffee and tea, and lots of good company. I'm usually busy in the office, but I'm always happy to talk to the students about campus life. I also teach extension courses through Abilene Christian College."

I left and walked to physics class, where I was in friendly rivalry with Lilly Mar, a Chinese girl. On test after test, Lilly and I alternately had the top score. Lilly's sultry voice was inquisitive and friendly. Gradually, I decided that I liked brainy girls a lot. Back at the Religion Center, I had become friends with a girl named Billie. She was interested in what I did and who I knew. One day, I mentioned my admiration of this girl in my physics class. To my surprise, Billie happened to know Lilly. I must have been more readable than I thought because Billie guessed that I had a huge crush on Lilly. Brainy girls absolutely turned me on! Well, Billie told me not to be so shy and to ask

Lilly for a date. The age-old problem of transportation arose. How would I solve this? I could invite her to one of the things on campus, like a movie over at the Quadrangle, or a concert at the University Center. So, one day after class, I approached Lilly.

"*Casablanca* is showing at the Quad. Would you like to see it with me?"

"Oh, Mike! I would like that, but my parents won't let me date a boy who isn't Chinese."

I didn't know what to say. I didn't anticipate such an answer. It was 1968, and I saw different races together everywhere on campus. Disappointed, I chided myself for taking my focus off studying. Billie was a disappointed matchmaker. I determine to stick my nose back in the books and let life slide past. The spring semester drew to an end, and I prepared to take a psychology course over the summer of 1968.

My third confrontation with discouragement (after the State Commission for the Blind, and the computer science course, Math 190) came a year later, and it was a verbal assault. I stayed offended for six weeks. This incident could have destroyed my newly resurrected confidence. In the summer of 1969 (after two successful semesters of math and psychology courses), I took electronics, my second physics lab. I wasn't taking anything else because I was apprehensive. Well, there was reason to be apprehensive. I had two lab partners. One was the quiet type. The other was a nightmare. As he built circuits and took measurements, he was talking to me and to whomever cared to listen. And I suspect that most people didn't want to hear any of it. Here's a sample of what he said on a regular basis for the first week. "Goddamn! Why did I have to get stuck with a blind man for a lab partner? Hell! I'm going to have to carry your load and mine, too. It isn't fair!" I waited for the professor to take control of his class; he never did. There would be no help from that quarter. I remember thinking that unless I did something soon, I would be run off the road just as I had been in the computer science course, and I couldn't afford to wait long. When on the second day he renewed his attack, I made my move. I reached across the table and grabbed the circuit he had just finished assembling. I quickly dismantled it, reassembled it, and laid it down in front of him—all the while looking, not at the circuit, but straight at him. I assembled it by touch. I said nothing. If I thought that would end it, I was wrong. He was surprised, but his tirade resumed as if I had done nothing. We got our first lab report back with a C grade. That didn't keep him from insulting me, although he had denied me any input into that report. To say I took umbrage at this unrelenting barrage of insults would be an understatement. Enough was enough! I erupted, telling him what an incompetent nincompoop I thought he was. "I intend to make an A in here, and I don't intend to let an idiot like you mess it up. Starting today, I take over! You don't know enough math to write our reports!" His colossal ego needed to eat crow. I didn't miss a chance to rub my superior knowledge in his face.

When the next few reports came back with good grades, I expected the situation to improve. Wrong again! We fought every day, and he backed down every day. I hated these fights, but my survival was on the line. I would not fail again! Trading insults with him didn't end the rancor. It ended without any harsh words being exchanged. It happened this way: One day, he turned on an oscilloscope and got a screen full of noise. He had no earthly idea what to do. I had never seen an oscilloscope, but I started asking questions and making suggestions. "Reduce the image down to a point." One of the buttons did that. "Okay, now move the point to the origin etched on the screen, then release the button to expand the point." The X and Y axes were etched onto the screen, and two rotating knobs moved the point to the origin. It worked! Suddenly a graph appeared on the screen. That marked a change in the atmosphere. His combative spirit vanished. Hostilities ceased. I was quite happy to address him as an equal. One day he said, "If we make an A in here, I'll buy you a steak." We got a B-plus at the end of the course. But this was such an unpleasant episode in my life, I was satisfied with a B.

Could I have handled this better? Yes. It disturbs me that I discarded the Golden Rule so easily. Once I was writing our reports, I should have ignored his insults. I didn't live up to my own standards of behavior. Beyond that, I let myself down in a second way. I didn't take the next two labs, a requirement for a major in physics. Before this, I had considered having a double major in math and physics. It didn't happen. I settled for a minor. Just remembering this incident makes me angry. The memory of the F in the computer science course, Math 190, had made my response to my lab partner ferocious. Without that memory firing my anger, would I have been up to the confrontation? Conclusion: Even failure is valuable. I see God's hand in how well one sad event can feed into a better one, or maybe two—even if I didn't handle events as well as I should have. The second good outcome came the following summer (1970), when I had my rematch with computer science.

But, before and between those two summers, I took more math courses, including vector analysis, linear algebra, introduction to abstract algebra, advanced math for science and engineering, and courses in mathematical analysis. My professor for vector analysis, Louis Brand, was memorably impressive. Born in 1885 in Cincinnati, Ohio, he had earned three engineering degrees from the University of Cincinnati and a PhD from Harvard by 1917. He wrote several texts on vector mechanics, vector analysis, and advanced calculus, the first one being published in 1930. (Some of Louis Brand's books have been republished in 2006, 2013, and 2020, giving testimony to their lasting usefulness.) After retiring in 1955 from the University of Cincinnati (where he had chaired the Mathematics Department), he had been appointed MD Anderson Distinguished Professor of Mathematics and chairman of the Department of Mathematics at the University of Houston. Professor Brand was in his early eighties when he taught my vector analysis course in the fall of 1968. He passed away just a few years later, in 1971. I heard from his students that he had developed procedures for the US Navy for landing airplanes on aircraft carriers. I don't know how accurate that story was, but it wouldn't surprise me.

While I was pursuing an education, my family wasn't standing still. Tracy was enrolled at Sam Rayburn High School, never once setting foot on school property. Except for a year in the third grade, he had always been homebound for schooling. Meanwhile, Kay was in her last year at San Jacinto Junior College in 1967–1968, majoring in home economics. Dad's employment with the Port of Houston, where he inspected ships, continued to be dependable and steady. No longer reading to me, Mom helped Tracy with schoolwork. In 1969, Tracy, who was now fifteen, joined a rock band, name long forgotten. Their first gig was in a Houston bar. Worried that Tracy might get mugged, Dad and Uncle Joe checked it out to see how wild it got. Nothing happened.

Halloween 1969 rolled around, and Aunt Betty's daughter Patricia came over to assist Tracy in putting on a spooky reception for the kids at the front door. Cackling and shrieking over a microphone, she welcomed groups of startled trick-or-treaters. After the kids picked up their spilled bags, Tracy's hand appeared to disperse candy. Tracy himself was hidden by the paneling that came halfway up the screen door. Studying in my room with the door shut, I tried to ignore all the screams and shouts. I succeeded, but furry little Bounce-A-Lot didn't. Unable to concentrate because of her frantic barking, I picked her up and walked into the living room for some candy. At that moment, Patricia screamed, and I heard a paper sack hit the porch floor. A weak whimpering filled the silence. Tracy opened the door and peered out. A little girl stood there.

"Oh, I'm sorry!" said Tracy.

Her mother stepped up onto the porch. "I think she just wet her pants."

After this incident, Patricia held back until she saw heads above the paneling. This didn't guarantee no tiny kids, but there were no more kids wetting their pants.

That Christmas, Mrs. Carl, a neighbor, rang the doorbell and gave Mom a platter of miniature pies encircling a container of rum sauce. We placed it under the tree, and Bounce-A-Lot claimed it as hers. We often saw her lying on that package. We all thought it funny to tease that poor dog. Tracy would scoot down the hall saying "Treat," and Bounce-A-Lot would leave her place atop the pies and start toward the hall. Seated close to the tree, I would reach for her private package, making sure that she could see me and clearing my throat to get her attention. Bounce-A-Lot's progress toward the hall would be rapid, so when she saw me out of the corner of her eye reaching for her package, her rear end would fishtail around while her feet were scrambling, trying to get traction. And she barked furiously as she whirled around. Often, we all enjoyed moving a sock around and around us as we sat. Bounce-A-Lot was quick, and sometimes she caught it. Dad used to ask her questions and move the sock, and her whole head would move up and down or sideways depending on the answer to the question. The onlookers always thought it very amusing.

I still did not live in the dorms, because by this time, I knew enough other university students from Pasadena that transportation wasn't a problem. But my ride's schedule often didn't match mine. This left me with lots of time between classes. To me, it is a sin to waste time, so I went to the library and did homework or read beyond my classes. Kay was at U of H my junior year (1968–69), so we often met for lunch and went to the library together. In my sister's company, I actually violated my rules and wasted some time. But mostly I studied, while Kay either read or wrote a letter. The letters went to Mark Hayter, whom she later married. He attended Stephen F. Austin State University, where he was majoring in forestry. After that year, Kay transferred to SFA. I naturally missed Kay's company.

I had very few social contacts, but during the same year that Kay was at U of H with me, I made an important friend. A guy named Peter was in two of my math classes. Despite my poor vision, I noticed him right away.

His wheelchair was always blocking my path. We started talking, and Peter offered to take notes for me, the way Kenneth had done in physics. He read my pure math proofs, and I listened to Peter read his. He stated conjectures and constructed proofs the same way I did. So, his suggestions exactly fit into my thought processes, and vice versa. Peter was very good to bounce ideas off of. We both had a very rigid way of presenting an argument. This made collaboration easy. The list of courses available to us was narrowing, and as a result, we were in quite a few classes together. Peter didn't allow anyone to push his wheelchair. He had been shoved down an escalator by a helpful but incompetent man. So, when Peter allowed me to push his chair around the building (even past the escalator), I was honored. Unable to see what was in front of his chair, I followed orders precisely. I listened carefully to his instructions, and I didn't push unless I was told to. Our communication went beyond mathematics. Peter had had polio as a child. As different as our disabilities were, our experiences were strikingly similar. Where our life experiences differed, it was easy for us to relate to one another's hopes and disappointments.

Eventually, we got around to girls. Peter was socially much more advanced than I, meaning that he had had more than two dates with a girl. Our experience deficit was how Peter came to be telling me the dos and don'ts of dating. I don't remember any of it except one story. A girl was in Peter's lap. Well, let me just skip the story and state the lesson, and he was about to learn a very important one. Don't play any jokes, especially of the prank variety, that might startle your date. The prank scared her, and she lost control and peed all over both of them. The date didn't go so well after that. Thanks to this story, I have avoided disasters.

As I headed into my last year (1969–70), all of my core subjects were behind me, and I was free to concentrate on mathematics. I wasn't quite brave enough to take four math courses at once. To make up for semesters in which I only took nine hours, I would skip vacations and take summer courses. I considered vacations a waste of time anyway. The next summer arrived (the summer of 1970), bringing the dreaded rematch with that computer science course. I prepared to put myself in that same trap and fight my way out. I thought I would face the same exact obstacles, but that didn't prove to be the case. The university now offered an undergraduate degree in computer science. So the course I needed was no longer in the math department. Also, the language would be FORTRAN 4, not Michigan Algorithm Decoder.

Unlike before, the students were not broken up into groups of three. Great! I would write my own programs this time. I determined to invade the computer pit and not budge. And I did! Camping out on the keypunch machines until my whole card deck was punched, I wasn't about to be run off the road again. The experience was totally different because the professor was very accommodating. In class he didn't point at the board and say "this" or "that," and outside class he was approachable. The text was readable, and I enjoyed exploring everything that FORTRAN 4 offered, even sections of the book not covered in class. This was my revenge match, and I spared no effort. At the end of the summer, I received the A that I demanded of myself, and an important piece of my education fell into place.

Although painful, this sequence of incidents proved necessary to my future. If I had dropped Math 190 as I wanted, I would probably have felt fortunate to escape something that, at the time, I thought unnecessary to my education. If I had dropped it, I probably would have skipped taking any computer science courses. Looking back on this whole episode, I almost missed being equipped for a future that kept me continually writing programs. I would have been unprepared for the events that came to dominate my life. I would have laughed at the very idea that I would have a career in the computer industry. Yet, it came to pass that I retired from IBM. I do not believe everything is predestined, and yet that doesn't mean God won't put a stumbling block in front of you, then give you the chance to make it into a trampoline. The twists in life are strange. I had started taking three math courses per semester and nothing else. Some of them were rings and ideals, advanced linear algebra, group theory, and more courses in mathematical analysis. This led to a string of semesters with a 4.0 GPA.

That fall of 1970, I still needed six hours to finish my bachelor's degree. There were a few math courses at the undergraduate level that I hadn't taken, but none of them were available at the right times. I got permission to sign up for two graduate-level math courses, but they were both discontinued because neither class had the required minimum of five students signed up. This left me scrambling to find something to take. I had more than enough math, so I looked at courses in other fields. I went through the list of open classes. A sociology course, population analysis, appealed to me, but nothing else on the list did. Overhearing me say that I needed one more course, Steve Smith made an agreeable suggestion. That's how I ended up taking an extension course in comparative religion through Abilene Christian College.

These two courses proved to be the most interesting, most informative courses I have ever had. The comparative religion class was taught by a PhD candidate at Rice University. At one point during that semester, both classes were studying India. They complemented each other so well that I told each professor what was being covered in the other class.

Because of the comparative religion course, I spent more time at the Religion Center, regularly eating lunch with the students who hung out there, and my social life was launched. One of the girls, Susan, took an interest in me. On my third date ever, she announced bluntly that not many girls would have anything to do with me. Then, she said I needed experience. It consisted of movies, conversation, dinner, and a peck on the cheek. Transportation didn't prove to be an obstacle after all; she seemed willing to pick me up in her car. But I was nagged by the thought that Susan was just taking pity on me. My confidence in social situations never quite recovered from what she said to me: "Most girls won't have anything to do with you." Susan wasn't manipulating me; she simply told me the truth as she saw it. For a long time afterwards, I was too easily discouraged. There was no second date with Susan, and we both graduated at the end of that semester.

In December of 1970, I graduated magna cum laude with a Bachelor of Science in mathematics and a minor in physics. I was twenty-three years old. I didn't buy a class ring or even attend the University of Houston graduation ceremony. I had seldom worn my high school ring and probably wouldn't wear a college ring either, so I wasn't inclined to shell out the money for one. My diploma was enough.

Bounce-A-Lot claiming her Christmas present, 1961. Author's collection.

Bounce-A-Lot opening her present, 1961. Author's collection.

Chapter 10

The Emptying of a Nest

I relaxed a little, having that first degree behind me, but I now faced a bigger challenge. Could I prevail in graduate school? From this point forward, the competition would be much stiffer, and because I had made up my mind long ago that I wanted a PhD, this would be a long struggle.

Enough time had passed that my high school acquaintances were no longer attending the University of Houston. Rides were getting harder to find. So, when a girl in one of my classes said she was from Pasadena, I arranged transportation with her for that semester. Aside from that one class, our schedules didn't mesh, so I remained at school when she went home. She did return for a late afternoon class, at which time I rode back to Pasadena with her. I still spent many hours at school, but the pressure was off Dad to provide me rides that semester.

Eventually, I didn't know anyone from Pasadena going to U of H. This meant I relied on Dad to get me there and back. In consideration of Dad, I decided not to schedule my classes across all five weekdays. I signed up for Monday, Wednesday, and Friday classes, staying home Tuesdays and Thursdays to do homework, which consisted of reviewing axioms and constructing either proofs or counterexamples to conjectures the teacher had challenged us to resolve. Attending classes only three days a week gave me more freedom. I didn't need to arrange for as many rides. But I would spend more hours at school. It was hard to relax at the university. At home, I didn't have to worry about being caught without a coat when a cold front suddenly blew in, but on school days, I was on campus sometimes twelve hours. On those days, I often did get caught with the wrong coat— sometimes none at all.

Bounce-A-Lot frequently came into my room to visit while I studied. I pulled open the bottom desk drawer, where I kept a pillow for her to lie on. She watched me, getting up when I did. I took many breaks from study to stoop down and pet her. When I left the room, she followed me, and I couldn't resist picking up that cute little dog.

Kay had transferred to Stephen F. Austin State University in Nacogdoches to be near Mark Hayter, who was studying forestry. A year later they married, and Mark became a forest ranger in Conroe, Texas. Tracy was finishing high school, still homebound. Hearing Tracy being instructed by his teacher was an amusing experience. Trying not to disturb them, I shut my door and spent my days puzzling over conjectures from class. I tiptoed around and tried to keep Bounce-A-Lot quiet. But she barked if she thought I was going to leave the room without her. So, of course, I had to pick her up and take her wherever I went.

One day I answered the phone. It was Lilly, that Chinese girl from my last physics class.

"Mike, I work in records, and when I saw your name among recent graduates, I looked up your grade point average. Your GPA is 3.696. You missed being summa cum laude by .004. Why didn't you petition to be allowed to graduate summa cum laude?"

I said, "I didn't know I could do that."

"Mike, there are people that are graduating cum laude because they petitioned. That's two levels below summa, and you were so close."

We chatted a while longer, and the call ended. I had mixed feelings about having missed being summa cum laude by so little. Well, I have what I earned, but nothing more. I was glad to hear from Lilly, and I would have asked her for a date, but in my mind her earlier refusal was final. It never occurred to me that a girl would ever change her mind, especially about me. I didn't read anything into her call other than friendly interest. Was it more than it appeared to be? I will never know, but years later, Lilly called me again, and she did let me know that she was open to going out with me. If I hadn't been in a relationship, I would have gladly gone out with her, but, as it was, I had to decline.

Mom, who no longer read to me, did housework, answered the mail, cooked, cleaned, and watched TV. Life had slowed for her, and she seemed much more relaxed—there were no ongoing crises demanding her attention. Tracy's worst ordeals were over. His problem now was to figure out what to do with the rest of his life, which would always be lived in a wheelchair.

■ ■ ■

That May was memorable for two reasons. The State Commission for the Blind, the entity that didn't think I could major in mathematics, informed me that an award was waiting for me in its office. On May 20, 1971, my State Commission for the Blind counselor presented me with the Recording for the Blind National Achievement Award for outstanding achievement in academics. Its board had selected me as being one of the top six blind graduates in the United States. He said that the top three recipients would receive their recognition at the White House from President Richard Nixon. I was one of the bottom three alternates, who were not invited to go to the White House. The letter the counselor read to me said that I had been included because of the difficulty of my field of study.

May was also the beginning of an amazing vacation. Since I hadn't yet moved onto campus, I still went places with the family. Dad and Kay's intended, Mark Hayter, shared driving duties on a trip to California. We started in the dark and drove all night to avoid the heat. We made very few pit stops, despite frequent pleas from the back seat. Seventeen hours later we arrived in El Paso, where we had intended to spend the next night, but when Mom saw the motel room, she said, "Let's keep driving." Overcome by fatigue, Dad finally stopped in mid-afternoon at a motel in Deming, New Mexico. We crashed immediately in our rooms. I don't know who woke up first, me or Tracy. He got into his chair and wheeled over to the window. The sun was on the horizon.

"Wow, that was a short night!" We proceeded to wake the others.

Dad was not very happy. "No, Tracy! We've only been here a few hours. That's not a sunrise, it's a sunset."

Everyone was grouchy. Tracy said, "No it isn't! That's a sunrise!"

Dad got out of bed. "No, boys, it's a sunset!" and he walked to the TV and switched it on.

Andy Williams's voice filled the room: "Exactly like you!" No one was in the mood for a love song. Dad flicked it off. He was right; it was evening. Bounce-A-Lot let us know that she needed to go out. So we all got dressed, Mom took the dog for a walk, and Dad went out for hamburgers. We were still tired, so after eating we went back to bed, and slept the night through.

Refreshed from our slumbers, we drove for another two days, again with very few stops. As on previous vacations, the mobile short-wave radio helped make the long, hot journey bearable. Our only scheduled stop was at the Grand Canyon, where we stared down, not quite able to comprehend what we saw. The Colorado River was a thin, silver thread far, far away. We returned to the car and continued driving. Is this trip ever going to end?

We finally arrived in Antioch, California, at Dad's sister Helen's home. Uncle Lou, who drove a milk run for Borden's, took a week's vacation to show us around Northern California. Over the next week we visited the Japanese Tea Garden, Telegraph Hill, and Chinatown in San Francisco; an old mining town; and Lake Tahoe. Tracy had been in a wheelchair for five years now, so when we visited the mission overlooking San Francisco Bay, Tracy stayed in the car alone because the mission was wheelchair inaccessible. Since he was seventeen years old, Mom wasn't as apprehensive as she used to be. Tracy wasn't quite alone; he had Bounce-A-Lot to keep him company. Up in the mission, I wore a heavy wool coat, yet I was so chilled by the breeze off the bay that I couldn't take in my surroundings. I wasn't aware of anything, except how cold I was. My teeth chattered, and I shook violently until we left. Mark Twain was right: "The coldest winter I ever spent was a summer in San Francisco." (Actually, Mark Twain never said that. But he might as well have.) I was never so glad to get back in the car.

Bounce-A-Lot enjoyed sniffing around in the Japanese Tea Garden. The twisting paths were confusing to me, and I was glad to leave. We didn't let Bounce-A-Lot go to the bathroom in the garden, and she was more than ready when we got back to the parking lot. While we all sat in the car watching, Mom took her to a patch of grass to tinkle. The police, who happened to be driving by, stopped.

"What kind of animal is that?"

"She's a long-haired Chihuahua," Mom said.

"Oh," said the officer.

He rolled the window back up, and the police car continued on its way. Everyone in our car, except me, witnessed the exchange and was amused.

In the town of Lake Tahoe, Aunt Helen and Uncle Lou took us into Harveys, one of the gambling dens of iniquity. Tracy was old enough to come with us, but again, the casino was wheelchair inaccessible. He sat in the lobby holding Bounce-A-Lot. She proved to be a big attraction; people kept coming over to pet her. Back outside, we drove around to see the sights. Everyone who could see thought Lake Tahoe very beautiful. Fringed with pine trees, it is the second-deepest lake in the United States, and the bluest we had ever seen. Truly magnificent!

We couldn't leave California without seeing the giant redwoods and the sequoias, including the famous huge General Sherman sequoia. We drove our car through a tunnel cut in a redwood tree, like you see on postcards, and we took our own photo featuring Mom and us kids. Oh yes, Bounce-A-Lot too! The main impression that lingers with me is how quiet the redwood forest was. There were no birds. The only sound was the wind in the trees. Redwoods contain a chemical that insects don't like. No bugs, hence no birds! We drove on to the sequoias in a deep valley. The tops of the trees were beneath us. It reminded us of a misty wood out of J. R. R. Tolkien's *Lord of the Rings* trilogy, and we left suitably impressed. It was on to Yosemite and Bridalveil Fall. We stood there silent, appreciating the cliffs around us shrouded in a fine mist.

The vacation over, Kay and Mark returned to Stephen F. Austin State University in Nacogdoches. In November of that same year, Mark and Kay married in a small civil service attended by family members only.

In 1972, Tracy graduated from high school and quit the band. They had been playing clubs around town for three years. That fall, Tracy started at San Jacinto Junior College to study commercial art. He made an early visit to the campus to see how wheelchair accessible it was. There were barriers a chair couldn't pass, so Dad bought Tracy a walker, and he revisited the campus with a new question to be answered: How hard would it be to make classes on time? This place was very large. He got tired, and for that reason, he didn't sign up for a full load. The day he registered, Mom stood in line at the bookstore to buy his art supplies while Tracy and Dad waited in the car. Why was it taking so long?

When Mom got to the front of the extremely long line, she exclaimed, "What a line! Why don't you get some help!"

"Yeah? Would you like a job?"

Mom walked up to the car and handed the supplies in through the window. "I'm working until 9:00 p.m. Be here to pick me up."

As she walked back to the bookstore, Tracy and Dad exchanged surprised looks. This was the beginning of Mom's new life. Kay and I weren't living at home anymore; I had moved into the dorms at the University of Houston. Although Tracy still lived at home, he didn't need Mom's help, so she wasn't helping anybody. Emancipated at last!

That year, Tracy saw Mom daily at school, sometimes meeting her for lunch. Two years later, he received an associate of arts (AA) degree, whereupon he went to work for Boots, a camera repair shop. Tracy continued painting in his spare time, until his bedroom walls were overflowing with them. Although he never found a job doing commercial art directly, his artist's eye gave him a magic touch with the Photoshop program. Three years later, he switched to Cheeseman, another camera shop.

Over the next two years, Mark decided he didn't want to be a forest ranger after all, so he entered Sam Houston State University in Huntsville to get a master's degree in American history. Kay had taken a job as a secretary with the Texas Department of Corrections (TDC) Windham School District, a non-geographical district created in 1969 to provide educational services to Texas inmates. On her way into the Walls Unit (a nickname for the Texas State Penitentiary at Huntsville), she usually passed through two security gates. Her office was on the second floor, a short walk from the electric chair. One day in 1974, Kay's building was evacuated because a prison break was under way. An inmate named Carrasco was holding hostages. Kay had just returned from lunch with Mark. The office radio was on.

"And now for local news, Mrs. Thelma Jones lost her Mexican 'chu who uh, who uh' yesterday." The whole office started to laugh.

"He answers to the name Squeaky. So, if you find Squeaky, call our switchboard."

At that moment, a prison guard rushed in. "Everyone needs to evacuate immediately. There's no time to collect purses. We need to leave, right now!" Of course, Kay snagged her purse and followed him across the street to the administration building. A Catholic priest sped past Kay on his way to negotiate, but Carrasco took him hostage too. Prison officials, not ready to deal with the media, didn't allow Kay or anyone else to make a call. Carrasco and two confederates held male and female hostages in the library building. The plotters had smuggled in three hand guns plus ammunition, all embedded in canned hams. These hams had been returned from off-site to the TDC kitchen as spoiled meat. Once there, one of the confederates got the guns out of cavities carved into the hams.

Two hours passed before a guard drove Kay home. Mark was surprised to see her home so early. The news media was just then learning about the events in Huntsville. Regena Cross was starting supper in Pasadena, when a TV news bulletin stopped her in her tracks. She knew that Kay was in and out of that library on a daily basis. Both sons were disabled, and now her only daughter was about to be murdered. On the verge of a heart attack, she telephoned in a panic. When Kay answered, Regena breathed into the phone, "Thank God!"

Eleven days later, the crisis ended in tragedy. Four fire trucks parked close to the exit from the Walls Unit. Carrasco negotiated his exit from

TDC. He would come out inside a moving shelter, which he demanded be constructed for himself, his two confederates, and the hostages. It consisted of two blackboards, mounted on rollers duct-taped to stacks of books. That night the FBI, with prison guards and Texas Rangers, blew down the shelter. The stream of water from the fire hoses was supposed to knock over the makeshift shelter, but one of the hoses failed. A firefight erupted, in which hostages were killed. That priest survived a gunshot wound to the chest.

At Mom's urging, Kay started looking for another job. In 1977, Kay and Mark both got jobs at the Conroe Independent School District. Except for a two-year stay in Round Rock, north of Austin, they remained in Conroe until retirement.

After Tracy received his AA in commercial art, he joined a band called Windjammer. The keyboard player's brother, Marty, ran sound and provided muscle for moving equipment. He usually showed up late, but one day Marty got there before the band. When he backed his truck up to the restaurant door, the Polish owner came running out and said in broken English, "You need move truck." Marty's vocabulary wasn't much larger than the restaurant owner's. When Marty was at a loss for a word, he stuck in a bathroom word, or to be more specific, a potty word. So to this Marty replied, "Okay, give me about ten minutes. I have a lot of shit to unload." The band arrived as Marty was unloading. The owner's wife came out with tears in her eyes.

In heavily accented English, she said, "Someone said 'shit' to my husband? Who said this?"

The band members looked at each other, embarrassed. Charley, the main singer, suspecting Marty, said, "Marty, did you say something to her husband?"

Offended, Marty said, "No! I didn't say shit to nobody!"

Of course, that was his way of saying "I didn't say anything." The wife didn't understand why the band members started to laugh. Finally, Charley explained that Marty wasn't insulting her husband. He just had a foul mouth.

In 1975, Tracy formed a band that lasted twenty years. Charley was still the singer; and our cousin Randy Richards, the son of Uncle Wilton and Aunt Christine, and now an electrical engineer at NASA in Clear Lake, was the bass guitar player. Mom worried less, since Randy was there watching out for Tracy.

Cousins at Christmas (*left to right*): Randy Richards, Tracy Cross, and Larry Richards, 1974. Author's collection.

Chapter 11
Living on Campus

Having a BS in mathematics reassured me that my future wouldn't be selling pencils or lightbulbs at the Lighthouse for the Blind. I intended to relax and start socializing. I thought I was wasting too much time waiting for rides. Wanting a broader campus life, in the fall of 1972, I moved onto the fifteenth floor of the Moody Towers. My roommate, Rick, from Philadelphia, seemed nice. When he discovered that I was a graduate student in mathematics, he asked for help with his homework. I didn't mind that. But I did mind his bawdy, racist jokes. Well, I had to make the best of it.

I found a group sponsoring a dance and signed up for it. The sponsors of that party set up the pairings. Everyone put their name into a pot, and those in charge would match them up with a person of the opposite gender. That night, when my name was called, a girl in a walker came out to meet me. Surprised and a little insulted, we both had been avoided by the "normal" people. She had the same bone condition that Tracy had. A genetic counselor would have advised us not to get too interested in each other. From the chatter around me, it became apparent that the boys were allowed to purchase a girl's name. Of course, the highest bid won. So, the girls at this party were auctioned off. They had little say in the matter; hence, many of the pairings didn't survive the bash that night. A few boys tried, without much success, to persuade the girls they had purchased not to form a new attachment. I heard some of these unpersuasive arguments and thought some of the words could be interpreted so many ways that the arguments were self-defeating. The language used was sloppy. In a mathematics class, a word can't appear in an argument without first being defined. Outside these classes, people hardly ever define a word before using it. This makes misunderstandings likely. You can't control how others interpret what you say, but you should consider your words carefully before speaking.

My discontent with my roommate was growing, and finally came to a head. It happened this way. The TV room on the first floor seated about fifty people. Because of my connection to NASA during graduate school (I'll discuss this further in chapter 12), whenever there was a space flight, I tried to be in the TV room during the national news. I wondered if I could see the TV screen, so I tried an experiment. Sitting in the front row, I looked at the screen through binoculars. It didn't work. Extreme tunnel vision and binoculars are not a good way to watch TV. I was the ant crawling around on an elephant. What I saw was such a tiny patch, that my brain couldn't integrate it into an image of anything. Disappointed, I put the binoculars away and just listened.

A few days later, entering my room on the fifteenth floor, I found Rick standing at the window. He put an object on the desk. I recognized the sound. He had been peering through the binoculars, and they had been trained at the girl's tower. I was embarrassed. If a girl noticed a guy staring at her through binoculars, she would look up the room number in the Moody Towers directory, find out who we were, spread the word, and if I appeared downstairs with binoculars, she would brand me as a voyeur. Reason told me that this was unlikely, but I was paranoid.

The day arrived for the changing of the garb; my laundry was dirty, and I wanted to spend the weekend at home. When Dad picked me up, I made sure to take those binoculars with me. Rick did ask what happened to them, but I said nothing. Fed up, I inquired downstairs about moving into another room. There was a guy on our floor without a roommate. We met, and the switch was agreeable to both of us.

Ken was very sloppy. Dirty, smelly clothes hung everywhere. I accepted the new situation without complaint. But this wasn't the complete picture. Next day, I got on the elevator to go to class. Everyone stared at me. We rode down in silence. Just before the doors opened, their curiosity overflowed.

"Why don't you look tired? How was your night?"

"Okay, why?"

"Didn't Ken's snoring keep you awake?"

"No."

"Well, he's had two other roommates, and they both left."

The doors opened, and I walked out. Two weeks later the buzz on the floor was that Ken moved out. Was there something about Mike Cross they didn't know? What chased Ken off? I enjoyed my new reputation, so I never told anyone why Ken left. On his way down to turn in his key, Ken shook hands and told me he was moving into a commune at the Church of the Redeemer.

I knew I would either have to pick a new roommate or have one forced on me. So, when I met Lee, another resident of the Towers, and found him to be a thoroughly nice person, I asked him to be my roommate. He moved in, and we became good friends. Lee studied all the time because he was working on a master's degree in chemical engineering. We always took the stairs down because the elevators were too slow. They kept stopping on the way down to let people on. I had a kick step all worked out and was pretty fast, holding the rail, dancing down the stairs. Saying he needed the exercise, Lee adopted my mode of travel but not the dance step.

Every morning, we raced down to breakfast, flashing our meal tickets to Silvia, the cashier, on the way into the serving line. Occasionally, I stopped and talked to her in my Uncle Lars voice. (My father's mother was Swedish. So often, when I am in a lighthearted mood, I speak in a pseudo-Swedish accent, pretending to be Uncle Lars.) The cafeteria staff always told me what they had as I slid my tray down the line. We didn't, however, climb fifteen flights of stairs back to the room. We sensibly took the elevator. Only once did I climb fifteen flights. I was so hot and sweaty by the time I reached my room, I had to take a shower.

Lee didn't often take a break, but when he did, we went places together. In Lee's company, I bowled for the first time. Enthusiastic, I knelt down to see the marks on the alley floor. Putting my foot on the fourth mark, I began my approach. I couldn't see the pins, but I could hear them fall. We bowled seven straight games. My scores were bad, but I enjoyed every minute.

At a party in the Quad, another dorm, Lee brought food and drinks to the table. I said I hated beer and would prefer a coke. He brought me a gin fizz. Afraid of getting tipsy, I drank slowly, and when Lee left to get more onion rings, I dumped my drink in the potted plant next to the table. "Oh, your glass is empty. I'll be right back." He set a second drink in front of me. We repeated this dance twice more that evening and then left. I don't think Lee ever caught on.

Another time, Lee offered to be my chauffeur on a hot date. We picked up my date and drove back to the campus, where she and I took in a movie and ate at a place off campus but nearby. When we took her home, I walked her up to the front door, administered the goodnight kiss, turned around, and ran headlong into a post. The collision shook the post, the lantern atop the post rattling around like a dropped coin. It spun around on its rim a few times, and finally settled into place. Lee, who had the driver's door open, doubled over laughing and fell out of the car. I wasn't hurt, just embarrassed. "Wow! Mike, that must have been a great kiss!" On the way back to the Towers, I imagined the scene through Lee's eyes and started to laugh.

At the Religion Center, I met a girl named Janet. Unlike Susan (who I had also met at the Religion Center and briefly dated during my undergrad years), Janet didn't think other girls would ignore me. Janet not only liked me, she attempted to chase away other girls that were friendly to me. I was not attracted to her at all. Janet told me to avoid one girl because she was a mutant. I felt like I was being stalked. Two guys got interested in Janet. Dressed up, she was quite attractive. But her tactics to chase away other girls only succeeded in driving away the guy she was trying to hang on to. I watched this, all the while sympathetic to Janet, because I didn't dislike her.

Over the next few weeks, I had a change of heart about Janet. ("O heart of man, how fickle art thou.") There came a day when I asked her for a date.

"There's a movie at the Quad. Would you go with me?"

"Mike, I'm sorry, but I can't. I'm seeing a guy named Tom."

"Janet, that's great! You have my best wishes. I'm always your friend."

Back in my room at the Towers, I breathed a sigh of relief. "What did I just do? I almost made a giant mistake. Bless you, Tom, whoever you are." Another year rolled by and Janet graduated.

Crazy things were happening at the university. These were the weird 1970s. A flasher on a motorcycle buzzed through campus, ending when he ran over an obstruction in his path. I believe that was worse than merely being kicked where it hurts. Ralph Nader visited campus. Vietnam protests were in full swing. Not maintaining your GPA sent you to Vietnam. A student failed a course and shot his professor in the hand.

Despite all the stuff happening, I wasn't apprehensive about walking across campus. One day, I went over to the Fine Arts Building to listen to a lecture open to the public. Walking down the path, I kept hearing someone behind me. But whenever I stopped and turned around, there was complete silence. No one was following me. But when I resumed my steps, I heard it again. Was it the birds? Maybe that Alfred Hitchcock movie had a basis in reality. I whirled around several times, trying to catch the followers. Finally, it clicked. I reached back and held my hair off my collar. I started walking, and this time, I didn't hear anything. That afternoon, I visited the campus barbershop.

Living in the dorms opened my eyes, a crack. I know now how ignorant I was then. I knew some facts about mathematics, science, and literature, but I had few life skills. I had never expressed any interest in learning how to cook, wash clothes, or clean house. When I attempted to help, nobody liked the way I folded clothes. The only bright spot in this bleak landscape is that I could wash and dry dishes and vacuum (provided someone had cleared the floors of stuff). Otherwise, I was a total loss. Kay and Tracy knew much more than I did. Kay could do all of the above, plus she had taken courses in fashion design and tailoring.

A partial answer to my dilemma was a dormitory meal ticket. Because I got hungry late at night, I fortified my pantry by taking cookies and brownies back to my room. There were, however, times when I had no ready-to-eat treats from the cafeteria. One such night I was very hungry, but I could find only a can of beans, a jar of tomato sauce, and a box of Skinner's spaghetti noodles. That night I showed how little I knew about cooking. I plugged in my popcorn popper, broke the noodles in half, put them in the popper, and poured the beans and tomato sauce over it. I sat back to wait. Ah, this was the life! To my dismay, it looked like a porcupine that had hemorrhaged to death. Now, I hadn't poured any water over this dead porcupine, so it started to smoke. I stared at it for a while, and when it continued to smoke, I got worried. A few minutes passed. At last, thoroughly alarmed, I gave up and buried it in the trash can.

One of the more interesting people I met in the Towers was George Fisher. He had muscular dystrophy and zipped around campus in a motorized wheelchair. His major was civil engineering, giving us both a scientific way of viewing things. He and I started hanging around together, going to campus events and comparing notes. We talked about not feeling quite accepted. We especially compared notes about the different religious groups on campus. Some groups viewed us as inferior. We both were told that we would be healed if we only had enough faith. We were still disabled, so obviously we didn't.

One night I got a phone call from the faith healer group. The voice said that they had been praying for me to be healed, but, since nothing happened, there was something wrong with my faith. I had heard them say this in speeches, but no one had confronted me until now. My response was to quote a verse from the book of James (5:16). To paraphrase, "The fervent prayers of a righteous man accomplish much." Turning the tables on the caller, I went on to interpret that verse. "Either your prayers about me are not fervent, or you aren't righteous." I didn't get any more phone calls. I don't think I changed any minds, but they didn't expect to be challenged. Every blind person I know has had a similar experience. Most are angered; others believe it and are whipped into submission. The rest of their lives are guilt-ridden. To be fair and objective, most Christians don't target blind people for such attacks (and it did feel like an attack).

My reply was perhaps too aggressive. The response I should have made falls under the category *l'esprit de l'escalier*, a French term for the situation of having thought of the perfect reply too late. Here's my "after-wit."

"You prayed for me to receive my vision, right?"

"Yes, we did." And they had.

"Then God didn't grant your request, either. So why do you think your faith is superior to mine?"

George got the same phone call from the same guy who called me. I told him my response, and he laughed long and loud. At least, for George, it was loud.

George also visited the religious groups, sometimes at the same time I did. We usually discussed what we had observed. I told George what I concluded from listening to voices. He in turn told me about the body language clues that I couldn't observe. Surprisingly, we often reached the same conclusions about what we saw and heard. George was my eyes. I was his better set of ears.

Our collaboration wasn't limited to the religious scene, either. He knew all of the girls I knew. I trusted George's observations and opinions. Other people told me what they wanted me to hear. I would have missed a lot of opportunities and made a lot of mistakes if it hadn't been for George. I made enough mistakes as it was.

I had just put my tray down at a cafeteria table and picked up a fork.

"May we sit here?"

"Of course."

Carol, a short blonde, and Cathy, a tall, thin brunette, sat across the table from me.

"What are you girls studying?"

Cathy said, "We are both majoring in sociology."

Cathy did most of the talking. Carol was the shyest girl I have ever met. I later told George about an imaginary conversation with her.

"Carol, do you ever talk to yourself?"

"No, I'm too shy."

That day at the table, they took turns describing themselves to me, no doubt in flattering terms.

George was watching us from a nearby table. The conversation moved on to music. They liked Carole King. That broke the ice. We ended up in my dorm room playing the *Tapestry* LP on my record player, and before they left, I had a date with Carol. George said later that Cathy seemed to be taking care of Carol. He said he liked Cathy better than Carol, and that I probably would too. That night, I didn't have a date with one girl; I had a date with two girls. Everything was dark. The news was full of Nixon's energy crisis. I followed them to the car as best I could. When they noticed I was lagging behind, I asked for assistance. Carol was too shy to touch me. Exasperated, Cathy said, "Can't you hold his hand?" When Carol didn't, Cathy did. That was one strange date. I was holding hands, but not with the girl I supposedly had the date with. The nightclub was dark and gloomy, and the place seemed deserted. Cathy was the designated driver, and I, as usual, was going to order a coke. George was right. I liked Cathy better. After a few minutes, we walked out having seen exactly one person.

It started to rain, and the girls wanted to run through the dark parking lot. I said, "I don't think this is a very good idea, but okay." Cathy started running, and I was attached to her hand. Something impacted me hard above my right knee, throwing me forward. I found myself on hands and knees, with my face almost touching the pavement. A sign had at some time been knocked down, and my right eye was within an inch of the edge of the metal sign. My leg was numb, and the right side of my face was bloody. I got to my feet, and the girls helped me to the car. Lying in the back seat, I took stock of my wounds. The bloody area was near my right eye, and I was not looking forward to stitches. The memory of those childhood IV treatments came flooding back, increasing my anxiety. Plus, I have always been unreasonably touchy about my eyes. Apologetic and worried, the girls sat in the waiting room while the doctor sewed me up. His specialty was going to be plastic surgery, so he practiced on me, putting in ten stitches where three would have sufficed. I was glad to hear this, but I was still nervous. Whenever I'm under this kind of stress, I tell jokes. When the girls heard me laughing, they calmed down.

Next day, I tried to take the stairs but couldn't. The area above my right knee was so swollen, I had trouble walking. Lee brought me a bag of ice, and I stayed in my room that day with my leg propped up and holding that bag in place. The relationship with the girls ended. For the next two months, I rode the elevator down and limped off to class.

Before George graduated, he founded the University of Houston Organization for the Handicapped (UHOH). He went to work for a small company writing COBOL programs. George was a success, but he made a mistake. He hired the wrong attendant. The attendant threw George into his closet, demanding that George sign over all his money if he ever wanted out.

George signed, but was left in the closet. Three days passed, and concerned about his absence from work, his boss went to George's apartment manager and together they entered the rooms and found him. George survived, and that attendant went to jail. I lost track of my friend, only hearing from him after long intervals of time. George lived into his fifties, unusual for those suffering from muscular dystrophy. George once told me that, misshapen as he was, no girl would ever love him. He died in his mother's home, where he spent his last few years.

Mike and his roommate, Lee, at Moody Towers dorm, 1972. Author's collection.

Chapter 12
NASA and Graduate School

The State Commission for the Blind's attitude toward blind people in the hard sciences had been turned upside down in five years. In 1970, the commission approached NASA at Clear Lake about jobs for me and three other students at the University of Houston and a student at Rice University. This set the stage for the next seven years (1970–76). I attended university during fall and spring semesters and interned at the Manned Spacecraft Center (MSC) / Johnson Space Center (JSC) over the summers (the Manned Spacecraft Center was renamed the Johnson Space Center during those years, in February 1973). The first summer, just before my last undergraduate semester at U of H, was spent in the Computer Analysis Directorate in 1970, shortly after the dramatic return of Apollo 13. I spent the next six summers in Building 30, Mission Control, as part of the Mission Planning and Analysis Directorate.

Tending to be engrossed in what I was doing, it was hard to switch gears and return to school in the fall. But, once back on campus, NASA faded from my mind. Of course, when astronauts flew a mission, I was glued to the radio and TV. During the school year, I was a pure mathematician, but at NASA, I was strictly applied. Luckily, I had a strong interest in both areas. As an undergraduate, I took many applied mathematics courses. And, of course, the physics training gave me exactly the right background for NASA.

Every summer at MSC was different. In the Mission Planning and Analysis Directorate—mathematical physics branch, navigation section—I derived mathematical models of spacecraft navigation situations. My section's task was to determine if proposed navigation schemes were good enough to allow a spacecraft to fly its mission and return safely to a predetermined target area. This is a natural time to talk about my importance, or lack of it, in the scheme of things at NASA. They were committed to redundancy management. None of the navigation schemes I proposed would have been accepted unless someone else had concurred with my results.

Unlike in the Soviet space program, NASA astronauts had the ability to perform onboard navigation. The equations supporting star tracker navigation were full of triple vector products, and it was one of my tasks to simplify those equations into a form that was more computable. When Apollo-Soyuz was being planned, I met the scientists whom the USSR sent to Houston to coordinate the mission with NASA. Since the Soviets didn't have onboard navigation, the Americans executed all the docking maneuvers. One of the Soviet scientists came over specifically to make sure they could interchange information during those maneuvers. We called him Victor the Vector Collector. At the end of that summer, NASA gave a party for the Soviets. The man arranging the party asked who spoke Russian. I thought they wanted someone with more than my one year of conversational Russian, so I kept quiet. But actually, he was looking for anyone who spoke any Russian at all. So I missed an opportunity there.

Another summer I worked on the planning phase for GPS, the Global Positioning System. The TDRSS, Tracking and Data Relay Satellite System, is a group of satellites in geostationary orbits around Earth. Their presence allows devices on Earth to receive precise latitude and longitude information. Another one of the tasks I was assigned over the summers was called "visibility studies." How ironic! Actually, the visibility of concern was the ability of a spacecraft's onboard antennas to see a radar station down on Earth that would provide an update to the spacecraft's exact position.

By the time the Apollo program was canceled, the space shuttle program was underway. I wrote requirements for part of the life support software to run on the onboard IBM AP-101 computers. There were four of those computers. Only one ran life support. The other three ran the onboard navigation. Why three? The answer was redundancy management. It was possible that any one of the three computers might go down or fail at any time, which would complicate things. But beyond the need to have hardware backups, there was, in the navigation software, an intricate process going on that also needed to be managed redundantly. During a flight, NASA would track the values of eighteen separate variables. Each of the three computers provided its own separate data stream of these navigational measurements. Ideally, the three streams would be identical, but, for whatever reason, that was not always the case. Each data stream might have a different level of deviation, or "noise." The three data streams were continually combined into a single stream (providing best estimates of position, velocity, acceleration, and vehicle orientation) that would be used to guide the spacecraft's navigation. To help ensure the accuracy of that single stream, at each current time step the corresponding entries from the three computers' data streams would be combined with a weighted history of that stream of measurements as of the previous time step. This weighted history would cancel out any random noise (deviation) that had crept into the three current data streams. The end result was a more reliably accurate estimate of those eighteen navigational variables at each current time step. The process of redundancy management provided at each time step one single clear data stream that would be used for navigation.

I enjoyed the summers at NASA, but my main thrust was pursuing mathematical studies. I continued in school and received a master's degree in mathematics in 1974, from the University of Houston. During this period, a graduate student in the field of psychology interviewed me. The Ivy League school she attended had noticed that Texas had a large number of blind people majoring in math and science. They were curious. I told her I thought the reason was that there was unusual opportunity in Texas. Johnson Space Center was in Clear Lake, a short distance from Houston and its universities. It would be nice to think I had cleared the path for some of those people to get a technical degree. One of the rewards for overcoming great odds is thinking that you might have encouraged others in their struggle to find a better life for themselves.

My coursework was primarily in three areas: abstract algebra, topology, and analysis. These last two areas had a strong University of Texas flavor, since several U of H faculty members had earned their PhDs while studying with R. L. Moore, a well-known University of Texas topologist, and H. S. Wall, an equally well-known University of Texas analyst.

Some of my classes were lecture based, while others were taught in a style based on the Socratic model, named for the Greek philosopher Socrates. The professor asked questions, but gave very few answers. His role was to direct the students as they investigated propositions. Typically, the professor stated the assumptions upon which all investigations were to be based. He then wrote conjectures on the blackboard and challenged the class to prove the statements or to find counterexamples to them. Most of the conjectures were true, but to keep the class on its toes, some were false. After the first week, professors seldom told us whether the conjectures were true or false. We left each class with a list of conjectures to think about. Next class, the professor would ask, "Does anyone have a proof or a counterexample for any of the open conjectures?" If nobody was ready, the professor might ask some questions to get us started, or he might give us more conjectures to wrestle with. But usually, someone would volunteer to present a proof or, less frequently, a counterexample. We would watch (or in my case listen) as the presenter made his case. He had to defend each line of his argument. When the presenter couldn't defend, the room sat silent, pondering the problem. Usually, someone in class suggested a way to get the argument back on track, and the presentation would continue. Nobody was penalized for getting help from classmates. Some of these presentations spanned two or more class periods, because these conjectures were complex.

The spirit of cooperation made the classes enjoyable. Everything was verbalized and exacting. I had no trouble following the presentations. Nor did I have any trouble making a presentation. I read my argument a line at a time, waiting for the professor to write it on the board. There would be a pause while the class thought about it. After a suitable time to ponder, the class would say "we agree," or someone would point out a gap in the logic. Most of my arguments went unscathed, but on other occasions, if I couldn't correct my logic, someone would suggest a better statement. This didn't happen more than twice, because I would run the arguments past Peter beforehand. (Peter, my undergrad mathematics student friend in a wheelchair, was now also in graduate school classes with me.) In any case, I didn't present unless I was very confident. By this time, I could critique my own logic very well.

The statements were exacting. In all pure mathematics courses, the professors were rigorous about the use of language. Where there was ambiguity, we disallowed all meanings but one. This gave rise to an agreed-upon vocabulary with which everyone's arguments were constructed. Early on, we learned how to deny a statement without over-denying it. For example, if "for each element x in set S" something is true, the bare denial is "there is at least one element x in set S" where that same something is not true.

Over the years in graduate school, my courses ranged over ring theory, group theory, rings and ideals, and point set topology, real analysis, complex analysis (aka complex variables), and module theory. Real and complex analysis are both very important in many fields of science and engineering. My master's degree in mathematics specialized in group theory. I enjoyed all those courses. However, my favorite area of mathematics is topology.

The first day in graduate point set topology, Dr. Cook spent the entire period writing axioms on the blackboard. Shortly before the bell rang ending class, he wrote a conjecture on the board. He said this conjecture happened to be true, something that wouldn't be the case for every conjecture he gave us. One of my classmates agreed to make me a carbon copy of his notes. Dr. Cook didn't state his conjecture correctly. Next class he asked for a volunteer to present a proof of that conjecture. I was quick to volunteer. "I would like to present a counterexample. Then, if you will let me rewrite the conjecture, I will prove the conclusion." Dr. Cook was surprised, and he looked at the statement on the board. The class assured him that he had stated it the way I had it in my presentation. Flustered, he said, "Show us what you have." I remained at my desk, and he wrote as I read out my counterexample, followed by the reworded hypothesis and theorem proof. I think I made an A that day. For the next few classes, whenever he wrote a conjecture, he always ended by looking over at me and saying, "Assuming that I wrote this correctly, it's a theorem." This embarrassed me.

Of course, some conjectures were false. This kept our level of skepticism high and gave us practice in finding counterexamples. At the end of the semester, I had presented thirteen proofs and counterexamples. Still, I was worried. Dr. Cook hadn't given any in-class or any take-home tests. The last day of class, I took my seat, expecting a terrifying final, but he conducted class as usual. At the end of the period, he walked to the door, turned, and said in a casual voice, "By the way, you all have an A." He walked out, and we all breathed a sigh of relief.

In 1975, I started a doctorate at the University of Houston, but not in the area of group theory. It was in analysis. My doctoral dissertation topic was "Functions of bounded sub-N variation." There are many ways to categorize functions according to how well-behaved they are. This is one of them: You can think of categorizing how torn-up or drivable roadways are. Is there a point on the road where a car would drop twenty feet onto the next portion of roadway, and a car going the opposite direction would have to jump straight up twenty feet to stay on the road? How many places like this are there? How big are the jumps? Are there infinitely many points like this? If you formed a sequence of the magnitudes of these jumps, would that sequence converge? These are a few of the simpler questions to ask.

My dissertation had not progressed very far before I decided not to pursue a doctorate any further. There wasn't just one reason for that decision. I had been a university student for ten and a half years. Most of the people I knew were younger than I was. I had started to wonder if there was a benefit to anything beyond a master's degree. For a blind man, this was an urgent question. Would a PhD earn me a better livelihood? I didn't know the answers to any of these questions. I wanted an answer before I got much older.

Then, something happened to change everything.

Chapter 13

Lightning Strikes

September 1976 brought many new faces to the Religion Center conference room for the Bible Chair program. Seats filled up with a mixture of students from the University of Houston and Rice University. The older faces talked animatedly, while the newcomers sat shyly, not saying much of anything. Dr. Rick Oster began the discussion by having everyone introduce themselves. I don't remember much about the next hour. What I do remember is what one girl said. Speaking from the corner off to my right, her comments about self-discipline and the spiritual life made an impression on me that no other girl had ever made. Her voice stood out as the most heartfelt in the room. I didn't remember the introductions. I thought, "I have to meet this girl." Smiling to myself and remembering the girl I had dated a few times as an undergraduate, who had told me that most girls would never have anything to do with me, I thought, "I hope her name isn't Susan." Oh, did I say that aloud? The guy next to me said he thought her name was Karen Williams.

After the meeting broke up, some students left, while others lingered talking. A girl passed me on her way to the door. I followed, hoping it wasn't the wrong person. I caught up with her outside as she walked toward Moody Towers. I decided she must live there. (I had moved out of Moody by then, but still had a meal ticket for its cafeteria.) I introduced myself to her. "Pardon me, my name is Michael Cross." My informant was right; her name was Karen. I asked if I could walk her to class. Karen accepted, and as we walked, I discovered that she was working toward a master's degree in education and that her BA was in drama.

Girls were being cautious those days because there had been a rape on campus. Karen said all of her classes were at night. Being a born-again opportunist, I offered to escort her to her classes, and then walk her back to the dorm afterwards. Over the next few weeks, we walked the campus together, ate together in Moody Towers, and went to Bible studies. When I stood within arm's length of Karen, I could see how beautiful she was. I wasn't the only one who noticed this. But the guys who had noticed eventually paired off with other girls, leaving the field to me.

Karen was unlike anyone I had ever known. There was a puzzle piece missing from my life's mosaic, and Karen was that piece. She didn't slip quietly into my world, nor was my attachment to her gradual. It was abrupt; she blazed into my world like a comet. Our first formal date was dinner at Michelangelo's Restaurant, an Italian restaurant in Houston. There may have been other people there, but except for the waiter, I didn't notice them. It was a romantic candlelight evening. As though to underscore the presence of someone very special, the food was a revelation to my pedestrian palate. (My sophistication stopped at SpaghettiOs.) We had antipasto. The main course was Veal Parmesan. We split a baked apple full of spiced wine, nuts, and ricotta cheese. As if the food weren't enough, being there with this knockout girl made this the evening of the decade. Of course, as a helpless blind man, I had to hold her hand; no chore at all, but that surely blew my credibility as a bodyguard.

That autumn of 1976 was a beautiful dream. We spent more and more time together. Karen didn't have a car. One consequence of this was that we started attending Fifth Ward, a Black church. It was the only Church of Christ that sent a bus to pick up students at the University of Houston. There were few white people in the congregation. An older gentleman introduced himself. I asked if he were a student. His face lit up. Karen later told me laughingly, "I think you made his day." Everyone there was very kind to us. We found other opportunities to be together. On weekends, we caught the bus and went exploring. Karen often asked me how I perceived things around me. This, too, endeared Karen to me. She was tenderhearted and open-minded. She didn't seem to mind describing my world to me. I think I was a riddle to her. Blind means totally blind, doesn't it? She later told me about a conversation with a friend back home in Baytown.

"There's this really cute guy at the Bible Chair who I think is blind. He runs into things. Other times he reaches for an object, like a glass, and I think 'Well, he saw that.'"

People at the Bible Chair were beginning to think of us as a couple, but as of yet, our parents knew nothing. One Friday afternoon I met Karen's father, Rollie Williams, as he picked her up to take her home for the weekend. "Yeah, he's blind all right. He stumbled on the way back to the dorm." Mom and Dad were hoping I would meet some girl just like Karen. Dad picked us up one Saturday and spirited us away to Pasadena. Everybody liked Karen immediately. Tracy and Kay let me know how much they approved. Although Karen and I saw each other during the holidays that year, we kept to our own family Thanksgiving and Christmas celebrations.

In December, something happened that made a future with Karen seem within grasp. The Texas State Commission for the Blind found a job opportunity for me. Lieutenant Governor Bill Hobby had started a Braille project at the Region 4 Education Service Center. One of twenty regional centers established by the Texas state legislature in 1967 to assist school districts in improving student performance, Region 4 serves school districts in the greater Houston area. The purpose of the project was to move print books to Braille faster. At the time, textbooks were transcribed into Braille by volunteers, averaging two years per book. This was unacceptable. Students were failing because they couldn't get books when they needed them. A few years earlier I had had an interview at a junior college for a position as a math instructor. I was given some flimsy concerns and the bum's rush out the door. This convinced me no career in academia awaited me. It was not fair, but that's the way it was. Industry, meanwhile, didn't want to pay for a PhD when a master's degree was sufficient for their purposes. These two reasons led me to a decision. Having been at university for ten years, I decided I had had enough of student life. I took the job and moved into an apartment two blocks from the service center. This allowed me to walk to work, and even go home for lunch. Late in January 1977, I asked Karen to marry me, and she honored me by accepting. Karen banished the dark from my life with one word, "Yes." I bought a ring, and we celebrated our engagement at Sasha's, a Russian restaurant. It was a cold, drizzly day, but we were in love, and the day was great.

On August 14, 1977, Karen became my wife. We flew off to San Antonio, where our honeymoon was in the La Mansion Hotel on the River Walk. I had come away without a suitcase. The white suit I had worn on the plane was out of place in San Antonio in August, and especially on the River Walk. Walking around in that suit, I was afraid to touch anything. So, our first act as husband and wife was to buy blue jeans and a shirt for me. The rest of that time was a wonderful dream. The landmarks in people's lives seem to be deaths of famous personalities. The major event that weekend was Elvis Presley's death.

Karen, with her new master's degree in education, got a teaching job at Cypress Creek High School in the Cypress-Fairbanks Independent School

District. Karen had teaching certificates in three areas, making her eminent-ly valuable to a school. These areas are English, German, and Drama. And Cypress Creek High School took full advantage of it. She taught English II, German I, and German II. Doing three dissimilar class preparations per day didn't leave Karen much free time, in fact almost none. She often sat up past midnight grading papers. She also was the German club sponsor.

In order to be with Karen, I sometimes went to school meetings and events with her. On one such occasion, we sat in a room full of foreign language teachers waiting for the department head, a French teacher. She arrived and adjusted the microphone. "Welcome to the Autumn planning session of the Cypress Creek High School Foreign Language Department. First, I will pass out the department guidelines for each language and grade level. Then I need to make a few remarks." As she talked, I became more and more alarmed. She didn't sound well at all. Her speech was slow and labored. It was a real effort for her to talk. This woman should be in an emergency room right now! Why didn't she sound worried? This was an educated woman. Why wasn't she concerned?

I leaned toward Karen and whispered, "She's having trouble breathing."

Then, it dawned on me. "Is she pregnant?"

"Yes, she is."

I relaxed and sat back smiling.

On those rare weekends when we could get away, we visited Karen's parents in Baytown or mine in Pasadena, two bedroom communities near Houston. Tracy was often there, since he lived in Pasadena. We saw Kay and Mark less frequently, since they lived more than an hour away in Conroe. Mark taught history, so he had the same demands on his time that Karen did. Kay's job with the school district administration kept her almost as busy on weekends as Mark. Tracy's old room was full of posters and paintings. At that time, Tracy earned his livelihood repairing cameras. Mom worked in the San Jacinto Junior College bookstore, further limiting our chances to see her. Dad inspected ships at the Port of Houston for fire safety. There was one more important member of our household, and, of course, Karen fell in love with Bounce-A-Lot, our long-haired Chihuahua, who was by now an old lady. Well, that sums up my house, except to say that conversation flowed easily in the house in Pasadena.

We spent lots of our free weekends in Baytown with Karen's parents, Rollie and Maydell Williams. Karen had three sisters, but we only saw Wanda very often. Her sister Susan lived in Houston on the west side. She was an accountant, and her husband was an electrical engineer at Texas Instruments. Linda, eighteen months younger than Karen, was in medical school in Galveston. Wanda, eleven years younger than Karen, was still in high school. She was the only sister we could count on being around when we visited. Mr. Williams, who had a master's degree in physics from Texas A&M and was head of the Humble Oil & Refining Co. (now ExxonMobil) research lab in Baytown, was somewhat reserved. Most of our early conversations were about physics and mathematics. The atmosphere in that house was much too serious. Nobody ever told a joke. It's not that no one wanted to tell a joke, but none of the girls in that house knew how to set up a joke and deliver a punch line. Pardon me, but I have to digress for a minute. The situation I'm describing reminds me of a joke. Sailors on a ship hadn't been ashore for six months. They had told all the jokes they knew, several times each. To save time, they assigned numbers to the jokes. A sailor would clear his throat and say "Number twenty-five," and everyone within earshot rolled around on the deck howling with laughter. There was one timid soul who had never even smiled. One day, he walked to the center of the deck and in a loud voice said, "Number six." There was no laughter. After a prolonged dead silence, the first mate spoke up. "Boy! Some people just don't know how to tell a joke."

So, given the somber atmosphere in Baytown, how did I break the ice? It happened this way: Mr. Williams was glued to the TV set whenever a Texas A&M football game was being broadcast. At halftime during one of these games, I cleared my throat and ventured to tell an Aggie joke. At first, there was no reaction, but then he started to laugh. This opened a broad new avenue for conversation. After that day, I was always kidding Mr. Williams about A&M. When in Baytown, we often went to movies with whichever sisters were there and one or both of Karen's parents. This was especially true during Thanksgiving and Christmas. One Thanksgiving we tried to convince Mr. Williams to see the first Christopher Reeve *Superman* movie. I made one last appeal, not realizing what effect it would have on him. "Oh, come on! Just pretend he's an Aggie!" He clapped his hand over his mouth and turned purple trying not to laugh. Finally, he exploded. Mrs. Williams, watching his attempt to restrain himself, started laughing too. She had never seen him laugh that hard. The laughter subsided after a few minutes, and Mr. Williams cleared his throat and said, "No." Disappointed, we left for the movie and to go out to eat afterward.

My family, in contrast, almost never went to a movie. Instead, they might rent one. Another contrast between the two families was that at my parents' house, talk was usually not serious. Tracy was Mr. Humor, the master of setup and delivery. This was despite Tracy's being in constant pain. There was very little bone between knee and hip in his right leg. I couldn't compete with Tracy's ability to tell a funny story, and didn't even try. Although Kay's husband, Mark, would try, he still was Tracy's most appreciative audience.

Karen and I had been married about a year when we decided to buy a house. Providence smiled on us. Our new house was on Haverhill Drive, only one block away from our old apartment. This made moving easy, and since the distances to our jobs didn't change at all, our daily routine wasn't much affected. The new house was in the shape of the letter L, with a long hall running from the living room to the rear of the house. This was good because I paced a lot while thinking through math or computer problems. The nicest room was a combination kitchen, breakfast nook, and dining room. The woodwork was blond. For Karen's birthday, I bought a Tiffany lamp, which we hung over the dining table. Karen was very pleased with the appearance of the table with green curtains behind it and the glowing Tiffany lamp shining down on it. This was our first house, and we were enjoying drinking iced tea in the screened-in back porch and strolling around the large backyard. I discovered a Satsuma orange tree and a Kieffer pear tree. The pear tree produced lots of fruit. It is a cooking pear, large and crisp to the bite. Its shape isn't pleasing, being gnarled, but its flavor is superb. We ate all we could, and gave boxes away to family and neighbors. I had a nursery plant a peach tree, but we sold that house before the tree could bear fruit.

There were, of course, times when we didn't drive across Houston to visit our parents, either because they weren't available, or we didn't have a large enough block of free time to fit in a round-trip and a visit. Our house was two blocks away from West 18th, a major street, and four additional blocks away from Northwest Mall. Walking those four blocks took us under Loop 610, which encircles Houston. We frequently went to the mall just to walk around, looking but not buying. One place in the mall we stopped by was Farrell's Ice Cream Parlour, specializing in fancy ice cream desserts. The "Zoo" sundae was enough ice cream to feed four people, but we finished it and waddled contentedly home.

These years saw two major movies draw huge audiences. They were *Close Encounters of the Third Kind* and *Star Wars.* A third movie came out but didn't make nearly as much money as the two I have mentioned. It was the cartoon (animated) version of *The Lord of the Rings.* Karen and I are both J. R. R. Tolkien fans and had to see it. Any movie I go to has to have lots of dialogue, or I consider it not worth my time.

Chapter 14

A Move to Austin

Even though I was helping students at the Texas School for the Blind by getting print books transcribed into Braille, I felt out of place at Region 4. My skills were wasted there. It was time to move on. In the summers of 1978 and 1979, Karen spent two weeks teaching at a German language camp in Junction, Texas. During the school year, she taught classes in German and English at Cypress Creek High School and teaching at the camp gave her college credit through Texas Tech and improved her German conversation skills. While they were practicing their German and having fun, I was stuck in Houston doing the daily grind at Region 4.

The first summer while Karen was at the camp, Houston experienced one of its periodic floods. The news was bad. Junction flooded too, and people died. The phone lines were down, and I was very worried. Being kept indoors by all the water, the German language campers were together even more than was planned. Since they were avoiding speaking English, they weren't listening to radio or watching TV. So Karen was surprised to hear how worried I was about her.

Karen's time at German camp proved to be fateful for both of us. That first year she met Frank S., who was finishing a doctorate in mathematics at the University of Texas. His wife, Mary N., a software engineer at IBM in Austin, visited him at camp on the weekends. At the camp Karen also met Vance, a linguist contracted to IBM, with whom I would later work. Vance and Mary N., who had a PhD in Germanic languages, were in the same department and worked together in a group that maintained electronic dictionaries in eleven languages. Given our shared interests in languages and mathematics, Karen's and my friendship with Frank S. and Mary N. was inevitable.

Mary had lost most of her hearing as a child, but despite this, she spoke eleven languages. Karen was drawn to her, and when she discovered Frank's connection to math, she felt the meeting was providential. She came home full of enthusiasm about German camp and the people she had met there. Mary N. later spent a few days with us in Houston, but poor Frank, who was a teaching assistant in the UT math department, couldn't join. The two women agreed they were sick of listening to their husbands talk about math. Karen tells me that in those days, I only talked about two topics: mathematics and religion.

When I met Mary N., I understood Karen's enthusiasm. Mary N. was very impressive. Although she still had some hearing, it was remarkable how Mary N. could follow conversations in multiple languages by closely watching lips. Mary's speech was not at all affected by her hearing loss.

Mary N. encouraged Karen and me to visit Austin, especially in view of my job dissatisfaction. Once in Austin, I felt the city calling me. Mary N. had a friend at Tracor, an Austin defense contractor, and Frank had another job lead for me. His father worked at Radian, a company that did a lot of environmental contracts. I picked up job applications at these companies and also from IBM. I was granted interviews at Tracor and at Radian but not at IBM, a company that had seven thousand employees in Austin. IBM sent me a quick, polite "no." Their letter said, "There is not a good match for your skills at this time." A similar letter arrived from Radian. The defense company, Tracor, was a different story. I talked with people in two groups, countermeasures and marine navigation. Countermeasures was military, and marine navigation was civilian. When I spoke knowledgeably about programming microprocessors, the head of the marine navigation group was interested. That group programmed microprocessors and installed them on ships. I went back to Houston encouraged about new opportunities. My offer came from the countermeasures group, based on my NASA experience. The head of the marine navigation group later told me if countermeasures hadn't made an offer, her group would have. Karen and I were both reluctant to move so far from our parents, but we ultimately thought that providence was knocking and that we shouldn't ignore the call.

Once I accepted Tracor's offer, the scramble was on. We made a quick trip to Austin and rented an apartment. Back home in Houston, we put our house on the market and rented a moving van. The first night in our new apartment, we slept on the floor. The van with our furniture arrived the next day, Monday, my first day on the job. Karen unpacked, and by the weekend, we were ready to explore our new city. The most interesting places were down around the University of Texas campus. A street called the Drag sported the University Co-op bookstore and lots of street vendors hawking their products. A brief stroll took us past tables of jewelry, artists, crafts, Vietnamese egg rolls, etc. Around the corner were more dives and eateries, like Mad Dog & Beans. The Mad Dog was a hamburger bun with hot dog links split in half and arranged on the bun like spokes in a wheel. Red beans and rice was also popular. But my favorites were the large milkshakes in a variety of flavors, peach being my pick. There was not much variety on the restaurant scene in Austin. Having become addicted to tandoori chicken in Houston, we were elated to find Indian restaurants in Austin.

Tracor had a picnic, and we met several nice people, among them Charlie James and his wife, Mildred. The next day, we walked into a church, when who should we meet but Charlie. After services we met the minister, who had been a missionary in Austria for seventeen years. Karen and I felt like this was where we should be, so we became regulars there.

We lunched one day at a Vietnamese restaurant on the second floor of a small shopping mall. The seafood soup cooked in the center of the table. I had five bowls of this spicy hot soup.

After the fifth, I asked Karen in a worried voice, "Did you feel that?"

"Feel what?"

"Did you feel the building move?"

"No, it's all that spicy soup."

But I'm sure the building moved. I could hear footsteps, and whenever I heard them, the floor vibrated up and down. I explained to Karen that a famous physicist named Louis de Broglie conjectured that all motion can be assigned a wavelength. The wooden floor was moving like a wave. She didn't believe me.

Karen picked up a pizza one day and was surprised that the girl who handed her the pizza was an acquaintance from high school. She and her husband were managers at a Pizza Inn near our apartment. Karen's friend called me "Steve." I had once told Karen that all my life people who forgot my name called me "Steve," no matter how many times I corrected their mistake. She didn't believe me until we got together with another one of her friends from German camp, who taught school in Austin. The whole time we were together, the friend called me "Steve." She even sent a Christmas card to "Mr. and Mrs. Steven Cross." I smiled, but didn't say anything. Well, Karen, sometimes you need to admit defeat and give up. I told her that if we had a son who looked like me, we should name him Steve because everyone would call him "Steve" anyway.

Memorial Day of 1981, we were downtown at an ice cream dip store when a cold wind blew in. Karen and I decided we'd better get back to the apartment without delay. As we parked, the skies opened and drenched us. That day is known in Austin as the Memorial Day Flood, in which homes along Shoal Creek were under water. Bodies were found in trees after the waters receded.

Tracor hired Karen for a position in the business department. Since she knew German, she was asked by a different department to translate contracts with the Luftwaffe from German into English. She was paid separately for each contract that she translated. Eventually, someone in that department learned enough German so that he could do the translations himself.

Tracor's main countermeasure was chaff, a ribbon-like decoy to be dispensed from military aircraft to confuse enemy radar. I wrote a missile guidance program, and although several engineers took a crack at it, the head of the department chose my program for its speed and small size. Our resident physicist made sure I knew about my contribution. Otherwise, I wouldn't have known because no one else mentioned it to me. I also designed a missile to be fired from a satellite to defend against a Soviet satellite killer. At the instant of firing, its impulse had to be zero; otherwise, the satellite would be knocked into a different orbit. This involved setting target conditions and solving equations I found in an aerospace textbook. I never touched any hardware; that was for others to do. I then wrote a program predicting the electro-optical signature of a new decoy the company was developing. The last project I worked on for countermeasures was for the navy instead of the air force. It was a mathematical tool evaluating a Bessel function in the complex plane.

I moved into an office just inside an area requiring a higher security clearance. Even so, my clearance wasn't high enough for me to be informed how my computer function would be used in the Trident submarine program. Sonar is my guess, but that reveals absolutely nothing. While in this restricted area, I frequently talked to the guard (who was stationed there to make sure the enemy didn't steal my program). Now anyone who knows me knows that I like to talk about food, and about some of our experiments, such as barbecued liver marinated in vinegar, German red cabbage, or Thai coleslaw. One day, I stopped work to eat lunch. The guard asked what I was eating because she had heard about some of the strange things I ate. She was quite prepared to see something unusual in my lunch box. So when I answered that it was bean curd and alfalfa sprouts, she started to laugh and dropped her gun. She didn't pick her gun up until she had stopped laughing. She might have shot somebody. There's a lesson here for all you secret agents.

Learn how to tell a good joke. Even more important, beyond resisting torture, learn how to withstand a joke.

One day, my old office mate was admitted into the restricted area. He asked if he could have one of my five-drawer file cabinets, to which I answered yes. We inspected the shelves to make sure they were all empty, and I handed him the key. The smirk on my face should have warned him that something was coming, but Joe was preoccupied with wrestling the unit out of the area. The guard stood holding open the door with the badge reader. Timing makes ordinary events humorous. When Joe leaned down to push the cabinet forward, I sensed that the time was right. I said, "Okay," paused for effect, and suddenly exclaimed, "Shove it!" At that instant, Joe was incapable of pushing anything. He collapsed against the cabinet, lungs deflated, and slid to the floor shaking with laughter. When he regained control, he stood and faced me. "You were waiting for that moment, weren't you?" The smug look on my face told him, I couldn't resist.

About six months after I started at Tracor, we found out that Karen was expecting our first child. Since Karen and I were pregnant, our lives revolved around reading books and listening to tapes. We even took Lamaze classes preparing for our first child. We bought a house near Tracor, on Kings Point West, at the eastern edge of Austin. It had trees and a huge backyard. Karen's parents drove up from Houston to be with us during and after the birth. Our son was born that fall of 1981. I wasn't sure I wanted to be a parent, but when I heard Steve's tiny voice for the first time, I was instantly transformed into a doting father. I walked around with a goofy grin on my face while holding Steve. He did look like me and ended up with the name Steve. This just made matters worse because when he was playing with the other kids at church social functions, people would tell Karen where I was when she was trying to find Steve. Suddenly, our house became a port of entry. It was a "see" port—everyone showed up wanting to see Steve. Karen's sisters were enthusiastic aunts. Our extended families had to take a number and wait their turn to invade our house. The smile on sister Kay's face told you what kind of mother she would have been had she and Mark ever had kids. We bought a camcorder and made lots of tapes. I played cameraman, pointing where I heard a voice, and sometimes the subject was actually in the picture. Fortunately, I was seldom operating the camera.

Steve was the first grandchild on both sides of the family. Tracy and Kay had no kids, and at the time, neither did any of Karen's three sisters. This guaranteed Steve lots of attention. Karen's father had four daughters, but no son. He came from a family of five boys. So he was really enthusiastic about a grandson. Karen's married sisters caught the fever. Susan's daughter Victoria is eleven months younger than Steve. We had a second son, Tony, born two and a half years after Steve. The next cousin, Clara, born to Linda, came four years after Victoria. Next, Victoria got a little sister, named for her Aunt Linda. But there were no more grandsons (after Steve and Tony) until Karen's youngest sister, Wanda, married. Karen's father was happy to have granddaughters, but when Wanda presented him with a third grandson, Daniel, he celebrated again. Wanda's daughter Amanda rounded out the grandkids.

...

The day came when a hasty meeting was called. Tracor had lost a huge air force contract, and people started disappearing. The handwriting was on the wall, so I transferred over to the business side of the company, where I wrote programs in COBOL. My new boss told me to rewrite two insurance programs that ran in about thirty minutes, entirely too long. My two rewritten programs each ran in thirty seconds flat. The boss man was very happy, as were the people charged with doing business analysis. But I wasn't happy. Again, my talents were being wasted. I was a design engineer. Although I didn't care for the job, I liked my boss, Frank Miller.

One day, I went to a restaurant with my new department. Everyone was jovial, laughing and joking. Before I had found the new position at Tracor, I had sent a job application to IBM and had been asked to come in for an interview. I hadn't immediately called back to set one up, because I liked my boss so much. Sitting there at that table, I heard my boss say something that changed my mind in an instant. It didn't matter that Frank said it in jest. What caused my ears to prick up was hearing him say that he was thinking about looking for another job. I remember thinking, "I'm a fool." That one careless remark opened my eyes and changed my life forever. I have wondered how God shows up in people's lives. I don't think He micromanages people. But, had Frank made these kinds of remarks before, and had God brought me to this lunch to hear Frank say that? I think He did because it was so life-altering, and I almost missed it. Also, my reaction to it was so instantaneous. I called IBM to set up that interview.

Karen went back to work when Steve was three months old. She was able to work part-time for six months, but her job at Tracor changed, and she was moved into the department doing data entry. Steve was often sick, and Karen spent most of the time she wasn't working sitting with him at the doctor's office. Her new boss told her that she would have to come back full-time at about the same time that IBM made me an offer. Karen decided to give her two weeks' notice so that she could stay home, raise a family, and support me any way I needed. And she read to me.

Gradually, everything settled down. Life became a feeding and diaper-change routine. I took my turn at diaper duty until Karen decided I didn't do a very good job of it. Steve was nine months old when Karen quit work to stay home. One piece of advice we got from all directions was "Decide how to reinforce behaviors that you approve." The way we chose to show approval was by applauding. A month after Karen quit work, I was in the breakfast nook with Steve. He asked for a cracker. I went to the kitchen counter and got a stack of saltines. Karen and I were very amused when Steve started clapping. Wait a minute here! Who was training whom? Talk about turning the tables! We were amazed to witness Steve's intelligence dawning. He was observing patterns in our behavior too, even as we were observing his.

For the first time, I was jealous of others for having normal vision. They could see Steve clearly, but my images were dim and blurry. I started to worry about being a blind parent of a sighted child. Plenty of books talked about being a blind child of sighted parents. But, about my case, there was nothing. I began to be critical of everything I did, feeling guilty as if I were cheating Steve. I recited to myself all the things other fathers did with their sons, and I would never do any of them. I would never throw a football to Steve. I wouldn't take him camping or teach him how to drive a car . . . on and on. My inadequacies as a dad were endless. At last, I voiced these fears to Karen. Like the wise woman Karen is, she assured me that Steve might be the better for having me as a father. The lightning that had struck me when we met was truly divine. Karen had a dimension that was stronger in her than in most women. Steve might grow up with that same strong com-passion. Again, I saw that Karen was, and still is, the right wife for me, the one woman in the universe that I should have married.

I was truly blessed. Not only did I have the wisest and strongest parents in the universe, my wife was stellar. Mom and Dad echoed what Karen was telling me. I relaxed, determined to be content with what I had. Yet, my feelings of inadequacy as a father did not vanish completely. They would periodically haunt me as I watched the boys grow up. My life was very satisfying. Both sets of parents visited us more often. Karen saw a new side of her father when he was with Steve. Mr. Williams didn't seem to be as reserved. Those darker thoughts that I had, though not painful, didn't entirely vanish. When I saw my father with Steve, I thought, "Dad is getting to do the things he would have liked to do with me." Then, I realized, "If you're patient and have a little faith, life will give you what you missed earlier."

Chapter 15
International Business Machines

When the defense contracting company Tracor lost the air force contract, I applied to IBM for the second time (two years after my first application there) and was granted an interview. That spring morning of 1981, Karen dropped me off for the interview at the original IBM building on Burnet Road. I was met by Joe Quintana from Human Resources, who in turn handed me over to Jim Windlekin, a fourth-line manager (who had first-, second-, and third-line managers under him). Jim escorted me to three groups under his supervision. I met a few managers and lots of faces within their departments. Of course, they were voices to me, not faces. I can't name anybody I met, but among them must have been the people I ended up working with. They asked me lots of questions. I mentioned to the Displaywriter group that I had written an editor on the Apple II, and they seemed interested. At the end of a very long day, Jim said they would think about where best to place me. I went home a bit overwhelmed, but very optimistic. Looking back on that interview, I think my having written an editor determined where they placed me.

As I was leaving the interview with that group, I bumped into someone I had met years before at the University of Houston job placement center. He spoke first. He didn't remember my name, just my major.

He said, "Abstract algebra, right?" I immediately remembered meeting him. I responded, "Yes."

"Wow!" he exclaimed and walked on past. He had dropped an abstract algebra course because he was totally lost.

IBM in Austin was a large site, housing seven thousand employees. So the fact that I didn't hear back for six months, I told myself, was a good sign. I had begun to think I would never hear anything at all. But in late October, Joe from Human Resources called and made me an offer, which I accepted. I expressed a desire to start in January, but he recommended that I start in November because the earlier start date would give me credit for that entire year, important for retirement purposes. I took his advice and showed up bright and early at the main building.

At an orientation class for new hires, a photographer snapped my picture. This photograph on a temporary badge would get me past most badge readers until my permanent badge was made. I spent the morning filling out papers and listening to a series of speeches. One of them stressed to all us newbies that security was taken very seriously. Each time you left your desk unlocked, or left a sensitive document out on the desk, your manager received a security violation with your name on it. If you accumulated three violations within any eighteen-month period, you would be fired immediately. Many was the night that Karen drove me back to the office just so I could check my desk. The paranoia never subsided. That made me a person of strong habits.

At the end of the orientation, each new hire met his host for the rest of the day.

My host approached and said, "Hello, Mike Cross."

"Ray Hernandez, what are you doing here?"

"Oh, I left Tracor about a year ago and joined IBM. Someone else from Tracor is here too, our friend Chuck, and now you make number three."

I stood there flabbergasted. Ray had worked in that marine navigation group at Tracor that had decided too late to make me an offer. He asked me where I would like to eat and named a few local eateries. After lunch at Bennigan's, a chain of Irish pub–themed restaurants, Ray gave me a tour of the IBM site and finally delivered me to my workplace in the Charmark building, which IBM was renting off campus.

That weekend, when I called Pasadena with my good news, Mom gave me good news of her own. Tracy had gone to work for Oshman's Sporting Goods.

I never stayed anywhere at IBM for a long time. A universally told joke is that IBM stands for "I've Been Moved." It is nevertheless true. The moves may be across the hall rather than across the United States, or overseas. Two weeks after IBM hired me, we moved into new offices in a building on the IBM campus.

My first two assignments were to write assembly language programs to perform regression tests on the Series/1 computer and to write functional verification tests for the Displaywriter word processor. It didn't occur to me that I would see history being made firsthand, but my first year at IBM would be revolutionary in the computer industry. IBM announced the Personal Computer (the IBM PC) in 1981 and started migrating software to it from other systems. The Displaywriter function (the word processor software application) running on the PC was called DisplayWrite. Until the Displaywriter was withdrawn from the market, I tested compilers on both systems. The compilers were for FORTRAN, Pascal, and COBOL.

My second department maintained eleven spelling dictionaries for American English, British English, Spanish, Portuguese, Italian, French, German, Dutch, Danish, Swedish, and Finnish. The six linguists in that department, including my friend Mary N., attempted to determine some common rules for structuring these dictionaries in order to have a common way to extract information from them. The rules had to apply to all eleven languages. Finnish broke every rule proposed at those meetings. Finally, IBM dropped support for Finnish, which eased things quite a bit. The department did more than maintain these spell-check dictionaries. In addition to spell-checking a document, we wanted to be able to check its grammar as well. I designed and implemented a database in support of that effort. It was a research tool, storing results and helping the developers evaluate the correctness of their grammar-checking algorithm. The group broke up when the dictionary mission transferred to Gaithersburg, Maryland.

The third department I worked in was a group developing a composite editor. My assignment within this group was to design and implement a freehand drawing function. I had an IBM PC/XT (the XT stood for "eXtended technology") with a 10 MB (megabyte) hard drive. At the time, this was the best storage and performance power available. Part of the challenge was to overcome the lack of speed in doing real-time graphics. In addition, it was obvious to my manager that I needed a much larger monitor, 23 inches or more. I had enough mathematical skill to create a good design, but not enough vision to evaluate the appearance of the graphics on the screen. The size of my font, which I needed for editing, was limited by the diagonal of the monitor. Without a large diagonal monitor, my eyestrain was tremendous.

As a result, IBM sent me to a National Federation of the Blind convention in Las Vegas. Flying alone, I anticipated transportation problems, but a surprise awaited me. I was met at the airport by people from the Mormon church, which had volunteered to chaperone the National Federation of the Blind convention attendees. I did manage during those three days to elude my Mormon escort and go to Caesars Palace for a steak. The dinner eaten, I wandered around, eventually getting lost among the gamblers. I couldn't hear anything over the whir and clatter of the slot machines. It drowned out all other sound. I found the slot machines and played them like a fiend. When the monster had eaten all four of my quarters, I stopped. Tired of watching all the crazy people pulling levers, I finally started walking, and when the sounds grew fainter, I was encouraged and kept moving in that direction. At last, I heard traffic noises and got a taxi back to the Holiday Inn. For three days, convention attendees examined magnification devices and large diagonal monitors. The wake-up call to catch my flight home was the sound of slot machines. No human voice on that phone call said anything. To sum up this trip, I left having seen several closed-circuit televisions for reading books but not having seen a computer monitor that would solve my problems.

Because of my involvement with graphics, my department next sent me to Boca Raton, Florida, to take a course in computer graphics. This time, two coworkers flew with me. The teachers were two professors from the University of Utah. The material covered was very familiar to me. I had dealt extensively with moving coordinate systems in university physics. During the five-day class, I made some suggestions about getting the inverse of a matrix. The suggestion was from an advanced linear algebra course I had taken back at the University of Houston. Suitably impressed, the teachers were completely puzzled as to how a blind man could implement computer graphics. Shortly after this trip, my department broke up without having produced a product.

My fourth department developed a word processor called DisplayWrite Assistant, which went to market and had a modest earnings history. My longest stay in any group was in my fifth department. It developed the database engine for the IBM OS/2 (Operating System/2, which ran on personal computers). I was the lead programmer for the data services component. It handled all data conversions and mathematical operations. I held that job through three releases of OS/2. IBM decided to also put that database engine on AIX (Advanced Interactive eXecutive, an IBM UNIX-based operating system) running on the RS/6000 (RISC System/6000, a family of servers, workstations, and supercomputers made by IBM in the 1990s; RISC stands for Reduced Instruction Set Computer). The AIX database was called the DB/2 database engine. We managed to avoid having two separate build processes for both Database Manager (in OS/2) and DB/2 (in AIX). There were, of course, a few operating-system-dependent routines that had to be built separately, but that was minor.

People around me came and went; my department changed managers three times. Most programs were being written in the C computer language, but management decided that future programming should be done in C++.

IBM paid for its developers to voluntarily take a C++ course at the University of Texas at Austin. I was persuaded by some of the people in a fellow department to sign up. Then things got very busy at work, and I also found out I was facing surgery. This prompted me to drop the course. I called the IBM woman in charge of university education for IBM students. When I explained my circumstance and that I had transportation issues, she said she would take care of dropping me from the course. Well, she didn't. So, at the end of the semester, I received notice that I had failed the course. I was very angry. I should have taken a vacation day to attend to this myself and not trusted anything so important to a third party. But this was her job, and she didn't do it. Instead, I had academic egg on my face. Since I didn't plan to go back to school for another degree, I dismissed it. The lady apologized, but it was done. I failed the only course I ever took at the University of Texas. My doctor decided against that surgery, meaning the whole situation never should have arisen at all.

The first real help with computer accessibility for the blind came in the form of a program called IBM Screen Reader/2, which was released in the early 1990s. The installer was on three diskettes. It worked right out of the box. Its voice was IBM ViaVoice, which is very easy to understand. My life was much easier from that point forward.

In 1992, my division moved into six pink granite buildings, each one six stories tall. These new buildings were very nice. My office moved from building number 901 to building number 903, and then to 905. My office was never below the third floor. My manager always assigned a department member to escort me out of the building during fire drills. The stairwells were supposed to stay lighted, being on an emergency system. During one such drill, the emergency lighting failed, leaving the stairwells in darkness. As people slowly descended, several complained about going down a dark stairwell. I spoke up. "Don't worry, I'll get you out." They all appreciated the irony.

I rewrote C routines, achieving gains in execution speeds even when those around me said my routines couldn't be improved. My graduate school experience with proofs and counterexamples prepared me to think about approaches that others dismissed without much thought. The speed gains were 50 to 80 percent. A side project of mine was to write profiles for PE2, IBM Personal Editor 2. These profiles allowed a user to generate syntax quickly in several different computer languages. I wrote profiles for

C, Pascal, COBOL, PC assembly language, and SQL (Structured Query Language for databases). In fact, each profile defined keystrokes to change the active profile on the fly. To my immense gratification, people around me started using my profiles to speed up writing programs while avoiding syntax errors.

A group of us from various departments at IBM frequented local restaurants. I introduced the group to Thai food, which quickly became an area addiction. The competition among us was to eat Thai fried rice with the most peppers. Richard won the contest. We sat and watched him eat his rice with six Thai peppers. The competition ended that day. Richard admitted that he could no longer taste anything.

The pink granite buildings presented me with a new opportunity. Conscious of spending most of my day in a chair at a computer, and of how much a sedentary life style damaged health, I decided to take advantage of being in a building that had six stories. Each day at quitting time, I went down to the first floor and fast-climbed to number six. I repeated this twice more, by which time I was drenched in sweat—not to mention that this drained me of energy. Nobody else did this; I mentioned it to a coworker, and he thought I was crazy. However, I thought not doing it was an opportunity wasted, so I continued my afternoon ritual.

Although the departments around me were busy, we did find time to have some wide-ranging discussions. In addition to computer science and mathematics, the other sciences were well represented at IBM. So, the subjects ranged far and wide. One of the topics I introduced generated strong opinions. I stated that mathematics is deductive, whereas science is inductive. Therefore, scientists could never know when they possessed the ultimate truth about the universe. The mathematicians and scientists, of course, lined up on opposite sides of this controversy. The mathematicians on the OS/2 team naturally all said that I was absolutely correct.

IBM offered its employees university-level computer science courses. Taught by university professors, classes were off-site and ran for five days. Each team of professors lectured for eight hours, only breaking for lunch. In the course on databases, we discussed the algebraic underpinnings of SQL (Structured Query Language). A lively discussion broke out concerning whether mathematics depended on special symbols or whether its axioms and theorems could be stated using only the English language. Since each special symbol has an English language definition, the obvious answer is yes,

English is sufficient for mathematics. Special symbols and notations, however, allow mathematical statements to be very compact and information dense.

Back in the office, I was thinking of how to speed up decimal division, when the database mission transferred from Austin, Texas, to Toronto, Canada. I moved again, not to Toronto but into another department down the hall.

IBM was a family-friendly company. The annual picnic was a half-day event with rides and food for the kids. The adults weren't forgotten. There were groups from the Austin music scene, and even some nationally known. One Saturday before the IBM picnic, when Steve was about eighteen months old, Karen was running errands, leaving me alone to feed Steve. I poked around and found a full plastic bag of prunes. I gave him one. He really liked it, so I gave him another, and then another. Karen returned, and we piled into the car and headed off to the picnic. We arrived at Century Oaks Park, which was set up like a theme park full of tents, food, drinks, Blue Bell ice cream, and lots of rides. There were clowns making balloon animals, and Steve got a fireman's hat when he went to see the fire engine there. I accompanied him on a few rides but wasn't confident that I could take adequate care of him on the bigger rides. That little boy loved it all! The afternoon was waning, and we decided to call it a day. Suddenly, Steve started to scream, and I heard a wet spluttering noise like someone was blowing a raspberry. His diaper filled up as we rushed to the car. It was obvious he was sick. We were reviewing everything he had eaten at the picnic.

"Oh, no!" I remembered the prunes.

"Well, how many did you give him?"

She knew by my guilty look that the answer was "too many." By the time we arrived home, Steve was happy again.

Steve listened to Grandpa Cross telling a story. When Dad said, "The end," Steve said in his musical voice, "That's remarkable." It was a few minutes before my dad could speak. I hadn't heard him laugh like that in years. Mom was laughing, too. Dad finally cleared his throat and asked, "Did you say 'remarkable'?" and started laughing again. "Steve, you're a smart boy." Dad always remembered to say uplifting things. Of course, I thought "remarkable" perfectly described the whole incident. How many three-year-old boys would say something like that?

In 1983, Karen became pregnant again, and Tony was born on Mother's Day in 1984. He didn't look like me or else I would have had to name him Steve too. Tony resembled Karen. I was calmer this time around, but I can't say the same for Karen. The birth notice we sent out said "DOS 2.0 IBM PC, itsy bitsy Mr. Precious Child." The house was again swamped with visitors wanting to see the new arrival. We were gratified that Tony and Steve would eventually prove to be good friends. There seemed to be less friction between them than brothers in most families we knew.

...

I wasn't happy with the amount of time I could spend at home, so we bought a house in north Austin, about three miles from the IBM site. This let me leave the house later and get home earlier. Tony turned one shortly after we moved into the new house. A year later, Luke's family moved onto the street. Tony also was friends with Brian, who lived on a nearby street.

I was ruminating on the challenges I may face as a blind father. A few questions were always on my mind: How much of a burden was I to those around me? Could I fulfill my responsibilities to them? In particular, could I help in the development of my children? I would never fully answer these questions. I watched my own father interact with Steve and later with Tony, wondering if I could do the same things with my sons. I expressed my fears to Karen, and she reassured me that there would be benefits as well as drawbacks. Would I fail my sons? Fearing that at some point in the future, I would wish I had known them better. I have heard accounts of parents who tried to be one of their children's peers, and that didn't work out so well. Then, in view of that, can you be an authority figure and a peer too? Since I couldn't resolve any of these questions, I had to be content with whatever I could do and accept the fact that I couldn't do everything. A great comfort was knowing that I was not alone in this process. Karen and I were bound together, for better or worse. She would be helping me adjust to the people around me, even as she helped them adjust to me. My family is fortunate that my blindness can't be inherited. Where genetic inheritance is a factor, marriages can become toxic. It can even poison a child's attitude toward his or her blind parent. I have seen it happen firsthand, though providentially not in our family. We were extremely lucky to be spared this thorny dilemma.

The boys shared a bedroom, and I usually went in at night to tell them a silly story. I walked in one particular evening with bare feet. The boys liked action figures, and Tony loved Legos. After stepping on several toys, I turned around to leave. Steve, who was lying on a trundle bed, was looking at me as

I said "Ouch!" He said, "You're just not tough enough to sleep in my room." I quickly left because I didn't want him to see me laughing. As they got older, I asked them to help me water our blackberries, find the newspaper, and tell me when to go up or down curbs and stairs. We all also danced to some of my favorite Creedence Clearwater Revival songs and listened to recorded children's stories. These were my main interactions with the boys at the time.

We met a couple at our new church, Michael and Marion Vose, and our boys became friends with their boys. Michael had a PhD in math and was teaching at Texas A&M. He decided to switch to computer science and get a second PhD at the University of Texas. He told me he could go further on less talent in computer science. When Michael finished his second doctorate in 1988, the University of Tennessee hired him. Before he and Marion left town, we took them to dinner at an Indian restaurant, where we all had sampler plates. I could tell that Michael was having a transcendental experience. When the waiter brought the check, Michael said, "I have glimpsed heaven tonight, eating in your restaurant." Then Michael turned to me. "Why did you have to bring us here? We'll never get any food like this in Tennessee." But he was wrong. Michael had several graduate students from India, so he got plenty of Indian food after all. (In May 1989, Karen and I visited Michael and Marion in Knoxville. On the way back to Texas, we stopped in New Orleans. We sat and watched on television, on June 4, the Chinese military massacre student protesters in Tiananmen Square. We couldn't believe it was really happening. The whole world was watching.)

Steve started school, and Karen volunteered a lot. There were no art classes at the elementary school level at this time. Karen created a catalogue for the library of all the school's art posters. She used the posters to create several art displays, and some of the teachers used them in the classroom. When Steve was eight years old, he joined a soccer team coached by our neighbor. His son Nick lived a few houses away. After the first game, Nick's father knocked on our door. "Steve has all the right instincts on the field. He can do anything he wants in soccer. He's very fast." Despite this praise, the team had a mediocre season. Two years later Tony joined a soccer team, but only played one year because he had asthma. By this time, several coaches had taken notice of Steve. Three coaches wanted him for their team. They all wanted him as a fullback (or sweeper), because he had the speed to chase down most forwards and take the ball back. Nick was a little older than Steve, and his brother Sam was about a year older than Tony. When Nick was in fifth grade, he became too old for the after-school program. His mother asked Karen to watch her sons after school for about two years. The boys became close friends and often came over even after they could stay home alone. Tony's friends Luke and Brian had moved away by the time Tony finished middle school.

Steve and Tony liked basketball but only played it with their friends. Our new house was on a circle, and there was a pole with a basketball net straight across the circle from our driveway. I tried shooting baskets but never came close. The boys could always get my dad to shoot baskets with them. Dad was finally getting the interaction he missed with me, but I was there and enjoyed witnessing their fun. On one occasion, Steve approached the basket at a run to shoot, but at the last second, Dad stepped up behind him and snagged the ball as it was about to go into the net. Steve couldn't believe he did that. Grandpa was pretty sneaky. Dad included Tony in everything.

Steve took art classes in middle and high school. Tony took an art class but decided it wasn't for him. He found his niche in band. He started with the clarinet and moved on from there to saxophone during high school. Tony was also active in scouting until he started high school. Steve and Tony enjoyed using makeshift swords to play pirates or Jedi knights with their friends. Everyone had a good time. As they got older, they started playing paintball. It required special equipment and had to be played in specific locations. Computer games hit the market, and of course, the boys had to play them, too. By this time, all three bedrooms had internet connections, leading to more computer games. The house was taken over with local area network (LAN) parties. Tony set up a LAN for three computers, one in each bedroom. The house got pretty noisy as the computer gamers played a variety of multiple-user combat games. The three computers interacted with one another in real time. This amounted to paintball on a computer.

Tony had been assembling computer hardware under my direction since he was six years old. I occasionally bought computer components recommended by coworkers at IBM. I showed Tony what to do, and he would put the parts on the motherboard. I had to put my hands on top of his hands and press down until he became strong enough attach the parts firmly. One day in high school physics class, the teacher responded to a question about the classroom computer.

"Well, it just stopped working. I guess I need a new one," the teacher said. However, no one ever saw him use it.

Tony asked if he could take a look at it. The class scoffed, but Tony popped the case open and said, "It sure is dusty!"

He blew the dust out, put the case back together, and turned on the power. It booted right up.

"You need to get some canned air and blow it out." Tony went up in everyone's estimation.

Tony, in his senior year, took a computer graphics course. In the fall of 2003, he entered the University of Texas at Dallas, majoring in electrical engineering. The next semester they created a new major—arts and technology—which is the field of animation and movie special effects. Tony switched majors and never regretted it. He decided to specialize in motion capture, which uses cameras to capture sensors attached to people or animals and create moving stick figures on the computer, which can be made to look like animated characters. After he graduated in the spring of 2008, Tony went to work for Motus Digital, an independent motion capture company in the Dallas area that subcontracted for other companies.

Tony spent a lot of time at work and with his many friends in Dallas, but he always enjoyed getting together with family during holidays and reunions. He found a kindred spirit in Tracy. They both had a weird sense of humor, a distinctive laugh, and were always the life of any party. They also loved swapping jokes and telling funny stories. They were both optimists. Tony saw Tracy and me overcome obstacles, and he felt that he could too.

Tony's visits to Austin always started with a big bear hug and a "Hello, Dad." He and I often went out—just the two of us—to get tacos, barbecue, or Thai food. Phone conversations with Tony usually drifted around to our latest food discoveries. One Christmas in Pasadena, while visiting my brother Tracy, who hosted us, Tony was surprised to see me because I had a beard, though it wasn't luxurious like his. Tony won the beard competition hands down. One Christmas, Tony and I visited the Galleria Mall in Houston to see the new Tesla on the upper floor. When we arrived at the dealership, nobody was around the Tesla, and I started investigating it by touch. Tony briefly looked at the Tesla, but then struck up a conversation with the salesman. A friend who customized dune buggies had taught him how to fix cars. Tony bought his own Jeep and customized it to go off-roading with some of his friends. He mentioned his Jeep to the salesman and showed him several pictures on his phone. The Jeep was well worth a look. It had roll bars, big mag tires, and other improvements. The salesman never got around to his pitch. As we left, Tony glanced back at the Tesla and laughed.

Throughout the boys' formative years, my focus was on providing a living for us all. And that is as it should be. Looking back, I wonder if I could have rearranged my time. The constant time constraint was that at both Tracor, and later at IBM, the turn-around times for work projects were demanding— meaning short. And they got shorter as the years went by.

It was selfish of me to think that I alone had missed a valuable part of life. Dad and I both had been deprived. All those things I chided myself for not being able to do with my sons, my dad didn't get to do with me, either. But he was doing them now. On a particularly cold and breezy winter afternoon, Dad and Mom came to a soccer game in Austin and complained that they had nearly frozen to death. Having only light jackets, they soon retreated to the car. Since Steve was running constantly, he stayed warm.

Steve Cross, Luke (Tony's friend), and Tony Cross, about 1989. Photo from Kenda

Steve, Tan, Mike, Tony, and Karen Cross, Thanksgiving at Waco, 2009. Author's

Chapter 16
Empty Nesters at Last

Over the fifteen years following 1992, Karen and I said goodbye again and again to parents, kids, and other family members. On visits to Pasadena, both boys followed Grandpa around, watching him work on cars and do odd carpentry jobs. By this time, Dad was retired from the Port of Houston, giving him more time for kids and grandkids. He took the boys kite flying, out for ice cream, and to the zoo. He had the circus in mind, but it never happened. He never got the chance to teach Steve or Tony to drive a car. The very next year was his last on Earth. Two weeks before the 1992 Barcelona Olympics, a nephrologist put a line in Dad's shoulder to start dialysis. They weren't careful and punctured a lung. The X-rays showed not only the damage, but something else as well. There was a spot on one of Dad's lungs. Because he had worked at the port, they thought it was probably mold and dismissed it. The doctor left for the Olympics and six weeks of vacation, and Dad decided this meant it couldn't be very serious. Later that summer, they took another look and decided it was lung cancer. Since Dad had worked for Anderson Clayton, we got a doctor at MD Anderson to take his case. He was operated on in October and when he woke from surgery, Mom took his hand and said, "Well, you don't have lung cancer anymore."

Dad was home recovering, and Mom was preparing for Thanksgiving. We thought the problems were behind us. About 4:00 that morning, Mom started groaning, and we all rushed in to see what was wrong. Dad wasn't supposed to exert more than ten pounds of force because of his recent surgery. We thought she had the flu. We were all wrong. Mom had had an aneurysm during the night. She continued getting worse, and we took her to the hospital on Saturday. We should have brought her in earlier. The three-day window, during which surgery to relieve the pressure can be done, had closed and there was nothing to be done. We waited and prayed. Mom lived, but couldn't speak. Meanwhile, Dad was driving himself into Houston for dialysis. It left him too weak to walk to his car, so he stayed at the hospital for hours waiting for his strength to return. Then he could drive himself home.

Christmas in Pasadena that year was not at all cheerful. Mom was still in the hospital and oblivious to everything. Her doctor said her blood didn't contain enough oxygen because she had blood clots rising from her legs. When a surgeon put a stent into the vena cava in her groin area, it filtered out the clots, and Mom was speaking complete sentences within thirty minutes. Her short-term memory was gone, and the compartment of her brain regulating emotion was barely functional. Her expression was usually deadpan, but that could have been shock or depression.

In January, Dad went to MD Anderson to have the lines inserted to support peritoneal dialysis, which can be done at home. The surgeon saw something suspicious on his liver. The cancer had metastasized. The oncologist at MD Anderson gave Dad a little over three months to live. Mark and Kay brought Mom and Dad to Austin to get a second opinion. The Austin oncologist reviewed the hundred pages of analysis, and said there was nothing they missed, and that Dad should get his affairs in order. Kay was looking at Mom's horrified face. Dad was resigned, but Mom asked in a tragic voice, "You mean there's nothing left to be done?" The doctor offered us one consolation: death from liver cancer is the least painful cancer death. Two months passed, and Kay quit her job with the Round Rock school district to be with Dad and support Mom. The end came three days after Dad discontinued dialysis. This gentle giant looked into the distance, said "Well, aren't you pretty," and died.

Sitting at my desk, I shuddered at a sudden premonition. Mom answered my phone call. "Well, he's gone. Ray died thirty minutes ago." The blow fell hard on us. Steve was eleven and Tony was eight. They were both deeply affected, as were we all. The funeral was well attended, not only by extended family, but by many church people, and Dad's coworkers from the Port of Houston. Mom's doctors still had her on medication for pain. She walked through the funeral as if in a dream.

We all worried how Mom, with her short-term memory loss, would cope. Tracy left his apartment and moved in with Mom, who could hardly care for herself. We all rallied around her, but Kay and I both lived a hundred and sixty miles away. Tracy worked all day, leaving Mom to fend for herself, which was not exactly ideal. So Kay and Mark returned to their former jobs with the Conroe school district. From Conroe, Kay could get in her car and be at Mom's house in an hour. But this wasn't good enough. One day, Mom fell on the concrete back porch. Managing to crawl into the house, she finally called Kay, who left work in a rush. Mom's leg from mid-thigh to mid-calf was swollen and huge. After this crisis was resolved, we convinced her to go into assisted living near Kay's house. Mom was now diabetic, and her vision was no better than mine. But she didn't complain, figuring that if I could bear it, so could she.

Meanwhile, Karen and I were preoccupied with the stress of life in Austin, with school and job. I moved into my sixth department on the sixth floor in yet another pink granite building. I was now a tools programmer. This meant that I no longer developed office products for the marketplace, but rather software supporting those who did. My new job was to write an application using the DB/2 database engine that I had been developing for the last six years. It tracked $20 million worth of computer hardware for the entire Austin site. A person would scan an orange sticker on a piece of hardware, such as a computer, with a barcode reader. Using my Java program, they would then send a batch of such scans over the web to the DB/2 inventory database application. My C programs allowed any IBM Austin department to check hardware in and out of the Austin computer warehouse. The warehouse staff were very demanding, and I spent considerable effort catering to their whims.

Steve now entered Connally High School, which had just opened and only had junior varsity sports. He was still playing select league soccer, and he was captain of the school soccer team even though he was only a freshman. The coach worked at another campus, and all practices were held after school. Some of the players lived off a nearby road with no sidewalks or streetlights. Steve made sure his mom took home anyone who didn't have a ride. He had lots of stamina, since soccer players run all game long. When the cross-country coach heard about Steve, three weeks remained in the season. She immediately recruited him to her team. His third race was for the district medal. He won! This was the school's first medal in any sport.

The year 1996 was another stressful year: Karen's father was diagnosed with a blood disorder, which turned into leukemia. He received experimental treatment at MD Anderson and died in 1998. The funeral was large because this man, who had helped a lot of people, was well-loved. The boys were again hit hard, but life goes on.

In February 1997, Oshman's laid Tracy off. He went to work part-time for Kwik Kopy, using his familiarity with Apple printers. In July of that same year, Tracy phoned me with good news. Curtis 1000, an envelope and stationery company, hired him because of his Photoshop skills.

In 1998, my department changed areas, moving into IBM Global Services. While there, I worked on several projects. The entire computer industry was consumed by the Y2K scare: the fear that when the year 2000 arrived, banking and other software would crash or start trashing their own databases. I was put on the Y2K team, as was everyone else at IBM. We all scrubbed the programs we owned; and when 2000 arrived, nothing happened.

My work got a lot easier when HPR, the IBM Home Page Reader, came along. It was a self-voicing browser that ran on top of Internet Explorer 6. Its voice was IBM ViaVoice. The special needs department contacted me and other blind programmers at the Austin site about being part of a weeklong focus group on HPR. The next release of Home Page Reader reflected our feedback. A still-later release added Desktop Reader, a nice screen reader program. It gave blind Windows users the ability to issue special keystrokes causing ViaVoice to read various parts of the screen. The user didn't have to be in the browser to use Desktop Reader.

Home Page Reader also had applications beyond the blind community. A Chinese woman in my department, although she had good vision, found Home Page Reader very helpful in her attempt to learn to speak English better. With HPR, the words in the document being read are highlighted, then unhighlighted, as the reading cursor jumps through the text. The highlighting is synchronized with the audible speech. That is, ViaVoice speaks the currently highlighted word. The speech dictionary underlying ViaVoice controls the pronunciation. This made it easy for my Chinese coworker to listen to the pronunciation and know exactly which word was being spoken. ViaVoice pronunciation was very good, so her speech improved markedly.

I tried hard not to let IBM invade my home life. My job didn't interfere with my being a father or husband. One weekend Karen and I went to Pasadena and Baytown alone. The kids were old enough to stay home, and a school activity kept them in Austin. On our return, a surprise waited for us. Winter came into my life that hot day. I walked into the living room and there she was, a small dog checking out her new surroundings. Her first family had moved into an apartment whose management didn't allow pets.

"Steve, what is this? I told you I didn't want a dog. What do we do with a dog when we travel?"

"Oh, Dad, give her a chance! Her name is Winter, and she is a white Pomeranian."

"She's an inconvenience."

In later years, I would reproach myself for those words. "Okay, she has one week." During dinner, Steve and Tony played with her. Eager to show us her tricks, Tony pointed his forefinger at her, cocked his thumb, and said, "Bang!" Winter fell over on her side and played dead. Feeling rejection, she was auditioning for her new family. "Can you dance, girl? Come on, dance!" She stood on her hind legs, danced, and walked all over the room. Her insecurity was so obvious, and why not? Her former family had just disowned her. Steve said she cried for a long time after his friend Brandon dropped her off and left.

I finally sat down on the floor to get acquainted. Winter approached warily. My reserve melted. "Hello, Winter." I held my hand out to her, and she sniffed interestedly and licked it. I was hooked from that moment. "Dad, Brandon told me she doesn't like to be held." I thought, "Yeah, but that's when she felt secure." Over the next months, the boys and I played with Winter a lot. When I came home from work, she met me at the door. She reminded me of Bounce-A-Lot. In her early days with us, she was anxious to play and do tricks. I held her often; she even went to sleep in my arms. I grew very protective of Winter. More than once, when I was walking her in the front yard, a big dog rushed over to attack her. A few times, I noticed the other dog before she did. My hearing is very good. I grabbed her up just in time. She went crazy when she saw the other dog. Over the years, this scene repeated itself enough that Winter came to see me as her protector, and she came to me whenever she didn't feel safe.

One night Steve came home late after a soccer game. Winter was very excited to see him. Carrying the dog, I followed Steve to his room. I held her out so she could lick him. It was a cold, dry winter night, so when her tongue touched Steve, there was a loud snap and an energy exchange due to static electricity. Winter trembled, and we all burst into laughter.

An off-white, pretty, fluffy Pomeranian needs a haircut more than most dogs. Normally, Karen, Steve, or Tony caught her and did it. But nobody was around, and I thought I was up to the task. Hey, being blind is no problem! So I did it. Well, everyone was mad at me. Winter looked bad. She had plenty of hair left, so Karen gave her a second haircut. It wasn't any better than mine. The dog knew she looked bad; she wouldn't come out from under the bed. She was probably afraid she'd be worked on again. Of course, I had to point out that Karen's haircut was no better than mine. Karen retorted, "Well, I'll just tell everybody you did it!" And we both laughed about that.

One day when I came home, Tony and a friend were sitting on the couch facing the door. Three things happened in quick succession, because they happened every day: I put my hand down, palm up; Winter ran to me and belly flopped onto it; and I lifted her straight up. Tony's friend laughed and said, "She just ran over and caught the elevator." It was funny because it looked like we had rehearsed the maneuver.

Often when playing, Winter "went jet," streaking around the living room. Hair shaking, to the boys she was a blur. In mid-flight, Winter would stop on a dime, executing a pirouette on one leg. She was a ballerina spinning in a swirling mist. It would have made a great video, but we never caught it.

Everyone was gearing up for the holidays. Tony wrote a Halloween story in which the witch kick-started her broom and flew away; Karen and I were very amused. Before we knew it, it was Christmas in Baytown, and everybody was talking and eating. No one paid any attention to Winter, but she was paying attention to everyone. Karen dropped a cookie, and Winter pounced and ran with it. She rounded the corner of the couch and disappeared. When Karen followed, she saw Winter sitting like the Egyptian sphinx, an innocent look on her face. Karen looked everywhere for the cookie. "Well, where is it?" Tony, who had witnessed all, started to laugh. "Winter is sitting on it." Everyone was laughing as Karen picked up Winter and retrieved the cookie, which she dumped in the trash.

From an early age, Steve excelled at writing. When he was sixteen, he entered a local short story competition for Christian writers. Set on the planet Mars during the Neo-crusades on Earth, the story title was "The Red Siege." It took third place. All the other contestants were older adults. So, it was natural that Steve eventually majored in journalism. In 2000, Steve started classes at Baylor University in Waco, where Karen's sister Linda was one of the campus physicians. On September 11 of his sophomore year, Steve's journalism class watched the twin towers crumble. I had just walked out of my office, and the area secretary told me what was happening. Work continued, but we all kept going by the TV mounted in the hall, which by then was giving 24/7 coverage. Despite the strong distraction, work never slowed down.

In 2001, I moved to my last department at IBM. As part of LTC, the Linux Technology Center, I evaluated Linux accessibility for the blind. Aside from a program called Emacspeak (a speech interface), there wasn't much. In 2002, two weeks after I qualified for early retirement, IBM laid off twenty thousand employees. I took advantage of their buyout offer. May 2002 marked my emancipation from the world of work. I was retiring after twenty years with IBM.

Karen, my wife of twenty-four years, sat to my immediate right, and my manager, Sharon, to my left. IBM offered two lunch options to those retiring with at least twenty years of service but fewer than twenty-five. The first was to have sandwiches for thirty people, and the second was to have a fancy lunch for ten. I chose the ten-person option because I was more comfortable with a smaller group. The ten I had invited trickled in, greeting old friends warmly and seating themselves. The gathering had the atmosphere of a family reunion. Seven of the faces were former colleagues from the OS/2 database team. I had known them for about fifteen years. They hadn't all been in the same room for a decade, having dispersed into other groups around the Austin site. I had run into them all at one time or another, walking between the six pink granite IBM buildings, but, surprisingly, they had mostly missed encountering each other. One of the seven, Dean, was in my first department, DisplayWrite. A second, Mary T., I met in my fourth department, DisplayWrite Assistant word processor. The last three, unknown to the others, were with me in the Linux Technology Center. One of the three, Glen, had been in Global Services with me in 1997 when the IBM Deep Blue computer defeated Garry Kasparov in a chess competition. I introduced these two groups to one another and said a few words about each person. There was a variety of backgrounds in the room—some biologists, a fellow mathematician, a music major, a biochemist, and the rest computer scientists. Several said that they were looking forward to retirement and were jealous. But, everyone there had more years at IBM than I did, so they all could have retired at any time they chose.

Elevators opened and waiters rolled the food out on two carts. Lunch was served to universal expressions of approval. One of the guys said, "This is the best meal I've ever had at IBM." As people ate, they caught up with each other, laughed, and told stories. The fare was filet mignon, stuffed crab, green beans, and potatoes au gratin. Even more than I relished the gourmet food, I enjoyed listening to the conversations around me. Karen knew some of the invitees, having met them at informal department get-togethers, so she was able to join in the talk.

The meal finished, coffee and generous slices of Italian cream cake were set before us. My manager rose and read letters from people who had worked with me over the years, some funny, some serious. The people attending didn't really have to say all those nice things; however, I deserved every word of it! She laid down the last letter and said, "And now, it's time to hear from our retiree, Michael Cross." I was about to be an ex-IBMer. My feelings were mixed, as I rose to my feet.

"I could not have spent these last twenty years at a better place than IBM. Each of you had something to do with that. You have all been a pleasure to work with. I have many pleasant memories of you and of IBM. I leave with some regret, but prepared to move forward. And if you ever want to know how retired life feels, just give me a call. You've got my number."

I sat down to applause and laughter. Goodbyes were heartfelt; I really liked these people. Gradually, the room emptied, and Karen and I rode down the elevator and walked out of the IBM world. I arrived home, took off my three-piece blue suit, and felt lost. Then I rebounded, and thought about the books I'd like to write and the people I'd like to help.

In November 2002, I agreed to enter the Criss Cole Rehabilitation Center for the blind in Austin. Karen wanted me to learn housekeeping skills such as cooking, cleaning, and the like. I was apprehensive, knowing that part of the curriculum was industrial arts. Yes, that's right! Power tools! Not only would I do that blindfolded, I would walk the streets that way too. Well, I could hardly see anyway, so the blindfold wasn't much of a disadvantage.

Two years passed, and Steve was about to graduate from Baylor with no job prospects in sight. By this time, I had been retired for about two years and was sitting at my desk at home. The phone rang. It was Steve.

"Dad, I got an email from a sociology professor who supplies teachers for the royal palace school in Thailand. One of the teachers was in a car wreck. The professor wants to know if I am interested in taking his place. Can I go, Dad?"

I could hear the excitement in his voice. "Yeah, Steve. Go ahead. I'll fix it with Mom."

A schoolmate with a car rushed him to Houston to get a visa and passport. Steve got the battery of shots and was in Bangkok ten days after our phone call. This school, the Chitralada School, was instituted fifty years earlier by the king to teach his oldest daughter. Nowadays, government officials and relatives of the royal family send their kids there.

In May 2005, Steve flew home from Bangkok, and we were all with Mom on Mother's Day. She died a week later of complications from gall bladder surgery. Her burial was on Tony's twenty-first birthday. As with Dad's funeral, faces from the painful past were there—including some dear ladies who, on different occasions, had taken Mom and either me or Tracy to the hospital. Also, some of Kay's coworkers at the Conroe school district came to honor Kay's mother.

A last goodbye, or at least that's what we thought.

Chapter 17

A Wedding in Bangkok, Thailand

On Monday, February 9, 2008, Tony drove in from Dallas to join us for the trip to Thailand. It would happen in two stages, the first from Austin to Los Angeles and the second nonstop to Bangkok. None of us got much sleep the night before we left. Airline weight limits on luggage made our last-minute preparations frenzied. We were allowed one carry-on each, which couldn't exceed 30 pounds. We packed the usual assortment of pills, with accompanying written prescriptions so we wouldn't be arrested as drug smugglers. Priority items like pills had to be in the carry-on bags, since we couldn't allow them to get lost in the other luggage. Despite everything we didn't pack, this alone was considerable. Of course, we were taking cameras, cash, traveler's checks, shoes, and a very few garments. The shoes were loafers for easy removal at the airport security, which we expected to be ferocious.

Our firstborn son, Steve, was to be married in Bangkok, Thailand, on February 23, 2008, to a beautiful Thai woman named Tan. She and Steve worked at different schools but went to the same church. Tan is a nickname. Her actual name is Jeeranan. Tony and I each had a suit in our luggage. We had thought of having suits made while in Bangkok, but the wedding would take place so soon after our arrival that we couldn't count on having suits made in time. Karen packed a few dresses, but beyond these few items, we would arrive needing clothes and toiletries. In addition, Karen had some worries about the food in Thailand. She can't have eggs or dairy, and all of us were worried about the water. Over the past three years, more than once Steve had been sick enough to go to the hospital. He was never admitted but treated and immediately released. As a precaution, Karen packed some food items such as instant oats and granola bars—things that she knew she could eat. This pushed some other things out of the luggage. A lot of thought went into not packing things we could reasonably buy once in Bangkok.

Why, you might ask, was our packing so spartan? Because our luggage was stuffed to overflowing with 22 pounds of candy! This was to be divided up into a hundred gift packages for the wedding guests. According to Steve and Tan, quality chocolate in Thailand is very expensive, so we bought it in the USA to transport all the way across the Pacific. Does that make it expensive? I would have to ponder that later.

At 11:30 p.m., Karen concluded that our preparations were complete. Our neighbor had agreed to keep Winter, our white Pomeranian, while we were gone. So we picked her up and went across the street to Judy's house. Karen and I lingered, talking to the neighbor and her son Sam, postponing the moment when we would put Winter on the floor and rush out the door. As I predicted, when that moment arrived, Winter started to whimper as though we had just dropped her off at a meatpacking plant. She wouldn't see us again for another sixteen days. We retreated across the street and tried to sleep. Everything was done at last. Our bags were on the living room floor, ready to carry out to the taxi we had arranged to pick us up at five o'clock in the morning.

Five o'clock fell on us violently, and we rolled out of bed groaning and ate a fast breakfast, some apples we had sliced up the night before. A knock at the front door announced that Jeremiah, our Nigerian taxi driver, had arrived. We dragged ourselves out the door, all bundled in jackets, because Austin on February 10 was about 40 degrees F. At the airport, Jeremiah dropped us at a point past which airport security wouldn't let him go. We paid him and began dragging our luggage into the terminal. As arranged beforehand, a wheelchair was waiting for me. I was a little embarrassed, since I can walk. However, not only am I blind, but my balance is unreliable. Thirty minutes before departure, we checked in our luggage and started through security. A man named George pushed my wheelchair up to the metal detector, and I divested myself of belt, keys, wallet, and some coins. I also handed over my white cane. Next was the pat down. George leaned down and whispered a warning in my ear. "He's wearing gloves, but he's no doctor." I started to laugh. Karen and Tony, as my companions and my attendants, went through security with me. This was an advantage to all three of us because we went through it at the same time as the pilot and crew. At the ramp onto the aircraft, I stood, and walked into the airplane hanging on to Tony as my sighted guide. Tony exclaimed, "Next time I fly, I want to be with Dad. We get on the plane with the pilot! What could be better!" Our luggage was stowed, and we fastened our seat belts.

The flight to the Orange County airport was uneventful and not very memorable. We arrived there at about 10:00 a.m. Tony called Karen's sister

Wanda on his cell phone and agreed on a meeting point. We loaded ourselves into her van and headed off to her home in Long Beach. We dropped off the luggage, and then it was back in the van to go to a California-style Mexican eatery. We walked into a small place with a few tables. They were doing a brisk take-out business. This being California, we ordered fish tacos and burritos. Tony ordered extra. The blond furniture wasn't fancy, but very cheery. And the food was good. It was not hot like TexMex. Tony and I were disappointed. Is everybody out here a wimp? Where are the jalapeños?

After lunch, we picked up Wanda's fifteen-year-old daughter, Amanda, at a high school run by the Brethren church. Her seventeen-year-old son, Daniel, came to the van for a quick hello and went off to tennis practice. I had flown to Los Angeles in 2001 for a California State University, Northridge, conference on technology for the disabled, so I was familiar with where Wanda took us next. It was a hamburger joint known for its 50/50 milkshake, orange sherbet swirled into vanilla ice cream. It was situated at the end of a pier in Seal Beach. Tony was seated across from me, enjoying the atmosphere and his shake. Tony and I got the half-and-half. It was orange and vanilla swirled together. We were reminded of a Dreamsicle. The girls were discussing clothes and jewelry. The shakes filled us up, but when we got back to the house, Bruce, Wanda's husband, treating us as if we had had nothing to eat, grilled some steaks.

After a great dessert of apple cake, Amanda and Daniel had homework to do, but Tony talked to them a lot. Daniel connected to Tony's website to see his latest animations. Alas, the laptop didn't have the resources to run the animations. Finally, I reminded Tony that they had homework to do. Anxious to talk to her cousin, Amanda asked Tony for help with World History. "List four factors that led to the French Revolution." I found out, on our return from Thailand two weeks later, that the answers we gave her were correct. Daniel, who was a senior, had homework in integral calculus involving trigonometric substitution. I talked to him about setting up the triangles to make the substitution and the inverse substitution at the end of a problem. He caught on immediately. That night I was almost too excited to sleep. And I needed a good night's sleep because the next day was going to be busy. We weren't flying out of LAX until 5:30 in the evening.

The next day was Tuesday, February 11. That morning we toured an aquarium, where the staff went out of their way to give me a hands-on experience with anemones, shells, and other things. But before the tour was over, I started to think it would become a hands-off experience, when at last Wanda led us to what she told me was the shark tank. As we knelt and reached into the tank to pet what I believed to be the "shark," Wanda told me again that I'm her favorite brother-in-law. "Oh, come on, Mike, stick it in deeper! He can't get it!" Well, I did, and the "shark" rose to the surface. I pulled back just in time. I think he almost touched me, but he wasn't going to get a second chance. Wanda thought he did, and I wasn't going to tell her otherwise. She was satisfied, and I certainly left very relieved. This gave me a new story to tell: my traumatic encounter with a shark. (Later, Wanda confessed that she had been teasing me, and that what I actually had touched was a stingray.)

After leaving the aquarium, Wanda drove us in her van past the Queen Mary. For lunch, we stopped at the Safari, a restaurant with African decor and food that was not African at all. Hmm! Maybe the chef drove to the wrong address and didn't read the sign over the restaurant door. I had a creole dish, so maybe there was a slight African connection through New Orleans. When Tony tasted the food, he forgave their mistake.

We finished lunch, then went to Trader Joe's, about which we had heard a lot. Karen can't have dairy or eggs and was thus pleased to find several vegan items not available in Austin. Meanwhile, Tony and I enjoyed a sample of New Mexico Pinon (Pinyon) Coffee so much, we determined to get a bag on the return trip from Thailand. Wanda left us browsing through Trader Joe's to pick Amanda up for a doctor's appointment. When she called Tony's cell phone to say a tire had blown out on her van, I thought we would be late to the airport. Luckily, she got a ride home in time to switch vehicles, unload and reload luggage, dash back to Trader Joe's, and rush us to LAX.

George, who had wheeled me through the Austin airport, had told us that the LAX airport would be chaos, but surprisingly, going through security went smoothly. It was almost a repeat of the experience at the Austin airport. Finally, we sat in our seats aboard a Thai Airways Airbus. There was lots of leg room. We all had put on our pressure socks to guard against deep vein thrombosis. The flight from LAX to Bangkok would be a direct eighteen-hour jump across the Pacific.

As I sat in my seat looking around and listening, I was very impressed. The back of the seats sported a screen for movies. Optionally, music was available on a headset, including a jazz album of the king of Thailand's compositions. It was quite enjoyable. Tony had a window seat immediately to my left, while Karen was across the aisle to my right. About thirty minutes after our departure, the attendants served dinner, the first of three meals. While I had ravioli, Karen had requested a vegan dinner online from Austin. I was more impressed all the time. The attendants came back around later with soft drinks, and some drinks not so soft. I kept Austin time on my watch; people began to settle down for the night around 10:30 Austin time. But before doing this myself, I had Karen escort me to the bathroom.

Although I am perfectly capable of going to a public bathroom alone, this was an airplane. I didn't want to open the emergency door by mistake and fall out of the aircraft. I thought about the man who had parachuted out of an airliner over Oregon with a lot of money and escaped. The authorities searched, but never found him. Well, I didn't have a parachute or a lot of money. And that was water down there, not dry land. Also, my encounter with a shark was fresh on my mind. Suspended somewhere above the Pacific, I was feeling pretty homeless. And my imagination, like the working poor, was putting in overtime, on at least three jobs. Once in the bathroom, I discovered that the design of an Airbus restroom was very different from that of a Boeing restroom. Hearing impatient voices outside the door gently critiquing each other's dance steps made me very aware of the passage of time. *Come on, Mike. Don't panic. Take a few deep breaths.* After an intense search, I located the flush mechanism. I stepped out, and Karen led me back to our seats. As we passed it, she pointed out the door I didn't want to open. I was right; I could have made a wrong turn with who knows what results. Hopefully, once we're airborne, that door is hard to open.

Back in my seat, I found it impossible to rest. The vibration of the aircraft, instead of lulling me to sleep, kept me keyed up. Since I'm not focused on vision, I'm more aware of other things, such as sounds and tactile sensations. The cabin got quiet, and then it got loud again. People don't think they snore, despite the reality that they could compete straight up with a tuba. It sounded like a bad orchestra. I put the headset on and unplugged it. Would this night never end! Worried about deep vein thrombosis, I stood several times to stretch. There was plenty of leg room; that wasn't the problem. I slipped my shoes off. I tried a number of other things, but sleep refused to come. I was too aware of my body. I noticed the snoring had died down. Time dragged excruciatingly by. Minutes seemed like hours. I checked my talking watch. It was close to dawn, Austin time.

Tony and Karen woke up and whispered, "Good morning." Just in time, too! I needed to go to the bathroom. The cabin started waking up. Anticipating a rush, Karen and I hurried. When we got back to our seats, the flight attendants were taking breakfast orders. I was feeling out-of-place and wondering how Winter was. My thoughts were back in Austin, and so when my turn came, I ordered the American breakfast, bacon and eggs. That coffee was really good! The food was gourmet, especially for an airline. There was lots of slurping and clinking of glasses in that cabin. We were eating breakfast, but it was night here halfway across the Pacific. I guess the journey was wearing on people, because I didn't hear any conversations.

Finally, everyone was finished, the dishes were collected, and everything settled down. Tony watched a couple of movies, and Karen saw a video about the Thai royal family. The music selection didn't appeal to me; and even though I had worked in the Apollo program, my interest in the Apollo 13 movie was low because I had seen it twice. So I lapsed into a daydream, as I often do when on an extended car trip. On those occasions, I can't look out the window, and I am discouraged from talking. Whether Karen or one of the boys is driving, my saying anything usually elicits responses such as these: "Don't distract me! I'm driving! You're going to cause a wreck! Would you like to go to the hospital? You're going to get us killed! Don't talk!" So I go into a dream state. But eighteen hours! This was going to tax my talent for escapism.

Time itself must have been tired because it dragged by slowly like it didn't want to go anywhere. I think it just wanted to sleep. According to my watch, we were eight hours from Bangkok. My journey was punctuated by another very good meal, another pit stop, and more dreaming. The cabin was quiet. We had another six hours to go, and people were hunkered down for the long haul.

With about three hours left, suddenly the tempo changed. There was a commotion at the rear of the aircraft. A voice broke in over the cabin speaker. "Is there a doctor aboard this flight?" It turned out that there were one, two, three, four of them. One of the passengers had overdosed on anxiety pills. He had started his journey in Toronto, Canada, and had popped pills all the way to Thailand; well, halfway at any rate. One of the attendants told Tony that the captain was considering diverting to Hong Kong, so we waited to see where we would land. The doctors stabilized the man, and we weren't diverted after all. At the Bangkok airport, the passengers were told to remain in their seats until the patient had been removed by paramedics. Finally, he was gone, and we all stood to disembark. We landed on Valentine's Day, at 6:30 a.m. Bangkok time.

When we disembarked, there was my wheelchair waiting for me. It got to Bangkok before the airplane did, but the guy pushing it didn't even look tired. Like the Pony Express, they must have changed guys. I listened to the sounds around me. It didn't sound like I was on Mars. I even heard voices speaking English. I relaxed just a bit. I had been afraid that Thailand was going to be a twelve-day obstacle course. Maybe not! It sounded promising. And then, there was Steve, pulling me erect out of the wheelchair and hugging me. Tan was there, too, smiling. We stood around awhile, waiting for our luggage. If the luggage didn't make it, the wedding would be considerably crippled. All that candy was in it! Most things we worry about don't happen. So we worry about everything, a tried-and-true prevention tactic.

The Bangkok airport was huge. We dragged all that candy forever, until we reached Steve's Toyota in a giant parking garage. Finally, we were being whisked away. This wasn't Mars, but it was a left-handed universe. The steering wheel was on the wrong side of the car. This, like most of the English spoken in Bangkok, was distinctly British. I turned to Karen. "Happy Valentine." It was also a milestone for Karen and me—on this day, we'd been married twenty-eight and a half years.

I don't remember much about the ride, except that it was long. Since I couldn't see anything outside the car, as usual I went into a dream state. After a long interval, we parked and walked to a hotel. Our room wouldn't be available for six hours, so we checked in our luggage and went to breakfast. Steve and Tan hadn't eaten. Steve had taken the day off from his school, where he was teaching third grade. Breakfast was at Au Bon Pain. Karen had a cup of tea, and I had French roast coffee and a pecan pastry. The rest had items similar to mine. I took stock of myself. After an eighteen-hour flight from Los Angeles and a sleepless day before that, I was surprisingly alert. We sat around a white metal table outside on the sidewalk talking, our voices raised slightly to be heard over the noisy traffic. None of us were tired. I guess seeing Steve and Tan gave us a little extra energy. Mind over matter maybe! Tomorrow was Friday.

Steve outlined the plan, "I took off tomorrow too, but I go back to school Monday. We've planned some tours for you. You can see the Grand Palace, take a riverboat cruise to Ayutthaya, see the bridge over the River Kwai in Kanchanaburi, get a Thai massage, and get suits made."

We finished and rose for the long trek back to Steve's Toyota. As usual, I gripped Karen's right arm slightly above the elbow. This is the classic sighted guide technique for leading a blind person.

We next went to a store similar to a 7-Eleven, but with a fair assortment of groceries. There I found A&W Root Beer, incontrovertible proof that this wasn't Mars. Our focus at this moment was supplying ourselves with the items we would have brought had we not packed 22 pounds of candy. There was one big item the candy hadn't displaced. What was it? It was, of course, our fear of eating and drinking in a foreign country. So bottled water was definitely on our list. Steve pointed out the French bottled water, which I was curious to try. Among the displaced items were toothbrushes, instant oatmeal, granola bars, safety razors (one for me and one for Tony), deodorant, Handi Wipes, and a few over-the-counter medicines. Karen wasn't at all sure she could eat what the rest of us ate. Pink Pepto Bismol tablets completed the list, and we were done.

To make good use of our time (our room not being available for another six hours), next we went to a shopping mall. It was a huge mall. Karen decided that I needed shoes, slacks, and a shirt. I tried on slacks in a dressing room. While I was in there, Karen handed me a pair of swim trunks. They were nice enough, but I had no intention of exposing my scrawny legs to public ridicule and amusement. However, I kept my thoughts to myself, and the purchase was duly made. Next, I sat on a stool while Karen and Steve brought me boxes of shoes to try on. At last, I selected a gray pair of walking shoes with two Velcro straps. Meanwhile, Tony was being similarly pushed around and treated like a mannequin. He picked out swim trunks from Australia, which almost fit him, but regretfully he laid them aside. The items we bought weren't as inexpensive as I was led to anticipate. Tan's sister TudToo and cousin Mai joined us. The shopping behind us, we went upstairs to a Japanese restaurant where we sampled a bewildering array of Japanese delicacies, none of which I can remember. I did have a glass of Thai tea. A most excellent drink! The total bill for the seven of us amounted to thirty-five dollars, American. Before returning to the hotel, we toured several shops on different levels of the mall. Karen "oohed and aahed" over a vast assortment of beautiful textiles. Many of the shirts and jackets sported images of elephants. This is because elephants, being the first army tank, played a major role in the defense of Thailand throughout its long history. Thailand is, in addition, shaped like an elephant's head.

Our twelve days in Bangkok whizzed by. We met Tan's aunts, uncles, and cousins. They entertained us royally. One of the shopping centers had a Mercedes dealership on an upper floor; we have a picture of a car with the skyline behind it. All of the elevators talked, and the freight elevator was big enough for the Mercedes. The food courts offered a great variety of excellent cuisine. I have never had Indian or Italian food to match these offerings. The mango lassi (a creamy drink with mango, yogurt, milk, sugar, and cardamom) was wonderful, as was everything else. And, of course, you can't find Thai food like this in the states. A Thai dish I couldn't bring myself to eat is pork prepared as cotton candy. Trying to eat it was a *Twilight Zone* experience. Another was a squid-flavored cookie, very popular in Thailand. The Burger King, 7-Eleven, McDonald's, Kentucky Fried Chicken, and Dairy Queen chains were not hard to find, offering lots of familiar items; however, there were also things on their menus that catered to Thai tastes, and were therefore not available in the United States. One of these items that we really liked was basil-flavored potato chips. The Dairy Queen there only served ice cream. An ice cream sandwich in Thailand was ice cream on a hot dog bun, something else I couldn't get used to. The fruit was amazing—with the exception of durian, which stinks.

Our accommodations were on the twenty-second floor of the hotel. The hotel lobby contained a shrine to the king of Thailand. In our suite, there was a microwave but no kitchen. Tony had a separate bedroom. An English newspaper was delivered to our room every day. Early each morning, street vendors set up on the sidewalks selling food and other services, including a man with an ancient sewing machine altering clothes on demand. It was unusual to have kitchen facilities. Everyone tended to eat meals in a restaurant or on the streets. By midafternoon, the street vendors were packed up and gone for the day. We took our meals at a restaurant next door to the hotel. In addition to Thai breakfasts, an excellent American breakfast with bacon and eggs was always available.

The tours were all interesting. On a trip to see the ancient capital of Ayutthaya, I talked to the tour guide while Karen and Tan looked at jade jewelry. When I mentioned that the boys were going to see the bridge over the River Kwai the next day, the guide said they would stop at the Tiger Temple and pet a tiger. That night, I told Tony I didn't want to hear that he petted a tiger. So, of course, that is exactly what he did. He said that the six-hundred-pound tiger purred when he petted it. Steve took Tony's picture doing it. Then they switched places, and Steve petted the tiger. So both my sons lacked judgment. They also rode an elephant, to which I didn't object. Then they saw a kickboxing match.

Tony and I wanted to be sure to have suits made while we were in Bangkok. The boys and I went to a shop called The Boss. I decided on a charcoal gray combination cashmere and wool suit in an English cut. Tony chose a chocolate brown with black vertical stripes, also cashmere wool blend, in an Italian cut. After taking our precise measurements, the proprietor offered us the standard Thai beer. I had never had a beer, and the boys convinced me to try one. After my first sip, my lips puckered and I exclaimed, "This is awful. Why does anybody drink this stuff?" Not the most diplomatic thing to say in the store owner's presence, but maybe he was in the back of the store when I said it. I hope so anyway. A week later, we picked up our suits. Neither Tony nor I had ever seen a suit that nice. We were both wishing we had more money so we could have another suit made.

We all went to the night bazaar, where I bought some Crocs and Karen bought two fancy Thai dresses, one of which she wore to the wedding. The wedding happened before we picked up the suits, so we wore suits from Austin. The wedding was an American ceremony, not a Thai or Buddhist wedding. Tan's relatives are all Buddhists, so the wedding ritual was strange to them. Tan was beautiful. We were surprised to learn that one of the members of the band that played during the ceremony was from Karen's hometown, Baytown, Texas. The wedding reception was on the sixty-seventh floor of the Banyan Tree Hotel in downtown Bangkok. Later, we were served more refreshments on the roof, which was the seventy-third floor. The view from there was spectacular.

Finally, our twelve days in Bangkok drew to an end. We were anxious to get home. Our last meal, eaten at the Bangkok airport, proved to be the best. I don't remember what I ordered, but rather what Tony ordered. It was *khao soi*, a dish from northern Thailand. I only got to finish what Tony gave me, which wasn't much. It was yellow curry covered with egg noodles drowned in lime juice. It has become the dish I always ask for at Thai restaurants. More and more restaurants in Austin have it on their menu, and I almost never fail to order it. The flight back was uneventful, and our luggage was 22 pounds lighter, minus the suits and dresses we had bought.

Winter was happy to see us when we returned. Judy said she had a sad look on her face, probably thinking that she had been abandoned by her family, so we gave her lots of attention.

(Steve and Tan moved from Thailand to the Austin area in August 2008, where they both earned master's degrees in education, Tan at Texas State and Steve at the University of Texas. They continue to work in K-12 education. Their son, Skyler Ray, was born in 2020 in the midst of the COVID-19 pandemic lockdown. Karen and I are grandparents! We are delighted to have them living close by.)

Tony Cross at the Tiger Temple, Thailand, 2008. Author's collection.

Tour bus, Bangkok, 2008. Author's collection.

Chapter 18

It Is Always Winter

Our house was now an empty nest—empty except for a fluffy little dog. No longer a frisky dog, Winter's health started failing in her thirteenth year. She frequently vomited late at night, and I would clean up and lay fresh newspapers around her bed. Karen was regularly subbing as a teacher at a middle school. Not wanting to disturb Karen's rest, I would finish the night in the room with Winter. Our vet said Winter had lost some kidney function and recommended a special dog food.

On a trip to Pasadena, we stopped for a break, at which time Karen led Winter to a patch of grass. When Winter leaped into the back seat of the car, she didn't jump high enough, and tore a nail. She cried, and we noticed blood. That night, in transit from Baytown to Pasadena, Winter—alone in the back seat—yelped and started to cry. We took her to a local vet, who bandaged her foot. He said he noticed a heart murmur and to mention it to our Austin vet. A year later, we noticed that she ran into walls and got lost on the way to her room. She had developed cataracts. I now became Winter's caretaker. I carried her everywhere and watched her closely.

The end came suddenly, on September 12, 2012. I sat up in bed. Winter must be awake. I swung my legs to the floor. Winter was lying limp beside my feet. I was immediately alarmed. I knelt and gently slipped my forearm under her torso until the palm of my hand was beneath her chest. I had a bad feeling about today. I lifted and carried her to the bathroom. Holding her in my left arm, I turned on the bathtub faucet with my right hand and filled a small plastic cup with water. I put it to Winter's muzzle, but she didn't respond. My heart sank. I didn't want to accept that I was looking at death. I carried her to the front door, where I put on shoes and took her out to the front sidewalk. Putting her gently down on the grass, I willed her to use the bathroom, like yesterday and the day before. The leash didn't move. It was cold. A front had blown in that morning, and my jacket wasn't warm enough. I picked her back up, already dreading the worst. "I'll try the water again," I thought. Back in the bathroom, before I could offer her any water, Winter took three quick breaths and died in my arms. Standing there helpless, part of me died too. I stepped to the door and called Karen. When she appeared, her voice told me what I didn't want to believe.

The day before, we had come home from church to find Winter unable to leave her bed. She wouldn't eat or drink. We left for a mystery writers meeting at 2 p.m. I didn't want to go, but we had missed the three previous meetings. I can't forgive myself for not staying home with her. My mind wasn't alert to what was said at that meeting. We left at 4 p.m. and bought a few groceries before going home. I sat with Winter on a leash under a tree in the front yard. She had revived enough to explore and sniff the grass. She walked round and round me, as I switched the leash from one hand to the other to avoid getting it wrapped around me. I sat there a long time, letting her do anything she wanted. She finally came to me and collapsed in my lap. Her energy was spent. Back in her bed, Winter lay there not moving. She wasn't hacking and coughing anymore. "She's finally over her bronchitis," I thought, "she's just weak." But it wasn't bronchitis; it was heart failure. In denial, I listened to a football game until 10 p.m. and then checked on her again. I brought water to her, and she drank a lot. Feeding her by hand, I broke the moist kidney dog food into small pieces. She ate a few and then turned her head away to let me know she wasn't interested. How dense could I be? I was ignoring major signs.

The saddest word in the English language is "goodbye." We would say it again and again, because much worse loss lay a few years in our future.

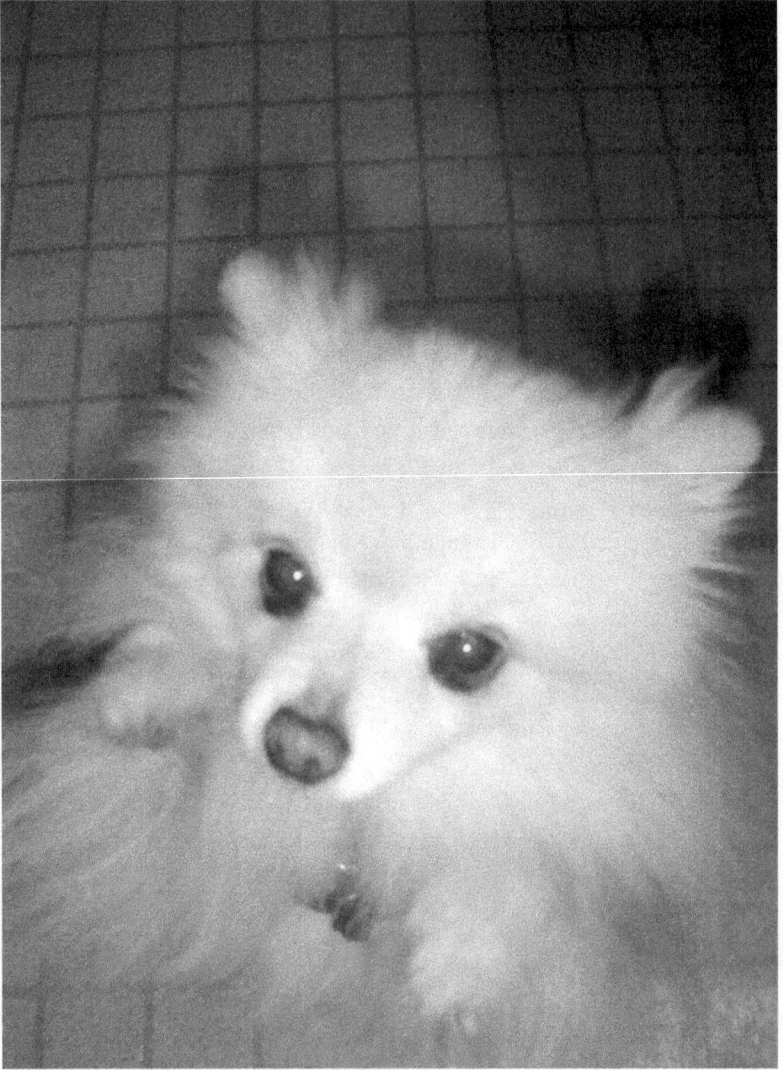

Winter. Author's collection.

Chapter 19

Shots Fired—September 10, 2017

The doorbell rang a little after midnight on a Sunday night. Despite the late hour, I was up because we had received a disturbing call from Tony's best friend in Austin, a boy who had been a high school classmate and fellow marching band member. There was no second call, and that was because David was driving to our house. I was full of dread. I was afraid that Tony had been in an auto accident.

When I answered the door, David walked in and said, "There's been a shooting, and Tony's truck is there."

My heart sank, although I had been expecting bad news.

I woke Karen, and we spent the rest of the night calling Dallas hospitals and the Plano Police Department. The Plano police had no way of knowing that we were who we claimed to be, and therefore were unwilling to tell us anything. I kept dialing Tony's cell phone, which went straight to voicemail. My conclusion was that either Tony was dead, or he might be in surgery. David stayed with us all night. It wasn't lost on me that this Monday was 9/11. David's father, Tom, volunteered to drive us to Richardson, since Karen was unfit to drive anywhere. We hurriedly packed and drove to Dallas. We arrived at Daniel and Brigitte's house in Richardson after noon. (Daniel had been two years behind Tony at Connally High School, and then a fellow student at UT Dallas, where they had developed a large group of mutual friends. After college, Tony, Daniel, and Brigitte had shared a house in Richardson. In 2014, Tony had been a groomsman in Daniel and Brigitte's wedding.) About twenty people milled around in the large living room. All were in shock, and some were crying. Walking into that scene, reality closed in on us, and we were crying too. None of us held out much hope that Tony was alive. Karen did not want to watch any newscasts, and I agreed with her. No one turned on a TV or a radio that entire week in Dallas. It would have been overwhelming. Most of all, we didn't want to see or hear a description of the crime scene.

Daniel drove us to the Plano police station, where we were ushered into the victim advocate's office. Three of Tony's friends walked into the office with us. A detective introduced himself and confirmed that Tony had passed. As Karen and I wept, the detective told us about the events of Sunday evening.

Tony had been at a Sunday football-game-watching party in Plano hosted by one of his friends, Meredith Lane. Everyone was in swimwear, there being a slip-and-slide in the backyard. Two guests were barbecuing on the back patio, while Tony and the others were gathered in the living room watching the Dallas Cowboys football game on TV. A car parked in front of the house, and Meredith went to welcome a new arrival. But the newcomer was her ex-husband. The neighbors heard a loud altercation in the front yard and called the police. Meredith went back into the house, and the ex-husband went back to his car. Tony was on the couch that faced the entryway. Suddenly, the ex-husband kicked in the front door and came in wielding an assault rifle. He shot nine people at the party, and only one survived their gunshot wounds.

Prior to the shooting, the ex-husband had gotten drunk and returned to a bar not too far from Meredith's house. When he brandished a knife and started to make threats and told the bartender and manager to watch the evening news, the manager told him to leave and go home. He replied he needed to talk to his wife. A Plano police officer arrived at Meredith's house in time to look through a window and see the ex-husband shoot his last victim. The policeman confronted the shooter when he came outside and killed him. In swimwear, none of the victims had identification on them.

One of the guests (a close friend of Tony's and of Daniel's) had left the party after the first football game was over to play volleyball for a couple of hours. On his return to the house, it was a crime scene. He called Daniel, who in turn called David, who came to our house in Austin.

The Plano police could not have been more considerate and compassionate. Nothing like this had ever happened in Plano. On Friday, Karen and I attended a memorial service for Tony in Richardson, Texas. That morning Karen and I sat in the front pew, surrounded by her family and mine. The preacher mounted the podium. The next six speakers variously described Tony as "big like a bouncer," with a "booming voice, iconic laugh, and infectious giggle." His "inside voice" was "for inside a stadium."

"He had the greatest beard, and his heart was even bigger than the beard."

"Tony was the gentlest soul I ever met."

"He was my sunshine, when I only saw rain."

"Tony never gave up."

"We should all live more like him."

"Tony was the peacemaker in our group, our social salve."

We heard many things that were new to us. Nobody should have to find out about his son that way. Karen was exhausted from weeping. The next day I attended Meredith's funeral. I thought one of us should be there. It was especially hard because Meredith was an only child.

David, who had stayed with us in the wee hours of the morning after the shooting, drove us home to Austin. My memory of that time is blank. Tony did not have a will, which made settling his estate long and difficult.

Six weeks after the Richardson funeral, we experienced a second major loss. Karen's youngest sister, Wanda, died in her sleep. The last time we saw her was in Richardson. Karen didn't get to go to Wanda's funeral in California because she was scheduled two days later for surgery. There were two more funerals for Tony that fall—one at our church in Austin and on the day before the church service, one put together by his friends in an adventure camp in Marble Falls, Texas. Tony's off-roading group, the Hillbilly Crawlers, and his Viking re-enacting group, Black Wolves, Dallas, organized a camp-out, catered a barbecue, and held the first Tony Cross Memorial Run, complete with T-shirts with a picture of Tony standing on his jeep. After most of the people piled into jeeps and off-road vehicles for a run on a trail ending at a high point, where we watched the sunset, everyone came back for a Viking funeral. A member of the Black Wolves made a speech and friends burned notes to Tony, items that reminded them of Tony , some of his Viking items, and his ashes .

Tony has since had two namesakes born, Luke Anthony (born in 2018 to Daniel and Brigitte) and Yari Anthony.

Are we angry? No! Who would be the target of our anger? The police killed the shooter. That spared us a trial that would have been a wound that would stay raw without any end in sight.

A year and a half after the shooting, Karen and I attended a wedding. David, who rang our doorbell in 2017, married his fiancée, Kima. They both had wanted Tony to be their best man. Determined that Tony would be there in spirit, David made a life-sized cutout from a photograph of Tony taken at Daniel and Brigitte's wedding back in 2014. As the ceremony unfolded, a groomsman carried the cutout down the aisle. We were honored to think that our son meant so much to the party.

On Mother's Day 2018, we celebrated a birthday without a dear son. Karen made Tony's favorite, a blackberry cake. We ate it while praying, remembering, and crying.

Years have passed, and we are still in grief counseling. Deep grief can drive a wedge between husband and wife, but it has drawn us much closer together. Steve has not gotten counseling, but he has expressed his grief by writing some beautiful poetry.

Grieving for a victim of a mass shooting is long term. We had been grieving Tony's loss for four years, when we got a long-distance phone call from my sister Kay. She and Mark were visiting out of state, so I was surprised to hear from her. I had a premonition that something was wrong. Kay was crying. Tracy had been found dead in his bathroom. The dog had been scratching on the bathroom door, whining. The husband of the couple living with Tracy opened the door to check on him because he wasn't responding to questions. He had recovered from a case of COVID-19 and then had a relapse. Tracy died of a heart attack caused by a blood clot. It was September 28, 2021, the day after Steve's fortieth birthday. In my dreams I sometimes see Tracy, no longer crippled but standing tall.

Kay and I were now the only ones left in our immediate birth family.

Cutout of Tony used at David and Kima's wedding, with Mike and Karen, 2019.
Author's collection.

Chapter 20

And There Be Gentle Dreams

The past sixty-five-plus years, if not gentle, have been at least interesting, and often more exciting than I could have wanted.

September is forever stamped in my memory as the cusp of change. This association is not surprising since when school starts, schedules are adjusted. Lives change in ways great and small. Students leave home. Parents become empty nesters. Faces appear; others vanish. New relationships begin; others end. August and September serve as bookends for chunks of life. Marching through time, we are buffeted by tectonic shifts—storm clouds and occasional rainbows. Some trap us; others liberate us.

The brain tumor in September 1955 was the storm that forever put me in a cage. The arch across my future was Karen, my brilliant September rainbow. But what September gives, it can take away.

Thinking these thoughts, I fall asleep—perchance . . . I am a small child watching the morning ritual. As Dad fries bacon and eggs, sunlight streams past him and splashes the wall a rich gold. The percolator breathes and blows a jet of coffee into the space helmet atop the pot. There are other sounds. "When the sun in the mornin' peeps over the hill and kisses the roses 'round my window sill . . ." [1] I stand there silent, seeing and hearing everything. All is right with my world.

As I sleep, the dream changes. My mind drifts back to voices from beyond the door, at my homecoming so long ago. My father's heart longs to catch even a whisper of Tony's voice from beyond the final door. I have to be content with a gentle dream, a world in which my son is enfolded with boundless love and kindness. In my dreams, can I join him even for a little

---

1. "When the sun in the mornin' peeps over the hill and kisses the roses 'round my window sill" is a lyric from a song titled "Mockin' Bird Hill." The lyrics were written by George Vaughn Horton (© Southern Music Publishing Company Inc.). The song was performed and recorded by Patti Page in 1951. The music for the song was based on an old Swedish waltz.

while in that better world? "Your sons and daughters will dream dreams."[2]
Why not a father? As I sink further, these two worlds fuse.

> *Tremulous ethereal melody,*
> *Floating, restful voices*
> *From the mist, something drawing close,*
> *Shimmering, ethereal melody,*
> *Drifting, restful voices,*
> *Softly calling me to awareness,*
> *From the rich pure light,*
> *Only remembered vaguely*
> *Something drawing closer*
> *Colors waking my senses,*
> *Gowned in green and gold, the tree of life towers majestically.*[3]

As Tony comes closer, an eight-year-old dad looks up at his adult son and
smiles. With perfect vision, I see his face for the first time.

---

2. This is a variation on a Bible quotation, from Joel 2:28—"Your sons and daughters will
prophesy, your old men will dream dreams, your young men will see visions."
3. Poem written by the author.

Appendix: Calculus Discussion

A *set* is a collection of objects. The objects could be marbles, but the sets that mathematicians are interested in are collections of numbers or collections of pairs of numbers. A subset of a set S is a smaller set, all of whose members (objects) also belong to set S. The union of two sets is a set, each of whose members belong to one or both of the two sets being united. The intersection of two sets is a set, each of whose members belong to both of the two sets being intersected.

After a brief review of the set Z of integers and the set Q of rationals (fractions), our Calculus 1 class focused on the set R of real numbers. R includes integers and rationals, but it also contains numbers like the square root of two, which are called irrational numbers because they are not the ratio of two integers. This is just a hint of what R actually is.

Definition (Upper and Lower Bounds)

The statement that U is an upper bound of set S, a subset of the real number set R, means that no number in set S is greater than U. Similarly, stating that L is a lower bound of set S means that no number in set S is less than L. Note that to have an upper bound, a set cannot be the set of integers, the set of all fractions, or the set R of real numbers. None of those three sets has an upper or lower bound. There isn't a biggest integer; there is always one bigger than the one you propose as the largest.

LUB(S) is the least upper bound of set S. This means that if U is an upper bound of set S, then LUB(S) is less than or equal to U. It is common to denote the least upper bound of set S by sup(S), otherwise known as the supremum of S. Likewise, GLB(S) is the greatest lower bound of set S. This means that if L is a lower bound of set S, then GLB(S) is greater than or equal to L. It is common to denote the greatest lower bound of set S by inf(S). This is known as the infimum of S.

These are more than definitions, because we assume without proof that any set S of real numbers with an upper bound has a least upper bound. We make the same assumption about a set S of real numbers with a lower bound having a greatest lower bound. Without the least upper bound axiom (i.e., assumption) and the greatest lower bound axiom, differential and integral calculus could not have been developed. Here is that axiom/assumption:

Completeness Axiom

Each subset S of R that has an upper bound has a least upper bound, and each subset of R with a lower bound has a greatest lower bound.

Before going further, and at the risk of putting the reader to sleep (if I haven't already done so), I will present a few definitions representative of those I dealt with on a daily basis in my calculus studies. This will give the reader an idea of who I've become.

Definition (Dedekind Cut)

L is a Dedekind cut of Q. This means that there exist subsets G and H of the set Q of rational numbers such that every number in set H is greater than every number in set G, and such that G does not contain a largest number; then either L is the least number in set H or L is the least upper bound of set G.

(Note that not every Dedekind cut of set Q actually belongs to set Q. Dedekind cuts were first defined by German mathematician Richard Dedekind.)

Definition (Formal Definition of the Set R of Real Numbers)

The set R of real numbers is the union of set Q with the set of all Dedekind cuts of the set Q.

The set Q of rational numbers is full of holes. Dedekind cuts fill those holes.

(Omitting the definition of real numbers seemed a grievous sin, hence I felt compelled to include it.)

The last two concepts needed for the further development of calculus are those of a function of a single variable and the limit of such a function. You can think of such a function as a dating or matchmaking machine, where you are not matching two people but two numbers. You put a number X into the machine (function) and it matches it to a number Y. The set of numbers you select to be inputs to the function is called its domain. The set of numbers that the numbers in the domain are matched to is called the range of the function. The set of all the pairs of numbers created by the function is called a relation; the numbers in each of those pairs are now related because they've been matched. A single-valued real function is a relation that doesn't make any bigamous matches; that is, no two of its distinct ordered pairs has the same first member. No input X gets matched to two distinct Y outputs. A relation that fails to be single-valued is said to have different branches, one for each bigamous match. The equation of a circle is an example of a relation with two branches. The matched pairs (X, Y) of a relation are said to be points of that relation. The collection of these points plotted on a graph usually looks like an unbroken curve, but not always.

Definition (Limit of a Function)

The statement that L is the limit of the real function f(x) at xo means that xo is a real number in the domain of f and for each positive real number epsilon there exists a positive real number delta such that if x is a real number in the domain distinct from xo with its distance from xo being less than delta, then the distance between L and f(x) is a positive real number less than epsilon.

With this, Calculus 1 was off and running.

Let me briefly say something about Calculus 2, which is called integral calculus, and vector calculus, which is Calculus 3. The process developed in Calculus 1 is differentiation, and the process developed in Calculus 2 is integration. These two processes are inverses of each other. The functions in Calculus 1 and 2 are two-dimensional; that is, they lie in the X-Y plane. The functions in Calculus 3, vector calculus, don't lie in the X-Y plane. Most of them lie in X-Y-Z space; that is, they are three-dimensional. Other functions in vector calculus lie in four-dimensional space or even higher. Calculus 3 develops both differentiation and integration in those higher dimensions.

About the Author

Michael R. Cross grew up in Pasadena, Texas, and now resides in Austin. In 1955, at age eight, he lost over 90 percent of his vision, but he remained in public school, eventually earning advanced degrees in mathematics from the University of Houston. Mike interned at NASA, and then had a career as a programmer, retiring after twenty years at IBM.